To my friend, Ashley —
May God continue
to bless you, your beautiful
family & may you & Ramsey
enjoy book for Ramsey's
high school graduation

In His love —
Patsy

Clean Underwear, Wild Elephants, and the Princess

Clean Underwear, Wild Elephants, and the Princess

Patty B. Williams

Copyright © 2001 by Patty B. Williams.

Library of Congress Number: 2001118447
ISBN #:   Hardcover   1-4010-2767-9
               Softcover   1-4010-2766-0

All rights reserved. No part of this book may be reproduced or transmitted in any form or by any means, electronic or mechanical, including photocopying, recording, or by any information storage and retrieval system, without permission in writing from the copyright owner.

This book was printed in the United States of America.

To order additional copies of this book, contact:
Xlibris Corporation
1-888-7-XLIBRIS
www.Xlibris.com
Orders@Xlibris.com

Though written for my daughter, this book is dedicated to both my children, Michael and Brooke, whose lives have enriched and blessed my life beyond measure.

Acknowledgements

My heartfelt appreciation is given to those whose encouragement inspired me to complete this book of devotions. Whether by comments, applause, written notes of appreciation, or even by admonishment for being behind schedule, the following friends and family members helped this book come to fruition. I am forever grateful.

Debbie Bigham, Bill Bigham, Bobbi Lester, Mary Jane Green, Peggy Spears, Carol Culbreth, FSU Extra Point Club members, Coach Cecile Reynaud, and especially to Carol Sinclair, my editor and friend in Christ, whose professional expertise and shared love of the Lord supported my humble efforts to publish this work, to Obie Deyo, my "other son" for his design and artwork on the book cover, and to my dear friend, Terrie Corbett, for her continuous encouragement and sweet words found on the hardback cover.

I also acknowledge with great appreciation and admiration the following whose words, thoughts, work or lives touched my heart and helped illustrate messages within the book. (referenced by devotional date).

Charles Kendall Adams (6/29), Mitch Albom (2/20), Gilbert Arland (7/5), Danny Baker (11/14), Elizabeth Barrett-Browning (2/14), The Beetles (12/29), Corrie Ten Boom (3/8), Sarah Ban Breathnach (1/18), Garth Brooks (6/8), William Jennings Bryan (2/6), Andrew Carnegie (2/9), Winston Churchill (2/8), Alan Cohen (10/13), Henry Drummond (6/10), George Eliot (5/31), Benny Fields (4/8), Henry Ford (2/10 & 2/11), Mavis & Merle Fossum (10/12), Robert Fulghum (3/29), Mohandas Karamchand Gandhi (6/23), Don Gibson (4/15), Ben Johnson (6/9), Spencer Johnson, M.D. (7/14), President John Kennedy (1/11), Elizabeth Kubler-Ross (5/4), Ann Landers (9/24), J. Lubbock (4/17), George MacDonald (5/8), Edna St. Vincent Millay (7/7), Doris Mortman (3/10),

Patty B. Williams

Howard W. Newton (2/7), Robert Nivelle (6/5), John Norley (4/27), Frank Outlaw (6/16), Patrick Overton (9/25), George S. Patton (2/13), Elvis Presley (12/16), Eleanor Roosevelt (7/27), Franklin Roosevelt (5/6), Frank Outlaw (6/16), Flavia Weedn (4/6 & 10/26), Oprah Winfrey (6/13) Unknown or Anonymous Authors (9/21,22; 2/17, 5/10, 4/8, 6/11, 17, 28; 7/3, 9/21,22)

Biblical References and acknowledgements

Thompson Chain Reference Bible [referenced as (NIV) in devotionals]
The Woman's Study Bible [referenced as (NKJ) in devotionals]
The Living Bible [referenced as (NCV) in devotionals]

Thompson Chain Reference Bible, Scripture quotations marked (NIV) are taken from the HOLY BIBLE, NEW INTERNATIONAL VERSION.NIV. Copyright 1973, 1978, 1984 by International Bible Society. Used by permission of Zondervan Publishing House. All rights reserved.

The Woman's Study Bible, New King James Version, Copyright 1995 by Thomas Nelson, Inc. Used by permission.

Scriptures quoted from *The Everyday Bible,* New Century Version, Copyright 1987, 1988 by word Publishing, Dallas, Texas 7039. Used by permission.

To the many friends and family members of Brooke and myself whose lives touched ours, we are grateful. Whether used as a subject of one or more of the messages or mentioned in a devotional, your presence in our lives have been a gift from God.

And, lastly, I acknowledge in loving memory, the following individuals whose lives inspired one or more devotionals: Mrs. Karen Hodge Bender, Mrs. Johnnie Green, Ms. Patsy Barber, Miss Roxanne Kelly, and Mr. Richard Wainwright.

Author's Message

Clean Underwear, Wild Elephants and the Princess begins on the first day the Princess begins her college experiences. It ends one year later.

If you are reading this devotional as a student, friend, relative or someone who just found the title of the book intriguing, I encourage you to read it one devotional, one day at a time. You may be surprised how the message on a particular day speaks directly to you.

My prayer is that God will bless your time reading his words and those of mine inspired by him. May your *Wild Elephants* be few and far between, may your U*nderwear*, for goodness sakes, always be clean, and may your dreams to become a Princess or marry one come true! Do I hear an amen?

Author

Forward

When Patty Williams sent her daughter Brooke away to school, she had three goals in mind. One was to support Brooke in her education, one was to motivate her to begin daily Bible readings and the other was to continue the parenting process. Knowing that a freshman in college is subjected to many more outside influences than she has encountered before, Patty decided the best way to carry on an instructive dialogue with Brooke and to get her in the habit of reading her Bible was to write a daily devotional series that she would find interesting and personal. She wrote the devotionals in advance and sent them ahead, asking Brooke to read them on the day for which each was meant.

These daily meditations bring Brooke's life back to her as Patty relates each one both to scripture, to family, and to friends. Some of them ask Brooke to recall certain discouraging scenes from her past and point out how she behaved in such a mature way for her years. Others recall happy moments when Brooke was secure in the love of her family. Patty's and Brooke's friends, family members, and acquaintances dance through the pages, as mementos of their influences on a growing girl and as illustrations of Patty's great ability to find the best in everyone.

There is no one better to have written this book for her child than Patty Williams who has experienced adversity, but who has always recovered with a stronger Christian faith and an even more positive attitude. Any young person who reads this inspirational book will be blessed by its down to earth, yet valuable life lessons. And parents will be moved as they experience the remarkable soul of a very special mother.

Carol Sinclair

Patty B. Williams

August 14th
(Nanny & Granddaddy's Anniversary)

Be Yourself

"To everything there is a season; A time for every purpose under the heaven." Ecclesiastics 3:1 (NKJ)

Today starts a lot of new changes in your life. I hope you start the day with a smile on your face, confidence in yourself and excitement in what lies ahead. As you start sorority rush, remember to be yourself. God made you who you are and you have every right to be proud of what you've become—not quite a princess, but almost!

Pray with me:
Thank you, God, for the opportunity of college life, for the fun times ahead, for the challenge of learning new things, and for the chance for others to see you through us. Amen

August 15th
(Justin's Birthday)

Roommates

"And now abide faith, hope, love, these three; but the greatest of these is love." 1 Corinthians 13:13 (NKJ)

As you start a new life of "roommates" there will be times when you will not agree and times when you will have to be the one to go the "extra mile." Remember that love is reflected in both feelings and actions. God tells us that true love is characterized as patient and slow to anger, kind and gentle, unselfish and giving, truthful and honest, hopeful and encouraging—you get the picture! Feelings and acts of love are not always easy, but they are always right.

Pray with me:
Lord, in times of disagreement and stress, give us patience and kindness. Help us to reflect the kind of love you would have us show. Amen

Patty B. Williams

August 16th

Words And Actions

"Now then, we are ambassadors for Christ, as though God were pleading through us . . ." II Corinthians 5:20 (NKJ)

It doesn't matter where you go or who you talk to, your words and actions reflect where you are in your relationship to God. Kind of scary, isn't it? Every smile can be important, every word significant, every action helpful or hurtful. You have a sweet spirit, and your words and actions have made a lot of people happy. I know God is pleased with you as one of his ambassadors.

Pray with me:
Oh, God, continue to touch others through us today. Help us to reflect your love in all we say and do. Amen.

August 17th

Chance To Bloom

"A wise Man will hear and increase learning, And a man of understanding will attain wise counsel." Proverbs 1:5 (NKJ)

You have learned a lot about friendship, love, and the realities of life the last two years. I've been proud of you and the decisions you have made. In many ways you showed wisdom beyond your years. College will offer you continued opportunities for the growth of wisdom in many areas, and I hope you will take advantage of each opportunity with great enthusiasm. You have always said you wanted to be smart. Now is your chance to bloom. I envy your new possibilities for growth. Use the wisdom you have already attained to buckle down and be what you want to be, and if you don't understand something be wise enough to seek counsel from someone who can help you.

Pray with me:
Dear God, please help us as we seek new knowledge and understanding in all things college life and the world have to teach us. Grant us wisdom and let it direct our lives. Amen

Patty B. Williams

August 18th

On Your Own

"My son, hear the instruction of your father, And do not forsake the law of your mother." Proverbs 1:8 (NKJ)

Well, you're on your own now. Is the freedom a little frightening? Have all those years of instruction from your daddy and me made a difference? This is what we've been working toward for eighteen years—trying to raise a responsible, mature, and wise young lady who can make the right decisions on her own. I guess we'll soon find out if we did a good job. We both think so, but then we've never really had to let go. Boy, is that difficult. Just remember, we trust you and know you're capable of wise decisions, but if you ever need us, we'll always be here for you.

Pray with me:
God, thank you for family, for loving parents, grandparents, and extended family members who love us and hold us accountable for our actions. Let us remember that our freedom comes with the price of responsibility to others, but most importantly to you. Amen

Clean Underwear, Wild Elephants and the Princess

August 19th
(The beginning day of my big Conference)

Fearful

"The fear of man brings a snare, But whoever trusts in the Lord shall be safe." Proverbs 29:25 (NKJ)

Think about me today when I am up in front of 600-800 people. Hope that I don't embarrass myself. I will be a little scared. You will have these days too—all too often during your next four years. You will be fearful of failing a test, fearful of not being accepted, fearful of being laughed at or thought of as being a "Geek." Fear can rob you of yourself, so be careful. Remember, God made us human. We are going to make mistakes and we're going to be laughed at at some point, but so what? Are you any less in God's eye? I don't think so. Think about it.

Pray with me:
Thank you, God, for the kind of fear that keeps us on our toes, that makes us study and practice and do the things we're supposed to do. Help us to remember though that we don't have to be alone when we're afraid. You're there to hold our hand and help us through whatever we have to do. All we have to do is ask. Amen

Patty B. Williams

August 20th

Riches

"There is one who makes himself rich, yet has nothing; And one who makes himself poor, yet has great riches." Proverbs 13:7 (NKJ)

"Money is only a small ingredient of both wealth and poverty. A person may be rich in material goods but have nothing of wisdom. God does not measure great riches by money." (From the Woman's Study Bible)

Our family, I think you will agree, has always been rich in many ways. We have prospered in love, cared for one another, shared the difficult times and celebrated joy (like the news of Uncle Billy's and Aunt Debbie's soon to be new baby). I hope you never take our riches for granted. Strive hard to do well in school so you have the opportunity to make good money—even to become wealthy, but don't forget where the "real" wealth is found.

Pray with me:
God, teach us the meaning of real riches. Keep us from worshipping the wrong things—like designer clothes, that pretty green Lexus, or Tom Cruise! Keep us mindful of all that we have and help us to be satisfied with, and appreciate, what we already have. Amen

Clean Underwear, Wild Elephants and the Princess

August 21st

Sadness

"Jesus wept." John 11:35 (NKJ)

The shortest verse in the Bible, but still powerful.

The night before you left for school I could identify with the sadness Jesus felt in this verse. He was saddened by the loss of a close friend. I was saddened by the pending loss of your presence. It's strange to have such mixed feelings of joy and sadness. I think you probably had the same feelings: sadness for the many good things left behind and joy for the anticipation of the good things to come. Aren't we fortunate to have "good things" on both sides?

Pray with me:
Lord help us to never be afraid to weep and show our feelings of sadness or happiness as Jesus did. Keep us mindful of others' feelings and give us the ability to be a comforter when needed. Amen

Patty B. Williams

August 22nd
(Aunt Shirley's Birthday)

Asking For Help

"When Jesus saw him lying there, and knew that he already had been in that condition a long time, He said to him, Do you want to be made well?" John 5:6 (NKJ)

The first step in overcoming problems, whether they are physical, emotional, or spiritual, is to admit you are in need and desire a change. Jesus asked the question, "Do you want to be made well?" In the same manner, you might ask yourself if you care enough about your problem to do something about it—even if it requires on your part some action, effort, sacrifice, or even suffering (The Woman's Study Bible)—Something to think about.

Pray with me:
Dear God, give us confidence in ourselves and trust in you to work out any problems we might have. Let us remember that there is no problem too big that we can't solve together.

Clean Underwear, Wild Elephants and the Princess

August 23rd

Compliments

"Pleasant words are like a honeycomb. They make a person happy and healthy." Proverbs 16:24 (NCV)

Isn't it always nice to get compliments? Doesn't it just start your day off right if someone tells you how nice you look? When you've worked real hard on a project or a task, do you feel the effort was worth it if someone tells you what a great job you did? Whether you're at home, in school, or on the job, you'll find that recognition is one of the greatest rewards you can give or receive. Believe it or not, but studies say that recognition is even above money in being a motivator.

Funny how we can look in God's word to tell us how to be good managers as well as good people, isn't it? As much as you like to receive "pleasant words," remember that others like to receive them too. Today, make it a goal to make someone feel good by giving them an unexpected compliment! (It'll make you feel good too.)

Pray with me:
Oh, Lord, help us to always be mindful of others' needs. Make our words pleasant to their ears and helpful to their spirit. Amen

Patty B. Williams

August 24th
(Aunt Susan's birthday)

Gifts

"We have different gifts. Each gift came because of the grace that God gave us . . ." Romans 12:6 (NCV)

I have often wondered what gift God has given me, not in terms of what I have received from him, because those are not hard to identify. The gift I'm talking about is the gift he's given to me so that I may give to others. We all have one, you know, the Bible tells us so.

I've always wished I had the gift of a beautiful voice so I could sing and entertain others, or the gift of being able to play the piano by ear without having to read or study music. At fifty years old, I'm still looking for that hidden talent or gift, whatever it is. In the meantime though, I'm going to continue to work at those things that I think God has at least given me the ability to do—like make presentations and do some writing.

What about you, don't you, even at 18, already have an idea of some of the gifts God has given you? If you don't, let me suggest a few—the gift of friendship. You know how to be a good friend. You genuinely care about others, and it shows. The gift of "gab"—You know how to talk to others whether they are young or old, rich or poor, black or white. The gift of discernment (judgment)—You look beyond the surface of someone or something and measure it for its true worth rather than just its "perceived" worth. Keep looking for that "special" gift God has given you, but continue to use those that have already been identified.

Pray with me:
Father God, (as Mike Crawford would say) we thank you for the gifts and abilities you have bestowed upon us. Help us to use them in the way you have planned. Amen.

August 25th

Forgive And Forget

"Love is not rude, is not selfish, and does not become angry easily. Love does not remember wrongs done against it." I Corinthians 13:5 (NCV)

It's difficult sometimes to forgive and forget when someone hurts us badly, isn't it? Not only is it difficult to forgive and forget, we often want to "get them back", don't we? Do you have a situation that calls for you to do what God has asked us to do—keep no record of wrongs?

Don't confuse keeping no record of wrongs with keeping no record of common sense. God doesn't ask us to forget a hurt to the point that we put ourselves right back in the same position to be hurt again and again. He just doesn't want us to let a hurt keep us from moving forward or keep us from loving a person in spite of not loving what they do or say. There's a big difference. I hope your "gift of discernment" will always help you to be able to distinguish between the two.

Pray with me:
Lord, you know we have had a difficult time forgiving those who have disappointed or hurt us. Help us to remember how much you have forgiven us when we didn't deserve it. Amen.

Patty B. Williams

August 26th

Promises

"Better not to vow than to vow and not pay." Ecclesiastes 5:5 (NKJ)

It's so easy to promise to do something and then not follow through, isn't it? It's not that we intentionally plan to break a promise, we just don't always put forth the effort needed to see it through.

I think God is trying to give us some practical wisdom in this verse. I think he is trying to tell us to think before we speak. See, when we say we're going to do something, others depend on us to follow through. When we're not responsible enough or committed enough to do whatever we vow to do, then He says it's better not to say we will do it. That way, we don't get labeled as an undependable person or a person who never means what they say.

Don't make the mistake that He only means the big things either. Often it's the little things that mean the most—like the phone call we said we'd make, the card we said we'd write, the party we said we'd go to, or the small favor we promised to do.

Just try and remember the times you've been disappointed when someone hasn't followed through on what they told you they would do. That helps motivate you to watch what you promise and then do what you promise.

Pray with me:
God, help us to think before we speak and to put forth the effort to do what we promise—whether it's a big thing or a small thing. Amen.

Clean Underwear, Wild Elephants and the Princess

August 27th

A Heavenly Resource

"I sought the Lord, and he heard me, And delivered me from my fears." Psalm 34:4 (NKJ)

When you were a little girl you were very timid, quite a contrast to your brother who was seldom afraid of anything. You didn't like the dark; you weren't keen on trying new things, and you were always afraid something was going to happen to me. All the reassuring I tried didn't seem to help much. I even encouraged you to ask God to take your fears away, but you continued to hang on to them for a long time. Then, almost overnight it seemed, you became much more confident in yourself and your fears seemed to start subsiding. I never knew what made the difference, but I guess I like to think that God answered your prayers.

I often ask God to help me with my fears and to help me through situations that I feel I need his help. I uttered one of those prayers this week when I knew I had to make a presentation that I wasn't sure would be received as it was planned. I hope you will always remember that prayers can be uttered at any time, at any place, for any purpose. Isn't that a wonderful resource? Don't forget to use it!

Pray with me:
Thank you, God, for being there when we need you. Help us remember that we're never alone, even in times of our greatest fears. Amen.

Patty B. Williams

August 28th

Clean Underwear

"But of that day and hour no one knows, not even the angels of heaven, but my Father only." Matthew: 24:36 (NKJ)

There is a funny age-old saying that supposedly mothers have always told their children: "always wear clean underwear because you never know when you might be in a car accident!" Kind of funny don't you think? Can't you just see it in the emergency room, commotion everywhere, broken limbs, blood, and the doctor, in the midst of it all, stops and exclaims, "would you look at this dirty underwear?" I don't think so!

I have been thinking, however, since my friend T.C. had his sudden stroke, how his and Carol's lives have now changed so drastically. It happened over night. That's a scary thought, isn't it? Yet we all know it could happen to us. We never know when an accident may occur, a sickness may put us in bed forever, or when our life or that of someone's we love may end. That's why God tells us to be prepared. Try not to have any regrets for the way you've lived life or treated people. Don't wait until tomorrow to do those things you know you need to do today. You're on a good path, Brookie Bear, of having no major regrets. I hope you will continue that path. (and remember, clean underwear does make your mother happy!)

Pray with me:
Lord, keep us mindful of what we say and don't say, do and don't do, so we will have no regrets in this life or in life hereafter. Amen

Clean Underwear, Wild Elephants and the Princess

August 29th

Jen

"Bear one another's burdens, and so fulfill the law of Christ."
Galatians 6:2 (NKJ)

One of the things that endeared Jen to me was the night she came over and brought you ice cream when she knew you had had a bad day. What a friend, what a sweet, and thoughtful thing to do. She was ready to share your burden, just like you have done for her in her times of need. That's what God intended us to do, yet so often we let other priorities and what others may think get in our way. I hope you will always remember how special that act of friendship was. It will help you one day make a special effort to do the same for someone else who may need someone to share their burden.

Pray with me:
Thank you, God, for those special friends in our lives who make us feel better just by their presence and willingness to help us through difficult times. We are blessed. Amen

"Brooke and Jen"

Patty B. Williams

August 30th

Pre-marital Sex

"I say then: Walk in the Spirit and you shall not fulfill the lust of the flesh." Galatians 5:16 (NKJ)

Not that you haven't already been faced with this decision, but college life will offer many more opportunities for you to make the decision about pre-marital sex. Sometimes it will be an easy decision and sometimes it won't—and for more reasons than just lust or love. I remember being totally shocked hearing a few of my sorority sisters talk about their sexual experiences, like it was no big deal. I also remember not being asked to a fraternity week-end because I wouldn't be as much "fun" as another date would be. I also remember being curious about all the "hype" and thinking maybe I was making a big deal out of waiting for marriage when it wasn't really that important to wait. I know things are different now from what they were when I was your age, but I don't think God's thinking has changed on the subject. As I've told you a million times, I never had to wonder why a guy asked me out. I still dated good-looking, popular guys, had a great college life, and married someone who cared that I waited. I don't think I was able to do that alone. I asked for spiritual help. I hope you won't forget that resource.

Pray with me:
Lord, you know we are weak in mind and body, especially when we want to be loved, accepted and popular. Help us to ask for the strength that only you can give to help us make the decisions you would have us to make. Amen

Clean Underwear, Wild Elephants and the Princess

August 31st
(Ashley's Birthday)

The Heart Doesn't Lie

"He made their hearts. He understands everything they do."
Psalm 33:15 (NCV)

Do you sometimes have your friends misunderstand what you say or do, or have you sometimes put a lot of effort in making something for someone and they don't seem to truly appreciate it? And, what about you, have you sometimes misunderstood what one of your friends or a family member has said and then found out later that what you thought they meant wasn't accurate at all? Well, that's pretty normal. Just remember, no one can deceive God. It's what's in your heart that really matters. That doesn't mean you don't need to work on your skills to better explain yourself if you are often misunderstood, or if you often misunderstand others. What it does mean is that you should always try to look in someone's heart rather than just hear the words that are said, or judge what is seen but not understood. I've heard that "the heart doesn't lie." Unfortunately, it sure can get us in a mess sometimes, can't it?

Pray with me:
Father, help us to avoid jumping to conclusions too quickly. Help us instead to look within to see the heart part first and then continue our assessment of what someone has said or done. Amen

Patty B. Williams

September 1ˢᵗ

Proud Parents

"I will tell of your goodness. I will praise you every day."
Psalm 35: 28 (NCV)

I know you are looking forward to being a mother one day, and I cannot begin to tell you the joys that will bring. Of course there will be difficult times, but the good will far outweigh the bad. You and Michael have given your dad and me so much to be proud of, and I don't think either of us takes that for granted, even though I'm sure you've both had days you questioned that. You always used to get embarrassed when you knew I used stories about you when I gave talks or Sunday School lessons. What you didn't understand most of the time was how I used those stories to "sing praises" about you. That's what proud parents do! I anxiously await you to experience that one day too—but not too soon.

Pray with me:
Thank you, God, for the experience of parenting—for the joys it brings and the opportunity for children and parents to grow together in love and understanding. Amen

September 2nd

Date Rape

"But she answered him, "No, my brother, do not force me, for no such thing should be done in Israel. Do not do this disgraceful thing."
2 Samuel 13:12 (NKJ)

I am amazed as I study the Bible how much the things that happened in Biblical times were so much like what happens in our present day time. This verse is from a story about a princess named Tamar who was raped by someone she assumed she could trust. It was a horrible experience for her, much like the horrifying experience of those who in our day are victims of date rape by someone they thought they could trust.

You, of course, are a princess to many, and God forbid that you should ever have to experience such a terrible act. If I, or your dad, or your brother, or your granddaddy could protect you forever, we would, but you know that is not possible. Please be careful of the situations you place yourself in, and remember emotions and alcohol are not good mixers, even with the nicest of young men who, under ordinary circumstances, may be trustworthy.

Pray with me:
Oh, Lord, keep us safe and make us wise in all situations. Give us courage and skill to defend ourselves if necessary and the wisdom to distance ourselves from precarious (dangerous) situations. Amen

Patty B. Williams

September 3rd
(The day, 18 years ago, when you were supposed to be born)

Making Mistakes

"For we all stumble in many things. If anyone does not stumble in work, he is a perfect man, able to bridle the whole body." James 3:2 (NKJ)

This is a given—you are going to make mistakes (stumble). Some mistakes will be big, some small. Some will embarrass you; some will make you angry with yourself; and some will make you feel guilty and ashamed. All will hopefully make you grow in some way.

I hope you will gain confidence enough in yourself and in God's word to believe that it's o.k. to stumble. I think maturity exemplifies itself in how we handle the mistake. Do you have the courage to apologize, the sense of humor to laugh at yourself, the faith to ask God for forgiveness? We will never be perfect; so don't be too hard on yourself when imperfections show up every now and then. Just learn from them. Do what you must to get over it, and move forward.

Pray with me:
God, you know we are a long way from perfection. Help us to strive for it, but not judge ourselves too harshly when we fail. Amen.

September 4th

Work

"The soul of a lazy man desires and has nothing; But the soul of the diligent shall be made rich." Proverbs 13:4 (NKJ)

From the time you were a little girl, you've always been busy doing something. You played for hours in your little kitchen and spent hours "teaching" all your baby dolls. You and Weston designed and ran your offices and built forts and houses in the backyard with pine straw and whatever other materials you could fine. You looked for jobs to make money—selling muffins, lemonade and giving backrubs. You've never been lazy—maybe a little lax in making up beds, cleaning your room and the bathroom, but not lazy.

You've had good examples of hard workers in our family, and I hope they will always be an inspiration for you. Remember there are riches to be found in feeling good about your work and what you accomplish, and those riches are often times more valuable than the money you'll make doing the work.

Pray with me:
Thank you, Lord, for the ability to work and to accomplish things for which we can be proud. Amen.

Patty B. Williams

September 5th
(The day your dad and I were married in 1970)

Walk With The Wise

"He who walks with wise men will be wise, but the companion of fools will be destroyed." Proverbs 13:20 (NKJ)

As we learned over the last few years, there are all kinds of friends, and sometimes those "friends" turn out to be so only in name. You have had wise friends who have been good influences and friends who have acted foolishly and not been good influences. You have probably learned something from both.

As unfair as it may be, you are often judged by the company you keep, and may also take on the mannerisms, speech and actions of the company you keep, so choose your friends carefully. That doesn't mean you shouldn't try to befriend those who are less "wise" than you, because how will they ever become "wise" if they never have the opportunity to walk with those wiser than themselves? You know what I mean. I am proud that you have had many different kinds of friends, and I am certain that your influence has been positive on each one.

Pray with me:
Lord, help us to choose companions carefully, to walk with those who are positive influences, and to be a positive influence on others in all that we do. Amen.

September 6th

God And I Together

"But Jesus looked at them and said, 'with men it is impossible, but not with God; for with God all things are possible'." Mark 10:27 (NKJ)

You will often find yourself in situations that you just do not think you can handle—physically, mentally, or emotionally. And, if the truth be known, you will probably be right. Look at the suicide statistics, the drug statistics, the number of divorces, domestic violence, etc. to see how poorly society handles adversity.

Isn't it a shame, too, that we wait so long to ask for help from the one person that we've been told can make all things possible. I am convinced that God has helped me through many heartaches and hard times, times I hope you never have to experience. Just know, however, that if you do experience those hard times, there's always extra strength to be found as close by as a prayer.

Pray with me:
God help us in our hour of need. Help us remember that all things are possible with you. Amen.

September 7th

Faith

"I tell you the truth. You must accept the Kingdom of God as a little child accepts things, or you will never enter it." Mark 10:15 (NCV)

This verse is really talking about faith, that little word that has such big expectations. It's that word that gives Granddaddy such a difficult time when it comes to believing in God. It's that word that often causes heartache when it is attached to people.

Think about it, though, where would we be without it? Would we worry every minute if we didn't have faith that tomorrow would come? What if we didn't have faith that people, for the most part, are decent and will do the right thing? And, when we're going through our most difficult times, where would we be if we couldn't have faith that things will get better?

Don't look for all the answers. You won't find them. Just look for the evidence that the faith you have is worthy of your risk and build from there. Look for the evidence of God all around you. Look for the evidence in the outpouring of love and actions from people who love and care about you. Look at the faith in a baby's arms reaching up and know that God gave a good example of how our faith should be.

Pray with me:
God, you know how easy it is for our faith to waiver. Please keep us on the right track. Amen.

September 8th

Greed

"Then Jesus said to them, Be careful and guard against all kinds of greed. A man's life is not measured by the many things he owns." Luke 12:15 (NCV)

What is it that we think would make us better than we are, more popular, classier, prettier, in a higher social status? Do you think that Honda Prelude would do it? How about a beach condo or a mountain cabin? How about a new outfit every two or three weeks? They do all sound nice, don't they?

Is it wrong to wish for all those things? I don't think so; it's just that I think God wants us to look at what we already have and not be too greedy—especially when there are so many with so little. I think he wants our primary focus to be on the things that really matter—like how we live, and how we love, and how much we really care about others. Just food for thought . . .

Pray with me:
God, we are truly blessed with so many things. Thank you. Help us to remember those who have much less, and keep us focused on the things that are truly important in your eyes. Amen.

Patty B. Williams

September 9th

Fruit

"Thus also faith by itself, if it does not have works, is dead."
James 2:17 (NKJ)

A recent devotion was about faith and its importance in life. Unfortunately, the trap some people fall in is thinking that as long as they have faith that's all it takes. I don't personally believe that. I believe that if you truly have faith in God and in people that you try to show that in your daily life by the way you live and the way you treat others. That doesn't mean we won't fail at times and sometimes we'll fail miserably, but at least the effort to try and try again should be there. Just like the tree that shows its worth by the fruit it bears, we must show our faith by the fruit we bear. That "fruit" is the type life we live and the way we treat others.

Pray with me:
Father, help us to exemplify faith in our daily works. Help us to live our faith instead of just talking about it. Amen.

Clean Underwear, Wild Elephants and the Princess

September 10th

Anxiety

"Anxiety in the heart of man causes depression, but a good word makes it glad." Proverbs 12:25 (NKJ)

As a little girl you never did too well with things that caused anxiety. Remember in elementary school when you ended up in the hospital with an asthma attack? I always attributed that, in part, to what was going on in your schoolroom with your teacher. She was a strong disciplinarian and would yell at some of the kids at times, and it frightened you. Once I talked to her though and she realized how she was coming across to the kids, she made changes, and you and she became best friends by the end of the year.

More recently, the anxieties you suffered in the last couple of years with broken relationships and broken friendships could have led to depression, but fortunately you had "good words," encouragement and support from others that obviously helped ease the heartache.

I hope you will always guard against letting anxieties build up to the point of causing unhappiness or depression. Use your head and your resources to help you through tough times.

Pray with me:
Thank you, Lord, for those who help us through hard times. Help us to remember also that others need words of encouragement at times too. Amen.

September 11th

Suffering For Doing Right

"Yet if anyone suffers as a Christian, let him not be ashamed, but let him glorify God in this matter." 1 Peter 4:16 (NKJ)

There will be times in the near future, as there already have been in the past, when you will suffer for doing what is right. There will also be times when you will question if it's worth your effort. I wish I could protect you from those times, but, of course, I can't.

I have been proud of the maturity you have shown in many of the situations where you have chosen the right thing to do over the easiest or more comfortable thing. I know those times were difficult, and I know I probably didn't acknowledge that as well as I should have. I'm sorry. I hope, however, that you never regret those decisions or the same type decisions you will make in the future.

God knew we would have to suffer at times for being His children; that's why he warned us. My prayer is that He will always give you peace in the right decisions and will tug at your heart when you start to make the wrong ones.

Pray with me:
Give us courage, Lord, to make right decisions even when it's difficult. Keep us headed in the right direction even when the road gives us many different turns from which to choose. Amen.

September 12th

Gossip

"But I say to you that for every idle word men may speak, they will give account of it in the day of judgement." Matthew 12:36 (NKJ)

Gossip or careless remarks can lead to so much hurt, disappointment, embarrassment, and sometimes broken relationships. Why is it so easy for us to participate in it at times? I wish I could say I never have, but I have, and sometimes I still do. Each time I feel guilty afterwards. I have to keep mindful, on a daily basis, to think before I speak, to decide if it's appropriate to "pass along" something I think or have heard—even if it's true. Will it hurt someone? What am I trying to accomplish by passing something along. Are my motives honorable? Would I say the same thing if the person were standing beside me? What if Jesus was standing beside me—whoa, now that's a different perspective! Anyway, it's something to think about, especially since God tells us that we will be held accountable—not just for one or two things we might say, but for every word. That's a big responsibility.

Pray with me:
God, you know our weaknesses and you know our hearts. Help the words we speak be reflective of what you put in our hearts. Amen.

Patty B. Williams

September 13th

Tithing

"For they all put in out of their abundance, but she out of her poverty put in all that she had, her whole livelihood." Mark 12:44 (NKJ)

You probably remember this scripture; it's from the story about the scribes who out of their arrogance gave a lot of money as an offering to God. The widow, on the other hand, who had very little, gave only pennies. The difference is that what she gave was all she had. The question, of course, is who gave the most?

I have told you many stories over the years about my experience with tithing. I think it is important, as well as what God has told us to do. It teaches discipline, budgeting, and giving for a purpose that supports others rather than just ourselves. I am still not giving in the amount I would like to be giving, but I try to be faithful in what I do give. You can start small; God will be happy with that first step—even if it's pennies. He's more interested in the spirit in which you do it. I'm going to work harder at it. I know he'll reward my efforts. I hope you will think about it.

Pray with me:
Thank you, God, for all the many wonderful blessings you have bestowed upon us. Help us remember to give back that which is needed to do your work. Amen.

Clean Underwear, Wild Elephants and the Princess

September 14th

Mr. Irwin

"The sun has one kind of beauty. The moon has another beauty, and the stars have another. And each star is different in its beauty."
1 Corinthians 5:41 (NCV)

I went to Mr. Irwin's funeral today (9/8). It was a nice service. He must have been a loved man, beautiful in his own way. I sat there thinking how I wish I had known him better. The minister talked about his sweet spirit and his ever-ready smile for everyone he met. What a nice compliment. I hope I can be described like that one day because I believe that's how God intended us to be.

I wonder if today was our last day if we would be pleased with what could be said about us. I guess I hope I have a little more time. I think I have some work to do!

Pray with me:
Lord, thank you for those who walk among us with sweet spirits. Help us to learn from them and then pass it on. Amen.

Patty B. Williams

September 15th

Living Within Your Means

"Pay everyone, then, what you owe him. If you owe any kind of tax, pay it." Romans 13:7 (NCV)

Don't you just hate to have to think about money all the time? Isn't it sad that it so often takes money to make us happy?

Debts are a bummer, too, aren't they, even though they are necessary at times? Usually, however, they are of our own making simply because we think we need something before we can really afford it.

I think the goal should be to keep debts at a minimum. Then you don't create extra stress you don't need. Strive to live within your means, and strive even harder to pay your debts whatever they might be. We are directed by God to do so, even though we may not be legally responsible to do so.

Pray with me:
God, please help money to be a blessing and not a curse. Help us to be good managers of everything we have. Amen.

Clean Underwear, Wild Elephants and the Princess

September 16th
(Aunt Vicki's birthday)

Freedom

"I am allowed to do all things. But all things are not good for me to do. I am allowed to do all things. But I must not do those things that will make me their slaves." 1 Corinthians 6:12 (NCV)

Freedom, that thing we long for so long. We look forward to what freedoms we'll get once we get to a certain point. When we are adolescents we look forward to the freedoms we'll have when we're teenagers. When we're teenagers, we look forward to the freedoms a car will bring when we reach 16. At 18 the freedom to see adult movies and walk in to a bar, even though we can't drink, is so appealing. The freedom to move away from home and make our own rules—gosh, what could be better? Then the ultimate—21, the time we become adults. We can make our own decisions, live our own life. Isn't it interesting that God gave us freedom long before we ever got to those certain points in our life? The problem is, of course, that there are consequences when you decide to exercise some freedoms. I guess our decision is whether the freedom is worth the consequence.

Some consequences are longer term and more severe than others, as you well know. I guess my hope is that you will always weigh your freedoms carefully. You have a good head on your shoulders and a good conscience. Use them both wisely.

Pray with me:
Lord it's so difficult at times to do the things we should and not do the things we shouldn't. When we're weak, help us, and when we're strong, help us to help others. Amen.

Patty B. Williams

September 17th
(Deborah's and Pop Bigham's Birthday)

Managing Your Time

"A time to weep, and a time to laugh; a time to mourn, and a time to dance." Ecclesiastes 3:4 (NKJ)

Have you learned how to manage your time yet? It's not easy, is it? I read something not long ago in my *Women's Study Bible* that might help.

"In managing your time, first, acknowledge that you have time—the same amount God has given to everyone. You, with God's help, must determine how to use it. Don't make the mistake of letting others decide your priorities and make your schedule. Remember that by using small bits of time faithfully, you can accomplish great things." I think "small bits of time faithfully" could be called discipline—such a tough thing, but so important. I hope you are working at mastering it.

Pray with me:
God, when we hear all the fun things calling our name, help us to remember that discipline is important. Help us become a master of our time so it doesn't become a master over us. Amen

Clean Underwear, Wild Elephants and the Princess

September 18th
(Uncle Robert's birthday)

Goodie Two-Shoes

"Those who do right do not have to fear the rulers. But people who do wrong must fear them. Do you want to be unafraid of the rulers? Then do what is right, and the ruler will praise you." Romans 13:3 (NCV)

"Goodie Two-shoes," that's what you called me, didn't you? I think that's how you pictured my years as a teenager. I guess in some respects you were right. I didn't get in to a lot of mischief that amounted to anything of great significance. Yeah, I skipped school and went to the lake. Of course I got caught, I went out and rode around with Richard when he wasn't supposed to be at my house. Phyllis and I sneaked out one night to meet Donald and Doug and, heaven forbid, I even drank too much beer at the Sig Ep house with Mike one time. Are you dying laughing at all the "bad" stuff I did? Well, actually, I'm not sure it was as much as being a "Goodie Two-shoes" as it was being a "chicken." I was always afraid of getting caught and afraid of what Mother and Daddy would say or do. I much preferred praises over being scolded. Choices, I guess that's what it comes down to, whether you're a teenager or an adult. I hope the decisions you make always include thoughts of the consequences. Sometimes the risk will be worth the fun, sometimes the price of getting caught won't be worth the risk. (the lake was worth the risk). Choose wisely!

Pray with me:
Thank you, Lord, for the freedom of choice. Help us remember that sometimes it's better to be a Goodie Two-shoes than have the burden of fear hanging over us. Amen

Patty B. Williams

September 19th

Rememberences Of You

"I thank my God every time I remember you." Philippians 1:3 (NCV)

I saw my boss's new baby last week. It brought back memories of you as a baby. I was so thrilled to have a little girl. I truly thought God gave you to me as a special gift. You brought such joy to a heart that had been hurting. Your dad and I were going through such difficult times. I'm not sure what I would have done without you. Michael adored you, too. I remember the pictures of the neighborhood kids coming over and Michael showing you off. You were a pretty baby. You even had hair. Then when you became a little girl, you liked all the little girl things, baby dolls, dresses, playing house and dressing up. I couldn't have designed you better if I had done it myself.

I read something in the paper last week that a mother had said to her daughter when the daughter asked if she was an "accident." The mother said, "an accident is a car wreck. You were a gift." I agree with her whole-heartedly. You weren't planned by your dad or me, but you were surely no accident. You were a wonderful gift sent straight from heaven!

Pray with me:
Father, we are so thankful that you are the master planner and not us. Help us to remember that when we are surprised along life's way. Amen

September 20th

Making A Difference

"Your love must be real. Hate what is evil. Hold on to what is good." Romans 12:9 (NCV)

There are things in life that you will see, hear and/or feel that will hurt, make you angry, or break your heart. Some of those things you have already experienced. Many of the things you won't be able to do much about. Others you will be able to do your small part that may make some difference. I think the important thing is for you not to give up or think your small part doesn't matter. It matters in God's eyes.

Race relations, world hunger, indifference to social problems, fear of getting involved, fear of taking a stand, where would we be in these issues if no one had ever done their small part in making a difference? Be realistic enough to know that you can't change or fix everyone or everything, but always remember that what you can do is important and it will make a difference somewhere along the way.

Pray with me:
Teach us, Lord, to be strong in our convictions, for our love to be real in all things we do and in all the lives we touch. Amen

Patty B. Williams

September 21st

Fixing Things

"But without faith it is impossible to please Him, for he who comes to God must believe that He is, and that He is a rewarder of those who diligently seek Him." Hebrews 11:6 (NKJ)

You know the struggles I have been through recently trying to "fix" all the things that are not right between Bill and me. Sometimes I think I'm so smart, and yet time and time again I end up more frustrated, more hurt, and more exhausted in spirit. Why am I such a slow learner? There are things that I cannot fix, no matter how hard I try or how sincere my efforts might be. Those are the times when I have to have faith to let go and let God take care of the situation. The following is one of my favorite writings. I hope you'll take its message to heart and be quicker to learn than I. I don't know who the author is, but he knew what he was writing about.

As children bring their broken toys with tears for us to mend, I brought my broken dreams to Him because he was my friend. But then, instead of leaving Him in peace to work alone, I hung around and tried to help with ways that were my own. At last I snatched them back and cried, "How can you be so slow?" "My child, " He said, "What could I do—you never did let go."

Pray with me:
God, help us to always do our part to fix what can be fixed, but when it's time to give it to you, help us to let go and trust you to fix it for us. Amen

September 22nd

Listening

"Pay attention to me and answer me. I am troubled and upset . . . ."
Psalm 55:2 (NCV)

"Listening without observing is like getting the words of a song without the music."

The above came from a Personnel Management booklet I read one time. Think about what it means. It's a great statement. How many times have you listened to people and missed the true meaning of what they were saying because you weren't paying attention or looking at them. Remember when you recently told me something that your dad said, and you told me you could tell he really cared because of the look on his face? When someone says something to you in anger, but he has tears in his eyes, doesn't that say something different than if he said the same thing with his teeth clinched and a frown on his face?

The greatest feeling anyone can have is to know that someone really hears what he or she is saying. Try to develop that skill and practice it on a routine basis. It will help you in friendships, in relationships with guys, in your marriage, with your children one day, and in your career. You already have a good start. Keep up the good work!

Pray with me:
Thank you, God, for ears to hear. Help us to remember to use our eyes and heart to truly listen. Amen

Patty B. Williams

September 23rd
(Uncle Billy's Birthday)

Uncle Billy

Later, the Lord said to Cain, "Where is your brother, Abel?" Cain answered, "I don't know. Is it my job to take care of my brother?" Genesis 4:9 (NCV)

I remember the night Billy was born. Mary Jane and I were so excited. We were at Honey's and Daddy Hardee's house, and I remember Daddy Hardee getting on to us for talking and not going to sleep. I remember Regina and I dressing him up like a girl when he was a little boy, and I remember how I looked forward to his coming to see me when I was away at college even though he was eight years my junior. I remember being excited watching him playing football in high school, and I remember Daddy with tears in his eyes, hurting for him when his engagement was broken three weeks before he was to be married. I remember how much he has always loved you and Michael and how he has celebrated with me in times of joy and supported me during times of sorrow. I remember at Bill's and my wedding when he told everyone, in a toast, that I was not only his sister but his best friend. That meant so much to me. I will always remember it. I celebrate this day of his birth. I know you do, too. I hope you and Michael will grow to have the same close relationship as we have shared.

Pray with me:
Thank you, God, for big and little brothers. Keep us mindful that we are our brothers' keepers, just as they are ours. Keep us close in relationship and in spirit. Amen

September 24th

Call My Dad

"Good sense will protect you. Understanding will guard you."
Proverbs 2:11 (NCV)

I have this little "ditty" in my journal book I keep that has some of my favorite writings in it. You may find it useful one day. I'm sure Ann Landers wouldn't mind your using it if necessary.

When our daughters reached dating age, we told them some boys would be gentlemen and others would be out for whatever they could get. If the girls ever felt backed into a corner, we instructed them to give the boy a dime and tell him, "Call my dad." "If he says what you're suggesting is o.k. with him, then it's o.k. with me."

Of course, you'd have to have at least a quarter these days, but it's a good thought! It would certainly break the tension of the moment, and if nothing else, it would give you both a chance to regroup your thinking.

Pray with me:
God, when we get in situations that are uncomfortable or dangerous, help us to use our heads before we risk hurting our hearts, our bodies, or others. Amen

Patty B. Williams

September 25th

Walking To The Edge

"Remember that I commanded you to be strong and brave. So don't be afraid. The Lord your God will be with you everywhere you go." Joshua 1:9 (NCV)

"When you walk to the edge of all the light you have and take that first step into the darkness of the unknown, you must believe that one of two things will happen: There will be something solid for you to stand upon, or you will be taught how to fly." (Patrick Overton)

This was framed and a gift I gave Nicole for graduation. I thought it was perfect considering what she was about to do with her life. I copied it because I really liked it. Now, each time I read it I realize how meaningful it is for any of us. We all are faced with the unknown at some time or another. If we only tackled those things we were comfortable with or familiar with, we'd never grow, would we? Even though I was not happy when you went to Wyoming, I was so proud of you for having the courage to do it. We grew a lot, didn't we?

Pray with me:
Lord, give us courage to learn how to fly, even when it's scary or difficult. Help us to use our head when learning and remember that you are there to hold our hand when we ask. Amen

Clean Underwear, Wild Elephants and the Princess

September 26th

Worrying

"So don't worry about tomorrow. Each day has enough trouble of its own. Tomorrow will have its own worries." Matthew 6:34 (NCV)

Are you worried about something? Can you do anything about it? If you can, then get on with it so you can stop worrying about it. If you can't, then ask God to help you have peace about it so you can spend your time more wisely.

Worry can zap a lot of energy from you. It can make you crazy. It can make you a grouch, and it can eventually make you sick. Now does that make a lot of sense? I don't think so.

Our greatest authority tells us not to worry, and who are we to question that wisdom? I hope you don't. You have much more meaningful things to do than worry. Do the best you can with a situation, and then let it go.

Pray with me.
Keep us doing what we need to do, Lord, so we don't set ourselves up for worry. Grant us peace when we've done all we can do. Amen

Patty B. Williams

September 27th

Constructive Criticism

"The person who accepts correction is on the way to life." But the person who ignores correction will be ruined." Proverbs 10:17 (NCV)

I hope you will always accept constructive criticism with grace and wisdom even though it will not always be comfortable or pleasant. In light of all we think we know, we still have so much more to learn, and sometimes others really do know how to do things better than we do. That's hard to accept at times, especially when it comes from someone we might not particularly like. Try, however, not to let your personal feelings get in the way of your good sense. Use all the good advice you can to your advantage. It will help you become a better, smarter person and, in turn, put you in a position to help someone else.

Pray with me:
Lord, help us not to let our foolish pride get in the way of accepting correction when we deserve it or need it. Help us to be smart enough to appreciate it and then, when the opportunity arises, pass it on to help someone else. Amen

Clean Underwear, Wild Elephants and the Princess

September 28th

Devils And Angels

"The Lord's eyes see everything that happens. He watches both evil and good people." Proverbs 15:3 (NCV)

One of my favorite stories about you was when you were about ten years old. You had been begging me to let you shave your legs and I told you you couldn't shave them until you were twelve. Then one day when you were at your dad's, either he or Mary, or both of them gave you permission to go ahead and shave them. That must have been terrible torture for you, because you knew I told you you had to wait.

Well, I guess your conscience was working because you didn't do it. Later, when you were telling me about it, you said, "Momma, it was just like in the movies, I had a devil on one shoulder saying, do it, do it, and I had an angel on the other shoulder saying, don't do it, don't do it. Of course, I had to keep a straight face, but I was so tickled and I did tell you you made the right decision.

I always pray that you, Michael, Amy and Obie will always have that angel jumping up and down or your shoulder or at least tugging at your heartstrings if you get headed in the wrong direction. Keep watch!

Pray with me:
God, we know right from wrong, but sometimes we have a tough time making the right choice. Keep us headed in the direction you would have us go. Amen

Patty B. Williams

September 29th

Life Is Tough Sometimes

"Cast your burden on the Lord, And he shall sustain you . . ."
Psalm 55:22 (NKJ)

I received an "E-mail" from Mary Jane today. This was one of the scriptures she sent me. She knew I was going to have a difficult day. She knew I was hurting and she wanted to give me some comforting words. I told her I would try to take them to heart instead of just reading them.

Life is really tough sometimes, and there are many times we don't understand God's plan. That's when we have to trust that he will take care of us when we aren't strong enough to take care of ourselves.

Don't ever be ashamed or too prideful to admit you are having a tough time, that you need help, or you just need a hug. God sends his angels and assistance in many forms—a sister, a brother, *a daughter*, a friend, a story, a day at the beach. All you have to do is ask and remember that he will take care of you.

Pray with me:
Father, you know when we hurt and when we need the strength you can provide. Help us to remember that you are as close as our knees. Amen

Clean Underwear, Wild Elephants and the Princess

September 30th

Recognizing Dreams

"Behold, children are a heritage from the Lord, The fruit of the womb is a reward. Like arrows in the hand of a warrior, So are the children of one's youth." Psalm 127: 3-4 (NKJ)

What an awesome experience to recognize your dreams being played out in front of your eyes, to see the terrific results of what you've worked for over the years. That's what I felt when I sat at the KD House and watched your sorority skits and watched you interact with your new friends, their parents, and your own family. I was overwhelmed with feelings of joy and excitement for who you've become and the possibilities I know lie ahead for you. I kept a lump in my throat and a tear in my eye all morning.

This is not meant to be one of those "mushy" devotionals, but it is one that is sincere. Remember that country song by Garth Brooks, *If Tomorrow Never Comes, Will She Know How Much I Loved Her*? I hope and pray that you and Michael will never have any question about how much you were loved and how proud you both have made me. I am a very blessed Mommy!

Pray with me:
God, for realized dreams we give you thanks and for future possibilities we ask your blessing. Keep us on the path you have prepared for us. Amen

Patty B. Williams

October 1st

Richard

Dear friends, we should love each other, because love comes from God." 1 John 4:7 (NCV)

Today is the birthday of my first love, the one I wrote poems about, laughed with, dreamed about, agonized over and still remember fondly. What a wonderful time of innocence and memory building. What a tremendous feeling to love and be loved, even if it doesn't end up the same way it started. Maybe it only ends in a sweet memory. Surely that's not so bad.

Hopefully you will have a lot of different relationships on your way to that perfect one. Don't miss out on any of them because of fear of being hurt. Don't miss "the dance." Sometimes the dance makes the sweetest memory.

Pray with me:
Thank you, Lord, for those people who will always hold a special place in our hearts. Let our sweet memories stay fresh so that we may encourage others to make their own. Amen

Clean Underwear, Wild Elephants and the Princess

The Dance

Patty B. Williams

October 2nd

The Spirit Within Us

"When life is good, enjoy it. But when life is hard, remember: God gives us good times and hard times. And no one knows what tomorrow will bring." Ecclesiastes 7:14 (NCV)

As I sit and watch the country music awards, it's amazing how many stories are told in a song, and it's amazing how many of those songs fit so many people. Aren't we so much alike to be so different? We make the same mistakes; we have the same type heartaches; we want the same things—the perfect guy, the perfect lady, the perfect love; we experience the same temptations—the songs say it all.

What's so interesting is how we handle things so differently. What makes the difference? Don't we all hurt equally, desire love the same, agonize over temptations alike? I think we do for the most part. I have to think that the difference is where we've been, how we feel about ourselves, and the place we are spiritually.

I know the places you've been. I know you don't think as much of yourself as you should, and I've seen you grow spiritually over the last few years. I hope, of course that you don't have to experience a lot of those things they sing about in the country songs, but when you do, and you surely will experience some of them, I hope you will handle them with all the resources I know you have. I'll be pulling for you!

Pray with me:
God, thank you for the blessings we've had from the places we've been and the growth we've experienced while we were there. Help us to use them to our advantage. Amen

October 3rd

Little Eyes

"Children are a gift from the Lord . . . ." Psalms 127:3 (NCV)

Tonight I am staying with Adam and Alyssa while their mom is at class and their dad is out of town. Alyssa wants to type you a note—*Hi, Brooke, how are you doing? I got my ears pierced. I have pink ice earrings.*

We tried to get Adam to type you a note, but he said since we weren't going to get rich with this book, he didn't want to type anything! Alyssa said to tell you that he really wants to marry you, but he didn't want to tell you!

Kids, aren't they wonderful? The laughter, the innocence, the potential—my, what an awesome responsibility we have as family and friends to help God's children grow. You and Michael have been fortunate to have so many people in your lives that have cared about you and positively influenced your growth. I hope your children are as blessed.

Remember, little eyes are often watching every move you make and little ears listening to every word you utter. Try to keep that in mind when they're around. You'll be surprised what an influence you can have.

Pray with me:
Thank you, God, for children and for the added joy they bring into our lives. Keep us mindful of their needs and our influence in the smallest things we say and do. Amen

Patty B. Williams

October 4th

Fall

"Give thanks to the Lord and pray to him. Tell the nations what he has done." Psalms 105:1 (NCV)

Fall is in the air. I can feel it. Do you remember that it's my favorite time of year? I love the leaves falling and changing colors. I just can't seem to get enough of it. It's amazing to me in all of life's disorder, all the things that we have going on, all the everyday ins and outs, that God can bring us back to serenity with a falling leaf or a faint hint of autumn briskness.

It's too bad that we sometimes get so wrapped up in living life that we forget to slow down enough to make that life worth living. I don't think that's the way God planned it. I think He wants us to work hard, but also wants us to take time to enjoy the beautiful world he created and the folks he put here to take care of it. You know I want you to do well in school, but I also want you to do well in life, so remember to balance your time. Study that Algebra, but every now and then, run outside and catch a leaf!

Pray with me:
Thank you, Lord, for all you have given us to enjoy, especially the fall! Help us to show our thankfulness by taking time to appreciate the beauty of the seasons and the beauty of your people. Amen

October 5th

Different Friends

"Lord, you have made many things. With your wisdom you made them all. The earth is full of your riches." Psalms 104:24 (NCV)

Last night I had a variety of my friends at a little party. Since they were friends from different "walks" of my life, I took a minute to introduce each of them to one another and tell how they each fit into my life. A nurse, an artist, an office manager, an administrator, a neighbor, an old roommate, a co-worker—all friends, but all very different, each touching my life in some way.

It was a fun evening. The party was a pre-Christmas get-to-gether to look at Christmas gifts and order the ones we wanted. The toys were especially fun. We laughed and talked so much the demonstrator could hardly get a word in edgewise. We also had lots of good fattening stuff to eat. It was just great.

Different friends from different backgrounds, different interests, different circumstances in their lives, but we could still come together and share laughter, food, and a good time. It's too bad the world can't be more accepting of differences, isn't it? We need to foster that idea every opportunity we get. Just like anything else, it's up to us to do our part. I hope you are as fortunate as I have been to have a variety of friends. It will brighten your life.

Pray with me:
Thank you, God, for all types of friends. Help us to learn something different from each one. Help us to love all of them in the way you have taught us. Amen

Patty B. Williams

October 6th

Aunt Dolly

"There are godly people in the world. I enjoy them." Psalm 16:3 (NCV)

Who are the people in your life that you look up to in admiration for their demeanor (outward behavior, conduct)? Do you think they have influenced you or made a difference in your life? You know Aunt Dolly has always been like a second Mother to me, kind of like Gloria was to you for many years. I don't ever remember a time when Aunt Dolly raised her voice or was too busy to help someone that needed her. I've always known that I was special to her, like you are to Gloria, but there is more to Aunt Dolly than just the way she has cared about me. She cares about others, too. I always thought she tried to do the right thing and tried to teach us to do the right thing, too. She didn't have bad things to say about people, she was a good mother, she could make great fried toast, and she went to church. I thought she was godly—still do. She holds a special place in my heart, just as Gloria does in yours.

Pray with me:
Father, today we ask you to watch over those special people in our lives. Keep them safe and help them to know that they are loved for who they are and for what they mean to us. Amen

Clean Underwear, Wild Elephants and the Princess

October 7th

Asking God For Direction

" I will try to do what you demand forever, until the end".
Psalm 119:112 (NCV)

I have a picture of you in my mind tonight in our old house on Byron Circle. You are placing blocks or something on the floor in the living room, one after another in a row, getting them lined up just so. I have no idea why, but you are certainly entertaining yourself. You are serious, meticulous, and determined. (cute, too, I might add)

I wonder why I remember that? It certainly isn't anything of any great significance, is it? Maybe it was one of those Kodak moments and I missed it. Maybe it was a vision of how you would be as a grown up, a serious engineer, a meticulous accountant, a determined scientist??? Nah—I don't think so. Maybe you'll be a serious teacher, a meticulous manager, or a determined counselor instead, what do you think? Your options are open at this point. I hope you will remember to ask God to get you focused in the right direction soon. I'll be praying for you.

Pray with me:
Help us, Oh Lord, to look to you for guidance and direction in all that we do. Help us to get focused and stay focused on the path you have planned. Amen

Patty B. Williams

October 8th

Commitment

"We want each of you to go on with the same hard work all your lives. Then you will surely get what you hope for." Hebrews 6:11 (NCV)

I'm writing this on the eve of the 7th which means I'm behind schedule. That seems to be happening to me a lot lately. Sometimes I just get worn out and would like to take off to the mountains and seclusion for a week or so, just to get my act together again. Haven't you felt that way before? The problem is that ole commitment thing that creeps up on us. It's hard to shake, isn't it?

Actually, I think God put it there just to help keep us on track. Commitment in daily school things, in the business world, in our friendships, and in our marriages is sometimes really hard. Even commitment when you love someone or something is difficult at times. When that happens, work hard to hang in there. Don't give up too quickly. Don't leave God out of the picture. Remember, he's your greatest resource of strength.

Pray with me:
Dear Lord, at times we get tired and commitment is the last thing we want to think about. In those times, let us pull strength from you. We thank you for being there. Amen

Clean Underwear, Wild Elephants and the Princess

October 9th

I See The Moon

"He made the moon and stars to rule the night. His love continues forever." Psalm 136:9 (NCV)

I know each time you see a beautiful moon you will think of Granddaddy, just like all his children and the other grandchildren do. What a neat thing to share! I'm thankful that Daddy took the time to make that special for all of us, to create a bond we all appreciate.

We should look for little things that mean something and then share them with someone we love. God created such beauty all around us, it shouldn't be a difficult task.

Tonight, when you look at the moon, think about me, too. I'll be thinking about you and might even sing . . . . *I see the moon and the moon sees me. The moon sees somebody I want to see. God bless the moon and God bless me, and God bless someone I want to see.*

Pray with me:
Thank you God for your wondrous creations and for the people we can share them with. We are truly blessed. Amen

Patty B. Williams

October 10th

Laziness

"The lazy person will not get what he wants. But a hard worker gets everything he wants." Proverbs 13:4 (NCV)

Studying is not the most fun thing to do, I know, but it certainly makes a difference when it comes to test taking time, doesn't it? Cleaning your room and balancing your checkbook isn't too much fun either, is it? Sometimes these things don't get done for legitimate reasons, but many times it's just because we're lazy. I know because I'm guilty!

I hope you'll guard against the "lazies." They can become a habit very quickly. Maybe when you feel them coming on you can try to examine the reasons why. Are you trying to do too much and you're worn out? Are you staying up to late? Are you worried about something? Are you getting sick? Who can do something about that? No, mommy is too far away. Besides, she turned that job over to you because she knew you were quite capable of handling it yourself! Good luck.

Pray with me:
Lord, when we don't have the enthusiasm for life and responsibilities that we should have, don't let the "lazies" catch us off guard. Keep us alert to what's going on, and help us to know when we need to take care of ourselves. Amen

October 11th

Paying Attention

"So I also will choose harsh treatment for them and will bring upon them what they dread. For when I called, no one answered. When I spoke, no one listened. They did evil in my sight and chose what displeases me." Isaiah 66:4 (NIV)

How many times do you listen to someone and don't really pay attention to their body language or the tone in their voice? This happens all the time in marriages and other close relationships, and it causes so much heartache and anger.

So, how do we get the song and the music? How do we really pay attention while we listen? Well, you can start with eye contact and then open your heart as well as your ears, especially when someone is upset or angry with you. Don't be thinking about your response before you listen to what they have to say. Ask questions to make sure you understand what they are saying. Keep an open mind.

Being a good listener is a wonderful attribute. I hope you will practice it every chance you get. You will endear yourself to lots of people.

Pray with me:
Lord, you listen to us constantly, when we're happy or sad, when we're hurt or angry. Help us remember to be as loving to our neighbor, friend, or family member. Amen

October 12th

Having To Be Right

"Always be humble and gentle. Be patient and accept each other with love." Ephesians 4:2-3 (NCV)

I've been reading a wonderful little book about relationships, called "*The More We Found Each Other,* by Mavis and Merle Fossum. One of the recent things I read talks about people who always have to be right. What those people don't notice is that other things they care about are being lost—like friends or more intimate relationships who get tired of their persistent need to be right.

When you stop and think about it, a good relationship is based on communicating our own thoughts and ideas to each other. Agreement is not always necessary. Our differences should give us an opportunity to view the world through someone else's eyes and mind. When one person always has to be right, those opportunities to learn are squashed. Why can't we just agree that there is more than one way to see or do something? Our job, the little relationship book says, is to learn how other people see and do things, because that is the way we grow.

Pray with me:
Lord, what a boring world this would be if we all saw and did things the same and how defeated we would be if the other person were always right and we were wrong. Help us to guard against being that person who always has to be right or being the victim of the person who always thinks they are right. Amen

October 13th

Being Happy

"Young people, enjoy yourselves while you are young. Be happy while you are young." Ecclesiastes 11:9 (NCV)

I just got the cutest book from my friend, Vicki. It's entitled *Are You As Happy As Your Dog?* It's just a tiny little book but it has so much wisdom in it. The author, Alan Cohen, talks about how happy his dog Munchie is and how Munchie is not afraid to show how much he loves him or how easy it is to entertain himself, or find joy wherever he is.

Wouldn't it be nice to know we could be happy with the really simple things in life like chasing a ball? Wouldn't it also be nice to know we could always express ourselves as freely as Munchie who wags his tail when he's happy, whines when he's sad, walks away when he doesn't want to play? Oh, to be as happy as Munchie, wouldn't that be great? I hope you work toward that. Start with a good attitude and count your blessings. That's a good start!

Pray with me:
God, help us to learn from your creatures. They must have something we're missing at times. Keep our attitudes positive and our blessings in mind. Thank you for life and all its opportunities for happiness. Amen

Patty B. Williams

October 14th

Saying Your Blessings

"Enter his gates with thanksgiving and his courts with praise; give thanks to him and praise his name." Psalm 100:4 (NIV)

When you were about 18 months old, you surprised your daddy and me when you folded your hands at dinner and "chattered" the blessing. You loved to talk, or at least try to, and you were putting two to three words together by that time. You also didn't like to go to bed at night and were lazy in the morning. Sound familiar? Some things never change.

I hope you're still saying your blessings. It's important not to take them for granted. We have so much when others have so little. Funny how we complain when we don't have the right kind of cereal and others would be so happy to have the crumbs of whatever we had. I know that sounds melodramatic, but unfortunately you and I both know it's the horrible truth. I know you're thankful, I just don't ever want you to lose that perspective.

Pray with me:
Thank you, Lord, that we are blessed with enough to eat and drink. Thank you, too, for the freedom we have to fold our hands anywhere at anytime and say our blessing. Amen

Clean Underwear, Wild Elephants and the Princess

October 15th
(Granny's birthday)

Granny

"Children's children are a crown to the aged, and parents are the pride of their children." Proverbs 17:6 (NIV)

You have been so fortunate to have grandparents that could and did share your life. Today is Granny's birthday, and if I remember correctly, she is in her eighties. I'll be happy if I'm still here at eighty and look and feel as good as she does.

Remember today to say a special prayer of thanksgiving for Granny and for your other grandparents and step-grandparents. They have all had their special place in your life, haven't they?

I think God gave us grandparents just so we'd know the real way to make biscuits, to listen for the red-eyed raccoon, to play cards and make cookies. I'm glad you'll have good memories to tell your children about one day when they are asking questions about their great-grandparents!

Pray with me:
God, for the blessing of grandparents and the love we share with them, we give you thanks. Keep us in touch with them in spirit and through the effort we make to let them know how much we care. Amen

Patty B. Williams

October 16th

The Princess

"A discerning man keeps wisdom in view, but a fool's eyes wander to the ends of the earth." Proverbs 17:24

At three years old, your favorite things were anything purple and "Strawberry Shortcake" everything! Do you remember? Funny how one of the things Bill remembered about you as a little girl was the cute way you said purple. That's the color of royalty, you know. Maybe that was the start of you becoming a princess!

And, my, what a princess you've become. Why, you were even courted by a few princes and were kissed by a few toads, weren't you? And you probably will kiss a few more of both before the Knight in Shining Armor comes along, don't you think? I surely hope so!

Look for the right one. Ask God for good judgement, and then be strong enough to back away if you know he's telling you it's not right. If you truly feel he's telling you it's right, then be willing to work hard to make it happen.

Pray with me:
Thank you, God, for pretend princesses, Strawberry Shortcake dolls and that beautiful color of purple. Thank you also for both the prince and the frog, because we learn and build memories from both. Amen

Clean Underwear, Wild Elephants and the Princess

"The Little Princess"

October 17th

Brokenness

"Many are the plans in a man's heart, but it is the Lord's purpose that prevails." Proverbs 19:21 (NIV)

Broken dreams, broken promises, and broken hearts, we never plan for them, but they sure find their way into our lives, don't they? To be such a blessed people with so much opportunity and freedom to do things right, we sure can muck them up sometime, can't we?

I am so glad that God can take all the things we muck up and some way use them for a better purpose. Even when we can't see it right away or question his abilities, he is working on it. I have that faith, even though I get very impatient at times.

I hope you will remember through those bad experiences, whatever they might be, that God will find a way to use them for good. So, don't fret for long. Get over it and wait for God's miracle.

Pray with me:
Lord, forgive us when we mess up in big things and small things. Continue to use the experiences for good somewhere. Keep our eyes and minds open so we can see your works. Amen

October 18th

Judging

"Who can say, I have kept my heart pure; I am clean and without sin?" Proverbs 20:9 (NIV)

It's so easy to point out other's fault, isn't it? Regardless of whether the fault is minor or huge, we don't have a problem seeing it in others. I wonder if we would be so quick to judge if we knew that the person was going to have the opportunity to judge us with the same measure? Not a fun thought, is it?

That's what I believe God tries to teach us. Don't criticize others when you have room to be criticized yourself. That should cut down on a lot of talk because I know of no one who doesn't deserve a certain amount of criticism for something.

Strive to keep your heart pure and non-judgmental, but when you slip, ask God to help you get back on the right track.

Pray with me:
God, you know our weaknesses. Help us to think about ourselves before we too quickly have something negative to say about someone else. Amen

Patty B. Williams

October 19th

Good-Byes

"There is surely a future hope for you, and your hope will not be cut off." Proverbs 23:18 (NIV)

Good-byes are so difficult sometimes, aren't they? I remember vividly when you were about 2 years old and your daddy had to leave to return to work in Chicago or Tennessee. You were with me when we took him to the airport, and the minute he got out of the car you started boo-hooing, your heart broken. You have always hated good-byes. You never liked Nanny and Granddaddy leaving when they came to visit and you would always let it show.

Getting grown-up doesn't change those hard good-byes, does it? Yet we all have to face them at one time or another. Whether it's good-bye for a short time, a long time, or a lifetime, they all cause sadness.

Sometimes the sadness is short-lived. Sometimes it takes longer than it should, but we finally "get a grip." Sometimes it hangs on so long it becomes unhealthy and keeps us from moving forward. That's what we have to guard against.

I think as Christians if our hearts and minds are focused where they should be, all other things and relationships become secondary in the overall scheme of things. We should be able to re-group and re-focus when those secondary things cause us pain, ask for God's help, and move forward from there. That doesn't mean it will be easy. It just means there is hope for the broken hearts, broken dreams, and tears. We just have to do our part and let God do the rest.

Pray with me:
Lord, you know our sadness, our broken hearts, and our weaknesses.

When we're too hurt or too weak to ask, please help us move forward and re-focus our attention on the plans you have for us instead of thinking all our plans are shattered with a sad good-bye. Assure us that you have many wonderful plans still in store for us. Amen

Patty B. Williams

October 20th

Pick A Pumpkin

"You love righteousness and hate wickedness; therefore God, your God, has set you above your companions by anointing you with the oil of joy." Psalm 45:7 (NIV)

You should see our offices across the hall. They are all decorated for Halloween. We have ghost and spiderwebs, pumpkins and witches. They are so cute. You know it takes so little to add a little joy to everyday life. Your Aunt Mary Jane and Deborah are so good at doing those sort of things. Just think of all they have done to add a little extra joy to a party, or to a room, or to our lives with a card, or a phone call, or a visit.

At some point everyone needs a little extra something to brighten his or her day. You have a knack for being creative and thoughtful, so I know you will use those gifts when you see a need—and you'll see lots of need during your next four years of college!

God just seems to know where to put people where they're needed at the right time, and I'm sure he's got some plans for you along these lines.

In the meantime, watch out for those goblins—especially those with deep voices, good looks, and good vibes! Tell 'um to go pick a pumpkin.

Pray with me:
Help us Lord to take time to add a little "spice" to life, to make things a little more joyful and brighter for others and ourselves. Use us to spread your joy for life and keep us mindful of those who need their spirits lifted. Amen

October 21st

Lives Changed Over Night

"Have faith in God, Jesus answered." Mark: 11:22 (NIV)

Faith, such a little word, but one that can hold up tons of weighty problems and worries that we have little or no control over. Do you feel like yours has ever been tested? If it hasn't, your day will come, so start with the little test of faith so that when the big test comes along you'll be better prepared.

You know my friend Carol and her husband T.C. are in the middle of a big test, and now I just heard that my boss, Patsy, is also being tested while she's waiting in the hospital to find out if she will have surgery on a tumor that may or may not be malignant. Wow, can you imagine? Lives changed overnight, what would you do? Of course, that question can't be answered until you're right there, right in the face of the problem, but you can start working on what you hope you would do.

If it were me, and it certainly could be one day, I hope I would start with a prayer to ask for a stronger faith. I would ask God to calm my fears, to give me physical strength to endure whatever might lie ahead, a good attitude to keep me mentally healthy, good medical staff with good hearts, as well as, good technical skills, and a good support group of family and friends. I think if I started there that would be the best that I could do. We might not can change a bad situation, but we can work on the way we view and handle it.

We will surely have some tests of faith ahead of us, but the thing we need to remember is that we don't have to take them alone. Don't you wish you could say the same thing for Algebra test?

Patty B. Williams

Pray with me:

Help us, Lord, when we have to face those big test of faith. Help us remember that you are as close to us during those times as you are during the times of smaller test. We are the ones who lose perspective. Please don't let that happen. Amen

October 22nd

Honesty

"Whoever can be trusted with very little can also be trusted with much, and whoever is dishonest with very little will also be dishonest with much." Luke 16:10 (NIV)

Remember the time we went to the beach and went to pay the bill and they had made a mistake of about two-hundred dollars to our good? I was teased unmercifully about bringing the mistake to their attention. It would have been so easy to get away with it, and they may or may not have caught their mistake at a later date.

In the realm of things we could be dishonest about, two hundred dollars is not that big of a deal. It would have been easy to rationalize that they got a lot of money from us anyway, that they would never miss it, that it was their mistake, but would it have been honest? Would the rationalization have taken away the guilt? What would Jesus have done in the situation? Isn't that the question we should always ask since we are supposed to be striving to be like him?

When you have children one day, you will understand how important honesty is from them. It's what the foundation of your relationship with each other is based on. Honesty in the little things makes honesty in the big things unquestionable.

Pray with me:
Thank you, Lord, for the ability to know right from wrong. Protect us from temptation when we are weak. Keep us mindful of the importance of honesty in little things. Amen

Patty B. Williams

October 23rd

Enjoying God's Nature

The meadows are covered with flocks and the valleys are mantled with grains; they shout for joy and sing." Psalm 65:13 (NIV)

When we went to North Carolina last week-end, the planted flowers on the side of the road were beautiful and the wildflowers were gorgeous. Nanny would have loved them.

This morning I'm sitting out on the deck. It's cool, leaves fall every now and then, and the squirrels have been running all through the trees. It's just great. Nature is certainly one of God's beautiful gifts to us, isn't it?

I hope you enjoy walking on the decks through the trees on your campus. I think I would spend some thinking time on one of those benches, if it were I. Don't forget to whisper a thank-you prayer when you're enjoying the beauty. Not everyone has the opportunity to enjoy all we've been blessed with to appreciate.

Pray with me:
Thank you, God, for all the wonderful things you have given us in nature and for the good health to enjoy them. Help us to take good care of your gifts and appreciate them daily. Amen

October 24th

Questioning God's Existence

"Jesus replied, You do not realize now what I am doing, but later you will understand." John 13:7 (NIV)

If you are a normal college student, you will eventually get in to some deep discussions about God and religion in general. Don't be afraid to join in on the conversation just because you feel like you don't know enough about the Bible. You know enough about your own feelings and the spirit that's within you.

You will also hear some convincing arguments like you have already heard from Granddaddy at times. That's o.k., it's alright to question. God gave us brains. He didn't expect us not to use them. Just remember, you will never have all the answers about God. You won't understand everything that happens. You will, however, be surprised to look back at a later time in your life and then understand some of God's plan. Some things we won't understand until God reveals them to us in heaven. That's where trust and faith come in to play. Listen to what others have to say, but don't think you have to have all the answers to know God is real.

Pray with me:
Lord, help us to be confident in our belief even when we don't have all the answers. Help us to show others you live in us through our actions, words, and deeds. Amen

Patty B. Williams

October 25th

Angels

"See, I am sending an angel ahead of you to guard you along the way and to bring you to the place I have prepared." Exodus 23:20 (NIV)

You know how much I always worry every time you get in the car going somewhere, especially if you're going to be on a long trip. I always ask God to watch over you, and even though I don't specifically ask for an angel, I'm sure that's what he must send. I know angels have been watching over your brother for years, sometimes doing double time, I'm sure!

I wonder what they do—put their hands on the wheel when you look away at that good looking fella for a few seconds, the seconds that could mean the difference between life and death? Do they apply added pressure when you slam on brakes because you were following too close and the car ahead of you stopped suddenly?

I'm not sure where the angels are, but I'm sure at times they've been there. I hope you don't depend on them too much. They have a lot of teenagers to look after, besides, God expects you to do your part to protect yourself and others on the road who are trusting you to be a good, alert driver.

Pray with me:
Lord, watch over and protect us and all those we love. Keep us alert to worldly dangers whatever they might be. Help us to remember to call on you to keep us safe. Amen

October 26th

On Loan

"A time to be born and a time to die" Ecclesiastes 3:2 (NIV)

One of my very favorite cards by *Flavia* says, *"If fate would so allow, I'd sit across the porch from God—and thank him—for lending me you."* I just love that thought.

And if you think about it, we are all here on loan. We never know when God will call us home. I don't mean that as a somber (gloomy) thought; I just mean that none of us has a guarantee on time.

What that says to me is to be happy for what I have, for where I am, and to not take life for granted. When you and Michael were loaned to me, I was blessed beyond measure. I have never taken that for granted—even during the young teenage years!

Pray with me:
Lord, you have blessed us so graciously. Thank you for lending us those very special people that make our lives complete. Amen

October 27th

Idols

"Whoever loves money never has money enough; whoever loves wealth is never satisfied with his income. This too is meaningless." Ecclesiastes 5:10 (NIV)

In the Disciple class I'm taking, we've talked a lot about how the Hebrew people used to worship idols. Idols can be a lot of things, you know. They don't have to be a stone statute. You can worship many things other than what we normally think of as idols.

Money is something many people worship, though it may even be subconscious. Money, to them, is the most important thing in life, and unfortunately it often takes precedence over family, friends, and God.

Don't think money is bad—neither is liking the smell of it! Don't think having a goal to make money is bad either. It isn't, in and of itself. Just remember to keep it in its proper place. For if you lose all else in its pursuit, what is left to help you enjoy it?

Pray with me:
Thank you, God, for the opportunity to make money and the freedom to spend it as we see fit. Keep us safe, however, from the temptation to be hooked on it. Amen

October 28th

Christianity

"In the same way, faith by itself, if it is not accompanied by action is dead." James 2:17 (NIV)

How do we know if someone is a Christian? Is it the one that goes to church every Sunday? Is it the one who spends much time at the church doing one thing or another? Is it the one who can talk so intellectually about the Bible and God, or is it the one who can speak so eloquently about God in front of groups of people?

I think the answer to the questions is that all of these people could be Christians; they could, however, not be Christians, also. Bob made a point in one of his sermons that if we are truly filled with the Holy Spirit, it will spill over in our day-to-day actions. He gave an example of someone's description of an active member of the church, one who performed many services for the church and belonged to a lot of church committees. The person describing him said, "but I sure wouldn't want to work for him." I think that says a lot about the spirit within that person, don't you?

We need to remember that we aren't Christians just on Sunday or just when we're working on a church project. We're also Christians when we're at work, aggravated at our roommate, mad at our boyfriend, ticked off at our parents, frustrated, having a good time—well, you get the picture. It's not always easy. That's why we have to ask God to help us remember.

Pray with me:
Lord, help us as we strive to be a Christian in our daily walk. You know we will fail time and time again. Keep a tight hold on us and don't let go, even when we do. Amen

Patty B. Williams

October 29th

On Golden Pond

"For this son of mine was dead and is alive again; he was lost and is found. So they began to celebrate." Luke 15:24 (NIV)

Terrie reminded me of one of her favorite memories of you when you were about four years old. We were all over at Nancy's and John's watching *On Golden Pond* and you were sitting in her lap. There was a part in the movie where the Grandfather was lost in the woods because he couldn't remember how to get home. Terrie had tears coming down her cheeks because it was such a touching part of the movie. You had heard us talking earlier about Terrie getting lost coming over to our house, and when you saw her crying you tenderly, and very intently leaned out, looked up in her face, and asked if she was crying because she had gotten lost coming to our house.

That was over fourteen years ago, but Terrie remembers that experience in detail. Even if you hadn't already captured her heart, you did that day.

Being lost is such a frightening thing, regardless of how old you are or where you are. Being lost in class because we don't understand something, or feeling lost because we don't fit in a group or a situation, can put us in an uncomfortable situation. It is certainly not the most fun place to be, is it?

God understands those feelings; so don't think it is too small a concern to ask for his help. It's a lot easier to handle those situations with someone at your side.

Pray with me:
Lord, when we find ourselves in situations where we feel lost or alone, please be with us, even if we forget to ask. Amen

Patty B. Williams

October 30th

Public Speaking

"So we say with confidence, 'the Lord is my helper; I will not be afraid. What can man do to me'?" Hebrews 13:6 (NIV)

Studies tell us that public speaking is one of the things that is at the top of the list of those things that frighten a person the most. Did you know that?

I know you have done public speaking already, but before your college days are over, you will be required to do more, and depending on the profession you choose, you may be called upon to speak often.

I think one of the things that has helped me the most in public speaking is remembering that people are just people. Regardless of who the audience is, God made us all. If I make a mistake, my humanness will show. Will that make me less in the eyes of the people I'm speaking to or in the sight of God? I don't think so. If I lose my train of thought or my place on the note cards, will that be the topic of conversation for the next week among my friends and co-workers? I doubt it.

When you have to speak, prepare. Ask God to take away your anxieties so you can be at your best. Be confident in yourself and think about whom you might touch in whatever it is you have to say. Then relax, be yourself, and have fun.

Pray with me:
God, when we speak in front of others, regardless of the topic, help us to be confident, prepared, and reflective of what you would have us to say. Amen

October 31st

God's Job

"There is only one Lawgiver and Judge, the one who is able to save and destroy. But you—who are you to judge your neighbor?"
James 4:12 (NIV)

Sometimes we think we know what someone should have done, or shouldn't have done in a given situation, don't we? Too often, too, we tell them so, or tell someone else.

When we're hurt or angry or frightened it gets even easier to say what we think about what another person has said or done, to make an assumption of their motives, to judge their actions, or worse, even to judge their character. We do it though, even when we know it's not our responsibility. We are weak when it comes to letting God do his job when we are affected by something someone says or does. It's something we need to work on constantly. I struggle with it. I hope you grow to be better at it than I am. Remember, God can handle the job. He doesn't need our help.

Pray with me:
Help us, Lord, to leave the judging responsibility to you. When we're affected by what others do that hurt us or make us angry, give us strength to only do what you would have us to do and leave the rest to you. Amen

Man Is Limited; God Is Not

"Jesus looked at them and said, with man this is impossible, but not with God; all things are possible with God." Mark 10:27 (NIV)

I can't imagine what it would be like to lose you or Michael. How does a parent ever get over such a loss? How does an average size man pick up a car and move it off his daughter who has been penned beneath a wheel? How does an alcoholic refrain from the temptation of drinking again or a drug addict from taking that last pill?

We, as humans, are so weak. Granted, some are stronger than others simply because they have more confidence in themselves, better support systems of friends and families, a stronger faith; but at some point, most everyone will have a situation he or she isn't equipped to handle on their own. They need more than a friend, a spouse, or a family member. They need the source of strength that is beyond human comprehension.

Man is limited. God is not. That is hard for us to understand, but the lack of understanding makes it no less true.

I hope you never have to call on God's strength to get you through a tragedy, but I hope you are secure in knowing that all things are possible with him, and if you need his strength, it's there.

Pray with me:
Lord, help us to know you are all powerful, that you are there to help us when we are unable to do it ourselves. Amen

Clean Underwear, Wild Elephants and the Princess

November 2nd

Treating Everyone Equally

"My brothers, as believers in our glorious Lord Jesus Christ, don't show favoritism." James 2:1 (NIV)

I remember when Michael was little he always seemed to befriend the child who was sitting in the corner or the one that didn't seem to have a friend. You have done that more often the older you have become. I think that is because it took you longer to gain confidence in yourself and therefore longer to think you had something to offer others.

Neither you or Michael were ones to shun others because they were not in the same social class as you, not the same race, or the same in personality or beliefs. I am proud of that, though at times I have to admit that it concerned me.

You, of all people, know how important it is to choose your friends wisely, but choosing wisely does not have to mean that you treat others unfairly or less than who they are in the sight of God. I think you have a good handle on that; don't change.

Pray with me:
Help us remember, Lord, that you made us all—rich, poor, pretty, ugly, fat, thin, smart, slow; let us treat each other as equals and know without question that you love us the same. Amen

Patty B. Williams

November 3rd

Not Doing The Things I Should Have Done

"Anyone, then, who knows the good he ought to do and doesn't do it, sins." James 4:17 (NIV)

When I pray and ask for forgiveness for doing things I should not have done, I also try to remember to ask for forgiveness for not doing the things I should have done. One is no greater than the other.

Haven't you experienced that gnawing little feeling you get when you don't do something that you know you should have done? It's so easy to make excuses for not doing those things that are uncomfortable, difficult, or take our precious time, isn't it? Sometimes those things are of no real significance other than it may get us in a habit of procrastination, but the things that really matter, that matter to God, those are the things we need to work hard to do.

I'll be pulling for you. I know it's not easy, but I do know it's important.

Pray with me:
God, help us to do those things we know we should do, even when it's hard for us. Help us remember, too, that you're there to work with us when we need you. Amen

November 4th

Drinking

"Wine is a mocker and beer a brawler, whoever is led astray by them is not wise." Proverbs 20:1 (NIV)

I know you have an understanding of why I feel so strongly about drinking. I feel even stronger about drugs. They rob so many people of so many wonderful things that life has to offer. They destroy or at least help to destroy relationships and build dependencies on resources other than God and self. They change personalities, and they end life. Surely that is not what God wants for us, or what we want for ourselves.

Once you are of age so you aren't breaking a law and risking consequences greater than your mother's disappointment, a social drink here and there should be no big deal. Drugs on the other hand could be a big deal the first time you try them. You've read enough and are smart enough to know that, I'm sure.

You have a good head on your shoulders, you have good reasons to be confident in who you are and what you will become. You also have an abundance of people who care about you and who hold you in high esteem. You have no reason to have to use alcohol or drugs to help you be something different than who and what you are.

Peer pressure doesn't stop with the teenage years, so stay prepared for it, and use all those skills I know you have to continue to be the Brooke God made. He did a great job!

Pray with me:
Thank you, God, for the freedom of choice to make decisions that affect our lives short term or possibly long term. Give us the wisdom and strength to make the right choices. Amen.

Patty B. Williams

November 5th

Knowledge

"Smart people want more knowledge. But a foolish person just wants more foolishness." Proverbs 15:14 (NIV)

If I were back in school and knew what I know now, I would work so much harder to gain more knowledge about everything I could. It's a shame the majority of us don't have that thirst for knowledge until our golden opportunity to learn has passed us by.

I envy your opportunity to learn new things and grow in overall knowledge of places, things, and people. I hope you will try to think about your coursework with an attitude of curiosity and opportunity for growth instead of having an attitude of, what is the least I can do and get through this course with a "B" or "C"?

Broad knowledge in a variety of subject areas will give you the ability to talk to all kinds of people with different interest. It will help make you a better communicator. Don't waste expensive tuition dollars just to obtain a degree. Get every ounce of knowledge you can for the money.

Just don't get too smart for your britches. I still need to be able to talk to you from my limited knowledge base!

Pray with me:
Thank you, Lord, for opportunities to grow through increased knowledge. Help us to keep open minds and enthusiasm to learn. Amen

November 6th

Pray Don't Worry

"She does not worry about her family when it snows. They all have fine clothes to keep them warm." Proverbs 31:21 (NCV)

I know you have had an extra burden this semester because you have worried about me and you have worried about your dad. We both love you for that concern, but you must remember that we each have resources available to us to help if we need it, and we're smart enough to ask for help if that becomes necessary. We also care enough about one another, despite our differences, to help when needed. We are truly blessed.

Pray for us when you are concerned, but don't worry. Trust God to answer your prayers and to handle what you can't, regardless of what it is or who it is about. I have to work at that or I would worry about you all the time. It's nice to know someone cares though, isn't it?

Pray with me:
Lord, calm our fears and our worries. Keep us mindful of others' hurts and well-being, but help us to know our limits in what we can do and to remember to turn it over to you when it's time. Amen

Patty B. Williams

November 7th

Asking For Guidance

" But the Counselor, the Holy Spirit, whom the Father will send in my name, will teach you all things and will remind you of everything I have said to you." John 14:26 (NCV)

Emily had dinner with us last night. We talked about when you girls were little and some of the insignificant things remembered, like my saying "Good morning, Morning," when I would try to get you up in the mornings. We talked about stopping to take a picture on the way home from St. George Island when I took you, Emily, and Ellen one weekend. Emily remembers how "cool" she thought I was because I let you girls stay out on the beach with your friends until after midnight. I remember worrying if I was being too lenient letting you stay out and how I would ever justify my actions had something happened to any one of you. Thank goodness you came in safe at the appointed time!

Sometimes you have to make decisions whether or not to do something based on your intuition, common sense, and faith. When I went beyond my comfort level with a little extra freedom to let you girls prove to me you were trustworthy, it was not easy. Fortunately, it was a good experience for all of us. I hope when you have similar decisions to make, you won't make them in a vacuum. Before you commit to something that makes you a little uneasy, send up a little prayer to ask for guidance. It could make a huge difference in your final decision.

Pray with me:
Father, every day we have to make decisions, some more significant than others. When we question what to do, help us remember that you are available to help. Amen

November 8th

Hanging In There

"Consider it pure joy, my brothers, whenever you face trials of many kinds, because you know that the testing of your faith develops perseverance." James 1:2-3 (NIV)

Today I had one of those experiences that helped me appreciate all the hard work we've been putting in at work the past few months. A lot of the different pieces of a project we were working on finally came together to make sense. At times it was tough to hang in there when we didn't see the whole picture, when we couldn't get the pieces to fit in our limited vision of the end result.

It kind of sounds like life, doesn't it? It sure is hard to hang in there sometimes when we can't figure out what the end result of our efforts will be, or don't understand the separate pieces of the big picture. I'm sure glad someone much wiser than I is in control, aren't you?

Pray with me:
Help us, Lord, to hang in there when the going gets tough for whatever reason. Stay in control even when we try to snatch it away. Amen

Patty B. Williams

November 9th

In Full Bloom

"I eagerly expect and hope that I will in no way be ashamed, but will have sufficient courage so that now as always Christ will be exalted in my body, whether by life or by death." Philippians 1:20 (NIV)

I will never forget the story your Aunt Mary Jane tells about coming to see us when we lived in Atlanta. When they pulled up in front of our apartment complex, they looked up toward our second-story windows and saw Michael, nude, jumping up and down on the bed in front of the window. Remembering Michael at five or six, that doesn't surprise me.

I certainly didn't condone displays of nudity when Michael was little, but in some respects it's sad that we have to lose that sense of unconcern in how we look, "in full bloom" to others. It's sad that we have to worry so much about how our bodies look on the outside when it's what is on the inside that really matters.

That doesn't mean that we shouldn't care, or take care, of how we look on the outside; it just means that our focus should be on the inside.

You are beautiful on both sides. I wish you could see that as much as others see it in you. Continue to ride your bike, eat right, and do all those things that are good for you and make you look better to yourself. Just don't lose the right perspective about what's most important.

Pray with me:
Help us, Lord, to be proud of who we are both inside and out. Give us strength and willpower to work on both parts to become the total person you would have us show to others. Amen

Clean Underwear, Wild Elephants and the Princess

November 10th

Susan's Shells

"O, Lord, what is man that you care for him, the son of man that you think of him?" Psalm 144:3 (NIV)

I talked to Susan, an old friend of mine, a few nights ago. She reminded me that she still had the shells on her dresser that you gave her years ago when you were a little girl. You endeared yourself to her with one little act of caring and sweetness. You parted with some of your prized possessions because you liked her and you wanted to express that in the only way you knew how at that age.

I hope as you go through life that you will continue to give your gifts of caring and sweetness. You may not have more shells, but you'll always have time, and the ability to communicate, and that creative mind that I've seen work so well—especially when you didn't have money.

I'll be waiting to hear future stories about how your thoughtfulness brightened someone else's life.

Pray with me:
Help us, Lord, to look continuously for ways that we can share ourselves with others in acts and deeds of caring. Amen

Patty B. Williams

November 11th
(Veterans' Day)

War

"So Joshua took the entire land, just as the Lord had directed Moses, and he gave it as an inheritance to Israel according to their tribal divisions. Then the land had rest from war." Joshua 11:23 (NIV)

When I was a little girl, I remember being afraid of war. Though World War II was over, I still heard talk about it, and I heard talk about the atomic bomb and the building of bomb shelters. It was scary.

You will study about the various wars in history and will probably, for the most part, be bored with it. Because you have been so far removed from them, they won't have the significance to you as they did for your Granddaddy and daddy who both fought in them.

I hope, as you study about World War II, that you will try hard to gain an understanding and appreciation of why that war was fought, why your granddaddy was compelled to enlist and fight for the freedom of our country. Try to understand what he and thousands of other soldiers did for us at the risk of their lives, and why now he is so easily brought to tears at the sight of the American flag flying high atop a crane on a construction site.

I hope you never have to experience war, or worse, lose someone you love in a war. I hope also, as you get older, that you remember to show your gratitude for the freedoms you have because someone fought for them. You can do that through interest, donations, and support of organizations that recognize veterans. It will be a way to honor your dad and your granddaddy.

Pray with me:

Help us, Lord, to never take our freedoms for granted. Bless those who so bravely fought to protect them. Amen

Patty B. Williams

November 12th

Disney World Excitement

"Be joyful always; pray continually; give thanks in all circumstances, for this is God's will for you in Christ Jesus." 1 Thessalonians 5:16 (NIV)

Do you remember the time you, Michael, Nanny, Granddaddy and I went to Disney World? You were both so excited. I can look at those pictures today and see the wide-eyed amazement in your eyes for all that you saw and experienced. I know you will love seeing that in your own children's eyes one day.

I hope to see and hear of that kind of excitement during your college life—when you get that "A" you worked so hard for, when you meet that special guy, get invited to *the* event of the year, or when something you do brings you unexpected accolades.

God wants us to live an exciting, joyful life. He planned it that way. Try to avoid those things that might rob you of those plans. Try hard to keep that Disney World excitement in your eyes and in your life.

Pray with me:
Thank you, God, for the opportunities we have to live the kind of life you want for us. Help us to guard ourselves against anything that would keep us from your plans. Amen

November 13th

Held Accountable

"But if the watchman sees the sword coming and does not blow the trumpet to warn the people and the sword comes and takes the life of one of them, that man will be taken away because of his sin, but I will hold the watchman accountable for his blood." Ezekiel 33:6 (NIV)

One of the things the legislature and the taxpayers want us as state employees to be is accountable for how we spend their money. If we spend it unwisely or throw it away on useless projects, they will hold us accountable for our actions.

In the same way, God holds us accountable for how we live. If we make poor decisions, use bad judgment, or go against his teachings, he will hold us accountable.

I venture to say that God also expects us to hold our friends and others we love accountable for their actions. If we know someone is doing something that is wrong or potentially harmful to themselves or others and don't try to stop them, I think we are doing less than God expects.

College life is a wonderful time to stretch your wings. It's a time of new freedoms and experiences for you and for your friends. As a Christian, you are your brother's keeper—a responsibility that you will often wish you didn't have. I hope you will have the courage to hold those friends and loved ones accountable if necessary. I can assure you it won't be easy, so start praying for help early!

Pray with me:
Lord, you know we will need your help to hold those we love accountable for their actions. Prepare us now so we'll be ready when the time comes. Amen

Patty B. Williams

November 14th

Because I'm Breathing

"And the Lord God formed man from the dust of the ground and breathed into his nostrils the breath of life, and man became a living being." Genesis 2:7 (NKJ)

I had a pleasant experience the other day while in the middle of a rather mundane task. I had gone to pick up a piece of furniture and was waiting for someone to bring it out to the car. A young man about your brother's age came out and greeted me with a smile and a "how are you today?" I responded in the normal way and asked him in return how he was. "Exceptionally well," he replied. I chuckled and asked, "exceptionally well, is that because it's Friday?" In a not so normal way he responded, "No, ma'am, that's because I'm breathing!" After I caught my breath and regained my composure, I told him how much I appreciated his attitude.

I think we should all respond more often like that young man, don't you? When you think about it, if you're breathing, everything on top of that is gravy. At least that's what Danny Baker, one of my favorite speakers said one time. I agree with him, and I think God would, too.

Think about how fortunate we are just to have life, much less life with health, love, freedoms, and happiness. I don't think I will forget that young man's comment for a long time. It touched my heart.

Pray with me:
Thank you, Lord, for the breath of life. Thank you, too, for all the "gravy" that you have given us to go with it. We are truly blessed. Amen

Clean Underwear, Wild Elephants and the Princess

November 15th

Perseverance

"Perseverance must finish its work so that you may be mature and complete, not lacking anything." James 1:4 (NIV)

Perseverance, often times a difficult task, is one that usually pays off in the long run. Whether it's studying until you "get it," working until the job's done, or playing until the game's over, it's not easy when you're tired, discouraged, or unmotivated.

When those times come along, try to remember that the harder you try, the more you can grow. Maturity comes many times with struggles and hard work. You can learn from most anything you experience—good or bad, but if you give up too easily, you miss out on that opportunity.

The next time you get discouraged about that math class or a particular problem, persevere. The more you discipline yourself to perseverance, the more mature you will become. Ask God for help when you find yourself slipping. Remember, he has more strength than you do.

Pray with me:
Father God, give us strength to keep on keeping on when we so want to quit. We are weak but you are strong. Amen

Patty B. Williams

November 16th

JB's Barbecue

"We did this, not because we do not have the right to such help, but in order to make ourselves a model for you to follow."
2 Thessalonians 3:9 (NIV)

I will never forget one night when you were about eight or nine years old and went with me to JB's barbecue to meet my singles Sunday school friends to eat dinner. When we got there the group was seated in long tables in a "C" shape around the room. I went in and immediately started making my way around the tables hugging and shaking hands with everyone. After a few minutes I looked around for you, and there you were, coming right behind me doing the same thing, but charming everyone with your charisma and sweet smile.

When you become a parent one day, you will quickly realize what an awesome task it is to try and be a good role model for your children. It's hard to watch your language, to watch your actions and reactions to things, and to be that person you want your children to respect, have faith in and love.

I know at times both your dad and I have failed miserably, but obviously we've done a few things right if judgment can be made by how you and Michael have turned out. We are truly blessed.

Pray with me:
God, you are the perfect role model. Help us every day to strive to become more like you. Help us as we live our lives to remember that others look to us as models. Help us to let them see you through us. Amen

Clean Underwear, Wild Elephants and the Princess

November 17th

Youth

"Children's children are a crown to the aged, and parents are the pride of their children." Proverbs 17:6 (NIV)

Isn't it funny how much time children spend trying to be adults and adults spend trying to keep their youth? Remember the birthday tea you had when you were three or four and all your little friends came all dressed up in their mom's clothes and jewelry? It was my most favorite party you ever had.

Though I loved the fact that you were such a typical little girl and wanted to be grown up, I never wanted you to do it too fast. I still don't. Youth is such a wonderful part of life, and I don't want you to miss any of it because you try to grow up too fast.

There is plenty of time for adult life, so don't rush it. That doesn't mean to be immature in your thinking or in your actions, nor does it mean that you should be irresponsible. It just means to be *who* you are *where* you are in life now. Let God take care of who you are and where you are in the future. Besides, I like you just like you are now. Don't take that away from me.

Pray with me:
God, we thank you for life as it is in the present. Help us not to take it for granted or to waste it on wishing for the future. Amen

Patty B. Williams

November 18th

Peanut Butter And Jelly Toast

" . . . and a little child will lead them." Isaiah 11:6 (NIV)

One of my favorite stories about Michael was when he was about five years old and asked for some peanut butter and jelly toast for breakfast. That was an easy order until he added, "and put the jelly on first and then the peanut butter." Now everyone knows that's not the way you eat peanut butter and jelly toast, so I preceded to tell Michael just that. He insisted, however, that that was the way he wanted it. In my not-so-wise motherly way I told him again that the peanut butter went on first and then the jelly. Again he insisted that he wanted the jelly on first and then the peanut butter. I patiently insisted that that was not the way it worked. He, not so patiently, whined and asked why it had to be that way. I, by now exasperated said, "I don't know why it's that way, Michael, it just is, and I don't want to hear any more about it." Silent for only a few minutes, Michael asked, " Did God tell you that?"

Now at five, your brother wasn't trying to be funny. He really thought God might have told me that the peanut butter had to go on first before the jelly. There surely didn't seem to be any other explanation.

That child-like faith, that confidence that God might actually have talked to me about that peanut butter and jelly, is what God tells us we must have. He knows we can't understand everything about him, so he gives us an example of the kind of faith we are supposed to have when all the answers can't be found. I know that is more difficult for some people than it is for others. I hope you can always have it. Look for understanding and strive for knowledge about God and the Bible, but remember you'll never have all the answers, and that's where the child-like faith comes in to play.

Pray with me:

Father, we are your children. Keep our faith strong when we don't have all the answers. Amen

Patty B. Williams

November 19th

Getting Back On Track

"Open my eyes that I may see wonderful things in your law."
Psalm 119:18 (NIV)

Have you experienced reading an assignment for long periods of time, knowing your eyes were open, but knowing your mind was closed? If you're not interested in something or if your mind is somewhere else, it usually doesn't matter if your eyes are open. For all practical purposes, they are closed. The problem is pretty much defined at that point, unfortunately the solution isn't. What can you do?

Take a break. If you're not concentrating, you're wasting your time. Try to get back on track. Try to change your attitude about the assignment. Think about the skills you were taught in learning how to study. Scan the assignment first. Look at any headings and then approach the assignment in smaller segments so you aren't overwhelmed. When you finish one segment, think about it before you go to the next. Look for something interesting, for one thing you can say you learned and want to remember. Ask God for help in concentrating if you need to, or for opening your mind if it seems to be closed. He's been through college with a lot of us, so he's used to it.

I'll be counting on you to get that assignment done!

Pray with me:
Lord, help us to know you're there for us in all kinds of situations. Open our eyes that we might see you wherever we look. Amen

Clean Underwear, Wild Elephants and the Princess

November 20th
(Nancy Turner's birthday)

Special People

"Honor your father and mother, and love your neighbor as yourself."
Matthew 19:19 (NIV)

One of my favorite memories of you is when you were about four years old and John and Nancy were our neighbors. You were dressed up, if I remember right, in some of my panty hose and high heels or something ridiculous like that. You were outside with me, and John came by and saw you. He stopped and asked if you wanted to ride to the Sing store with him. I couldn't believe it. Only someone who loved kids would have done that. It endeared John to me.

I think God puts special people in our lives at just the right time. John and Nancy were so good to me when I was single and you and Michael were young. Then, even though they moved away to another neighborhood, we remained good friends, and when John died, I was with Nancy almost immediately at the hospital. I'm sure God planned that too. Then you and Kim became good friends at a time when you both could share your "guy" problems and give each other advice. Somehow I don't think that's all been coincidence. We have been blessed.

I wish for you good neighbors and friends always. I know you will be a good neighbor and friend in return.

Pray with me:
Lord, for all the blessings you have bestowed upon us, we give you thanks. Amen

Patty B. Williams

November 21st

The Game

"Therefore we also, since we are surrounded by so great a cloud of witnesses, let us lay aside every weight, and the sin which so easily ensnares us, and let us run with endurance the race that is set before us." Hebrews 12:1 (NKJ)

Tomorrow we will be putting on our garnet and gold as we've done a million times before. We'll start our bantering with Gator friends and family members early, and we'll begin feeling that nervous, exciting knot in our stomachs about the time our feet hit the floor. Isn't it a great time to look forward to, to be excited, and to anticipate a year long of bragging rights? I hope for that as much as you do.

I hope another thing, too. I hope that through all the garnet and gold, all the bantering back and forth, all the excitement and nervousness, that what comes shining through most is what God wants others to see through you. Remember it's easy to get ensnared in things that are out of God's will for us. Remember what the game is suppose to be—a game—and when it's over, be in a position to say that you played as well as a fan as you expected the Seminoles to play as a team.

Pray with me:
Lord, help us remember that even in the football stadium others see or don't see you in our words and deeds. Keep us close. Amen

Clean Underwear, Wild Elephants and the Princess

November 22nd
(The day President Kennedy was assassinated)

Sinful People

"You have heard that it was said to the people long ago, 'Do not murder, and anyone who murders will be subject to judgment.' "
Matthew 5:21 (NIV)

You were not born yet when President Kennedy was assassinated, but people of my generation remember exactly where they were and what they were doing at the time they heard the news. It was unbelievable. I was in English class in the 11th grade. I remember my teacher putting her head down and crying. It was so sad.

Not only was a President lost that day, but so was a husband, a father, and a son. In a split second, the terrible act of a sick man affected the life of a whole country—such a waste.

We have so much; we are such a blessed nation, yet we still are sinful people. Go figure!

I am glad that God is a forgiving God; if he weren't, I'd be in deep trouble. I cannot imagine my harming anyone for any reason intentionally, but I have committed my share of sin just like everyone else I know. I ask God daily to forgive me.

Always try to do God's will, but know you will fail at times, and when you do, acknowledge it and ask forgiveness.

Pray with me:
Forgive us, God, when we fail. Help us to ask forgiveness and learn from our mistakes. Amen

Patty B. Williams

November 23rd

Getting Beyond The Actions

"Even in laughter the heart may ache . . ." Proverbs 14:13 (NIV)

People react to things in many different ways. Some people, when they are nervous, will laugh. Some, like me, will cry at happy things and not cry at sad things. Some people who have inferiority complexes behave arrogantly, and some who are very sad act very happy.

We have to try and remember to diagnose those actions of others that don't seem to fit the circumstance. In other words, if someone is acting like nothing is wrong and she is happy when you know she should normally be sad, try to get beyond the actions to see the heart. She may need your help but just doesn't know how to ask for it. If you are smart enough to figure that out, you'll be smart enough to help her, I'm sure.

I think good examples of acting one way and feeling another are included in some of the experiences you had with Adam. You knew how much he truly cared for you, but his actions, because he wasn't mature enough at 15 or 16, or adept enough to express his feelings appropriately, ended up hurting you when what he really wanted to do, I think, was love you. It was a heart matter, not an intentional act of hurt. Maturity comes with being able to discern the difference.

Pray with me:
Lord, give us the ability and sensitivity to look beyond actions to find the feelings, even when it hurts. Amen

Clean Underwear, Wild Elephants and the Princess

November 24th

Making Commitments

"Commit to the Lord whatever you do, and your plans will succeed." Proverbs 16:3 (NIV)

I either read or heard from someone that if you want to get something done, you need to tell someone so you will be committed to do it. I followed that advice before I started writing this book of devotionals. I told Patsy at work. I even confessed why I was telling her, because I knew it was a big commitment, and I needed to use all the tactics I knew to help myself stay focused and committed.

I also asked God to help me, and I know that without that help, I would not have the discipline to continue the commitment.

We need to think about committing more of the things we try to do to the one person who can help us the most. We don't have to wait for something big. What's wrong with committing that English paper or the study time for the math exam? Think what new thoughts to write about might come to mind if you commit your thoughts and words to God.

I think you have some exciting and memorable times in store for you during your college life. I hope you will think about the commitments you want to make about it to yourself and to God. I know it will help you to stay more focused.

Pray with me:
Lord, help us to remember that we don't have to tackle assignments or life by ourselves. You're always there to help us if we ask. Amen

Patty B. Williams

November 25th

Disappointment

"Hope deferred makes the heart sick, but a longing fulfilled is a tree of life." Proverbs 13:12 (NIV)

Disappointment can be an awful feeling, especially disappointment in people we love. Reality, however, is that it's going to happen and certainly more than once.

Probably the most difficult disappointments are those we don't understand, those things that people do or don't do that we have no control over, that just drive us crazy trying to figure out. Those are the times we have to count on hope and prayer that things will change. If we give up and have no hope that things will improve, it only makes us feel worse, defeated.

Remember that we all are imperfect. It takes some longer than others to start working toward what God has planned for them. Our role is to help when we can and to back off when we can't, to keep hope alive and to ask God for help—not when all else fails, but rather at the first sign that his help is needed.

Pray with me:
Keep us from being defeated by disappointment, Lord, and to remember that we, too, disappoint others and need forgiveness just as those who disappoint us. Amen

November 26th

Governed By The Spirit

"But now, by dying to what once bound us, we have been released from the law so that we serve in the new way of the Spirit, and not in the old way of the written code." Romans 7:6 (NIV)

The Old Testament is full of rules and rituals that Christians back in those days had to follow if they were believers. When I read some of them, I was amazed that they had time to do anything else. Some of the practices were disgusting, like killing animals and eating strange food. I am so glad that in the new testament we are expected to live governed by the spirit rather than governed by rules and rituals of Old Testament days.

What does that mean for us today? Does it mean we don't need rules or laws to keep us on the right track? I don't think so. What it means to me is that just because there is no rule telling me that it's against the law to hate my brother or despise my neighbor, my heart tells me it is wrong. Granted, there are many things that society has decided is wrong or socially unacceptable that I don't necessarily agree is God's thinking.

What I do think is God's thinking is that His spirit is always in us. That's why we get those pangs of guilt when we do something we know is wrong or why we get those warm, fuzzy feelings when we are doing things in His will. I know you will work hard at keeping those warm, fuzzy feelings; so will I.

Pray with me:
Lord, keep us grounded in your spirit even when we stray. Help us to find our way back if we get on the wrong track. Amen

Patty B. Williams

November 27th

Thanksgiving

"Let us come before him with thanksgiving and extol him with music and song." Psalm 95:2 (NIV)

As you know, this has not been our best of years—break-ups, divorce, friends who have become very ill, death, and even our Seminoles lost to the Gators! It doesn't get much worse than that!!

Isn't it very easy though to look around and quickly see so many wonderful things we still have to be thankful for? I hope on this special day that you will take an extra minute or two to count your blessings and thank God for them. I will.

These are a few of the many things for which I am thankful:

Life and health
Two beautiful, healthy children
Freedom
Love of family and friends
A good job
A nice home
Plenty of food to eat and clothes to wear

I could go on and on just as you could. I encourage you to give your list some thought.

Pray with me:
Lord, keep us in a mindset of Thanksgiving always, and help us remember to give you the credit for all things great and small. Amen

November 28th

Family And Friends

"Enter into His gates with thanksgiving, and into His courts with praise. Be thankful to Him, and bless His name." Psalm 100:4 (NKJ)

The day after thanksgiving, and I'm still stuffed! What a wonderful time we shared with family and friends. What a great time for Jeff and Carol and me to sit back and enjoy our children and who they've become. What proud parents we are. How thankful we are to have people in our lives who love and genuinely care for one another, and how thankful we are to have more than enough food to eat.

Though it's not a pleasant thought, it's important that during a time when we can so easily see the bountiful blessings we have to be thankful for, that we remember those who are not as fortunate. We have a responsibility to not only remember them, but to do our part in making their lives better. You aren't too young to start thinking about what you can do.

I read something the other day that I thought was right on point. It said someone asked God why he didn't do something about starving and suffering children. His response was that he certainly did do something, he created us!

Pray with me:
With all our blessings, Lord, let us not forget those who don't even have the basics to sustain life. Help us to look for ways to do our part to make their lives better. Amen

Patty B. Williams

November 29th

Being Content

"I am telling you this, but it is not because I need anything. I have learned to be satisfied with the things I have and with everything that happens." Philippians 4:11 (NCV)

We make plans and end up in places where we intended to be. We also make plans and end up in places where we didn't intend to be. Regardless of where we end up, we have a choice about how we'll react, how we'll respond to the situation. We can choose to respond negatively or positively. We can grow through the situation, or we can deteriorate. We can continue to be who we are, or we can pretend to be someone else. We decide.

I've decided that I am too blessed to be anything less than content wherever I am in life. That doesn't mean I won't hurt or that I won't be sad at times, nor does it mean I won't wish to be in a different situation. What it means is that I will always try to trust God to take care of any situation he puts me in or lets me put myself in. I hope you will too.

Pray with me:
Keep me focused on you, Lord, so that all other things will be put in proper perspective. Amen

November 30th

Tug At Our Hearts

"He gives strength to the weary and increases the power of the weak."
Isaiah 40:29 (NIV)

Have you found yourself in situations that weren't pleasant and asked afterward what happened or how you got yourself there? Do you think about how you might have handled the situation differently?

Sometimes when I feel really bad about how I handled something, I try to think about what I did wrong and why I did it that way. Sometimes I don't like the answer because it points to my weaknesses. Other times it points to plain selfishness. Pretty bad, huh?

I think that's one of those things we need to think about more often. We need to try and stay prepared just like we need to be prepared for peer pressure. We can ask God to help by asking him to tug at our hearts when we start down the wrong path in a situation and then help us to learn ways to respond better.

Pray with me:
Keep us alert, Lord, to situations that are difficult to handle. Give us wisdom and the ability to communicate so that we will be pleased with our responses. Amen

Patty B. Williams

December 1st

When The Time Comes

"Commit your works to the Lord, and your thoughts will be established." Proverbs 16:3 (NKJ)

When you were a little girl you liked routine, or at least liked to know where you were going, what was happening, or what to expect. As a grown up young lady you still wish you knew what the future holds—who you will marry, what you will be doing to make a living, what your children will be and what they will look like.

It was interesting at Thanksgiving to listen to Mitch, Michael, Christine and Matt talk about their goals and how they've gotten where they are at this point in their lives. It was interesting to see how far they've come since they were eighteen. I hope you aren't too concerned about not knowing, at this point, what you want to do with your life. I want you to be focused on a plan sometime in the near future, but for right now I want you focused on adjusting to school, learning responsibilities, learning how to live and communicate with others and learning how to discipline yourself when it comes to studying.

When the time comes to become more serious about a profession, don't overlook asking God to help direct you. He knows better than anyone else what your greatest gifts are and how they can best be used. I know he has wonderful plans for you, and I'll be anxiously waiting to see those plans unfold.

Pray with me:
Lord, keep us focused on you so you can direct our paths. Help us remember to ask for help when we need it. Amen

December 2nd
(Aunt Mary Jane's birthday)

Aunt Mary Jane

"But if a widow has children or grandchildren, these should learn first of all to put their religion into practice by caring for their own family and so repaying their parents and grandparents, for this is pleasing to God." 1 Timothy 5:4 (NCV)

In addition to your brother, I know you have always wanted a sister. I'm sorry you didn't get that opportunity, but maybe when you have a sister-in-law one day, that will become a special, sister-like relationship for you. That's what I will hope.

I was lucky to have both a brother and sister even though there were times when we were young that I wished I didn't have either. Isn't that funny, considering how close we all are now?

Mary Jane and I were so different growing up. I thought she was a priss, and she thought I was a brat. We were definitely on two different wavelengths, except when we were little and she cooked me dirt pies, and I ate them. They were so good!

Today on her birthday, I will say a special prayer of thanks to God for not only a special sister, but also a special friend and a special aunt for you and Michael. We are truly blessed.

Pray with me:
Thank you, Lord Jesus, for your gift of siblings. Thank you for the love and special bond we share with each other and with you. Amen

December 3rd

Experiences

"....O Lord my God, I will give you thanks forever." Psalm 30:12 (NIV)

Today was my day to have your car checked out to make sure there was no unseen damage as a result of your accident last week. It was an inconvenience, but one I certainly put in perspective. It could have been the day I was checking you out of the hospital, or worse; it could have been the day I was sorting through your things to give away. I know how fortunate you are that you, nor your car, were hurt badly. We were blessed that it was only a terrifying experience and not much more.

Hopefully it was also a learning experience, not just in terms of how to drive in severe weather, but how precious life is and how quickly it could have changed or been over in a matter of seconds.

When you think in those terms, it kind of puts all those other little things we worry about in their proper place, doesn't it? I have thanked God and his angels more than once that you were spared from injury and even death. Don't forget your experience too quickly. It should help you be a better driver and a more thankful child of God.

Pray with me:
Thank you, Lord, for guardian angels who watch over us. Help us to do our part so they don't have to work overtime too often. Amen

Clean Underwear, Wild Elephants and the Princess

December 4th
(Christine Long's birthday)

Christine

"Only be careful, and watch yourselves closely so that you do not forget the things your eyes have seen or let them slip from your heart as long as you live. Teach them to your children and to their children after them." Deuteronomy 4:9 (NIV)

Before you came along I claimed Christine as my little girl. I didn't know God was going to bless me with my own, and she was the closest one to me. I loved keeping her when she and Michael were little. I would secretly take them to have their pictures made together and then surprise Jeff and Carol when they came back. They were so cute together, and she was so sweet and quiet. Michael, of course, was always bouncing off the walls, looking for fun and chattering incessantly. Christine was probably in total amazement. No wonder she was quiet!

Now they're both grown up, handsome and beautiful, both full of charisma, working and enjoying their lives. They still even love their parents and like to be with us. I guess we did something right!

On her birthday I'll be thinking about my other little girl and hoping she is having a good day so far away from us. I'll hope she remembers how much she's loved and how many people are proud of her accomplishments. I will also be thinking about the perfect daughter I still have close by and hope that she, too, remembers how much she is loved and how proud so many are of all she has accomplished. My two Kappa Deltas—my two girls who are beautiful inside and out. The world is blessed.

Pray with me:
Lord, thank you for little girls, for special daughters and special friends. Watch over them and keep them safe always. Amen

Patty B. Williams

December 5th

Differences

"But He said to him, 'Man, who made me a judge or an arbitrator over you?' " Luke 12:14 (NKJ)

I often wonder why it takes some people longer to grow up than others, or why some people have such a struggle finding themselves or relating to others. We know that environment plays a part and sometimes there are physical or psychological problems that may also play a part of which we may be unaware.

Do you become impatient with those people sometimes? Do you judge them by what your standards are, or by what you consider normal? I know I have made that mistake. Just because some things seem natural for me, I think it should be the same for others, and it's not. God did make us different, and we need to remember that.

We need to work on trying to resolve, compromise, or enjoy our differences instead of letting them cause problems. That's not always easy, and sometimes the differences are too great to work out. I guess my hope for you is that you won't give up too easily in trying to discern which differences in friends or other significant relationships are the ones you can live with and which ones are the ones from which you need to walk away. Don't be afraid or feel like a failure if you have to walk away. God will use those differences in another place for both of you.

Pray with me:
God, you have made us all beautiful in our own way. Help us to recognize that in others as well as in ourselves. Amen

December 6th

Times Alone

"Now those who are such we command and exhort through our Lord Jesus Christ that they work in quietness and eat their own bread."
2 Thessalonians 3:12 (NKJ)

Quiet time, alone time, thinking time, I think we all need that every now and then. It helps me re-group, get my thoughts and myself together and get prepared to jump back in the rat race.

I hope you can enjoy times with yourself like you used to when you were little. You could spend hours with yourself and your baby dolls in your little kitchen or pretending to be in the working world. I think we should be secure in who God made us and enjoy our own company. I think He would want that.

When you have those alone times, I know you know that you are never truly alone. You have numerous loved ones and friends close at hand, and God is no more than a thought away. That should be a comfortable, secure feeling.

Pray with me:
Lord, help us to take advantage of time with just you and ourselves. Help us to use the time wisely. Amen

Patty B. Williams

December 7th
(Pearl Harbor Day)

Pearl Harbor Day

"And you will hear of wars and rumors of wars. See that you are not troubled; for all these things must come to pass, but the end is not yet." Matthew 24:6 (NKJ)

I know Pearl Harbor Day doesn't hold a lot of significance to you at your age because it happened over fifty years ago, and you can't really understand its significance to you at this point in time.

It was the time in history that the Japanese bombed Pearl Harbor and as a result brought the United States into World War II. This day is significant to our family because your Granddaddy and many others went to war to fight for the freedoms we enjoy and take for granted today.

I hope when you study Pearl Harbor Day that it will be important to you to understand the scope of the event, if for no other reason than to learn what it meant in Granddaddy's life.

Think about the difference in priorities for Granddaddy and Michael at the same age. Think about how the experiences Granddaddy and others had that influence their thinking today and that we can't comprehend. It might make your learning easier and more interesting. I hope so.

Pray with me:
Thank you, Lord, for those who sacrificed for us that we might enjoy the freedoms we so often take for granted. Amen

Clean Underwear, Wild Elephants and the Princess

December 8th

Wisdom

"Wisdom is the principal thing; therefore, get wisdom. And in all your getting, get understanding." Proverbs 4:7 (NKJ)

I wish I could instill in you how important wisdom is. As this scripture says, wisdom is the principal thing. It is what shapes your life and helps you make the right or wrong decisions. It helps you be conversant in life, and it helps you put the events of everyday life in order.

Please take advantage of this time in your life to learn and understand things better than I do. I so envy your young mind and all the brain cells you have to fill with new things you know nothing or very little about.

Take lessons from Granddaddy in being curious and interested in many things. I am still amazed at all the different things he knows something about. It's because he reads, and he still seeks wisdom and understanding. Nanny used to surprise me, too, with the things she knew, and you can't imagine how shocked I was one day to find out she never actually finished high school. She was a smart lady because she stayed curious and sought understanding, too, even after becoming a Nanny!

Know that I am counting on you to seek that wisdom and understanding of which I know you are capable. Just don't forget your roots when you become wiser and richer one day.

Pray with me:
Lord, like Solomon, we ask to be wise. Give us understanding hearts and minds in all that we do. Amen

Patty B. Williams

December 9th

Words Of Instruction And Wisdom

"My son, give attention to my words; Incline your ear to my sayings. Do not let them depart from your eyes; Keep them in the midst of your heart." Proverbs 4:20-21 (NKJ)

One of my greatest fears when you and Michael were little was that something would happen to me and you would not remember me. I guess part of that fear came from the realization that I had forgotten so many things of my own youth. Yet it's funny the things that I remember about Mother or Daddy, things they said or did that aren't even significant.

The manners that Nanny insisted upon, correct use of the word "get," not "git," the forbidden use of profanity, the "yes, ma'ams" and "no ma'ams," are small things but things that helped shaped me into who I am. The fear that Daddy placed in Mary Jane and me about lying is probably the reason I couldn't tolerate it with you and Michael. I couldn't imagine that you would even think that lying was an option out of a situation.

I guess my hope is that somewhere along the line your dad and I have given you guys some words of instruction and a little wisdom that will stay in your hearts and minds forever.

Pray with me:
Thank you, God, for parents who love us enough to instill values and insist on certain standards of behavior—even when we don't appreciate it. Amen

Clean Underwear, Wild Elephants and the Princess

December 10th
(Punkie's birthday)

Names

"O Lord, our Lord, How excellent is Your name in all the earth, who have set Your glory above the heavens!" Psalm 8:1 (NKJ)

Nicknames are funny sometimes, aren't they? I don't ever remember calling Punkie by her real name. She's just always been Punkie. You will probably always be Brookie Bear and Michael will always be Pookie Bear. Fortunately for you two, you are only called those names around friends and relatives—though if you make it big one day, we might have to tell the rest of the world!

Names are important. There have been studies conducted to validate this fact. Names have an impact, the studies say, on how you feel about yourself, how successful you are, and what type person you are. I'll never forget being in a parking lot one day when a man was having a difficult time trying to manage a little boy about four years old. The child was running around, not paying attention, and generally just being out of control. Then I heard his father holler "Michael, get over here". I wanted to go tell him it was okay, that his son was normal, that the behavior just came with the name!

I'm glad you have a pretty name and that you have always liked it. Ashley Brooke is sort of princess-like, don't you think? I guess you know a lot of responsibility comes with a pretty name—I'll leave it at that.

Pray with me:
Lord, you know us all by name. Help us to always act in a way that will make us proud of who we are. Amen

Patty B. Williams

December 11th
(Kim Williams's birthday)

Finding The Right Profession

"Give her the reward she has earned, and let her works bring her praise at the city gate." Proverbs 31:31

As a little girl you loved to play office, especially with Weston. You two could get in a world all your own. You were quite good at it, too. At times when you were pretending to talk on the phone, if I hadn't known better, I would have thought you were talking on a real call.

Now as a big girl your practice over the years has paid off. You have worked a real job most of the year and have gotten rave reviews. I have been so proud of you.

I hope you put some thought in to what you want to do as a profession. Rather than just fall into a job, I hope you'll consider the strengths and talents you have and try to find something that lets you use them to their fullest potential.

Work will most likely be a major part of your life. Try to find something that you enjoy and feel like you can make a difference in the world or someone's life. You have such an opportunity before you. Don't let it pass you by. Use the resources at school to help you make some decisions. Talk to people about their professions and do some research into areas you think might interest you. You are smart, sweet, pretty, have charisma and a level head. Those attributes go a long way with employers, so get busy thinking about where you want to be in three or four years. Ask God for help. He's your best student advisor.

Pray with me:

Thank you, Lord, for a free country that let's us choose our professions. Thank you, too, for the opportunities we have to prepare ourselves for the work you have planned for us. Amen

Patty B. Williams

December 12th

Anxiety And Worry

"Anxiety in the heart of man causes depression . . . ." Proverbs 12:25

It would be nice if we didn't have to experience anxiety, wouldn't it—or would it? If we didn't ever experience anxiety, we would never experience the relief of having it lifted, would we?

I know you often times are anxious about different things, which of course, is normal. I guess the one thing I would always hope for is that you don't hide your anxiety and not face it or not talk about it with someone. If you do, then it might quickly become a source of a much bigger problem that you aren't equipped to handle.

Don't ever be afraid or embarrassed to show your fears or anxieties. I can assure you that whatever they are, or will be in the future, someone else has already experienced them. Don't waste life's precious hours on worrying or being anxious about something that maybe someone can help you with, or at least help you realize that you can't do anything about it but forget it and move forward.

God does not want a life of anxiety for us, nor does he want us to put ourselves in situations that will result in anxiety. He wants us happy and full of joy so we can pass that along to others. Work toward that. I will too.

Pray with me:
God, you are always there for us when we need help—maybe in the words of wisdom from a friend, a mom, a dad, or a counselor. Help us to have the courage and wisdom to ask when we need it. Amen

December 13th

Kindness

"She opens her mouth with wisdom, and on her tongue is the law of kindness." Proverbs 31:26 (NKJ)

I think one of the greatest attributes a person can have is kindness. Kindness covers such a wide spectrum of traits. Think about the people you respect and admire the most. Isn't kindness one of their personality traits? Think about the people that you aren't as fond of or don't enjoy being around as much. Is kindness missing in their personality, or at least missing to some extent?

When someone is kind they choose their words carefully; they think before they speak. They sympathize and emphasize with others. They are gentle and would let themselves be hurt before they would hurt others. They love.

God has taught us all to be kind. We just too often miss the mark. It's something we have to work on. I have always felt that you and Michael were both kind children and now kind young adults. That is an attribute of your dad, too, and I hope of myself. Still, we all need to work at it daily. That, I'm sure is God's intent.

Pray with me:
Lord, help us when we miss the mark, whether in kindness or any other attribute. Help us to get back on track quickly. Teach us to be the kind of children you designed. Amen

Patty B. Williams

December 14th

Helping Others

"The person who gives to the poor will have everything he needs . . . ." Proverbs 28:27

I know when you don't have the "right" thing to wear or exactly what you want to eat it makes you grumpy! I suppose that's pretty normal for an 18-year-old. It's pretty normal for a 50-year old, too!

When I buy you and Michael nice things for Christmas it makes me happy because I think it will make you happy, too. I can't, however, forget about all those children that won't have a bunch of nice new things for Christmas. Some, I'm sure, won't have anything at all.

I always try to give to charitable associations at Christmas and throughout the year, though I never feel like it's enough. Of course, if everyone did a little, it would be enough.

I hope as you are out doing your shopping you will think about others who are much less fortunate than we are. You don't have a lot of extra money, but you can always throw a quarter or so in the salvation army bucket or go through your clothes and give those away that you don't wear any longer. Someone would greatly appreciate a warm sweater that you don't like.

God gave us the responsibility and resources to help others. We need to ask his guidance in finding ways to do that.

Pray with me:
Thank you, Lord, for enough to eat, for warm clothes, a bed to sleep in at night, and people who care about us. Help us to take care of those who aren't as fortunate. Amen

Clean Underwear, Wild Elephants and the Princess

December 15th

Questioning God

"Remember the wonders He has done, His miracles, and the judgments He pronounced." 1 Chronicles 16:12 (NIV)

I know there will be many times in your life that you will question the existence of God. As I have told you often, even in these devotionals, it is okay to question. God gave us brains. He wants us to use them!

I think what you have to keep in perspective is how you use your brain when it comes to questioning God. Don't use it just to think about his possible non-existence or how he could let such and such happen if he really loves you. Use it to also look at all the wondrous things around you and question where they came from, why they exist, how they just evolved if there is no God. Question the perfection of a newborn baby, the uniqueness of a snowflake, the knowledge of the animal kingdom.

There will be legitimate reasons to question biblical teachings you've heard all your life. If you have a need to pursue those things you don't understand, God will understand. Just remember that even though science can explain some things, it hasn't been able to explain everything, and many things in the Bible have been validated by archeology. If some things can be validated, is it possible that many of the other things are true also? Seems to me that faith is called for regardless of what you believe.

Pray with me:
Help us, Lord, when we struggle with those things we don't understand. Give us courage to question wisdom to discern the truth, and knowledge in our hearts that you are there. Amen

Patty B. Williams

December 16th

So Wrong, Yet It Feels So Right

"And do not lead us into temptation." Matthew 6:13 (NKJ)

There is a country song that has some lyrics that go something like—"How can it be so wrong and feel so right?" It's talking about a relationship, of course, the one that shouldn't exist, but does. It might very well be a relationship of the heart only, not a physical relationship, but it's one that exist just the same.

Sometimes you can figure out pretty easily why the relationship exists. There's a mutual physical attraction, the atmosphere encourages it, you're lonesome, you feel loved or cared for, you meet one another's needs that someone else can't, or won't. The possibilities are endless.

The question is what do you do about it? The simple answer is—you run away as fast as you can. You make yourself forget it. You just say, "NO"! The reality is most of the time it's not that easy. So then, what? I wish I had the answer for you. I don't. I've been there. I can only offer some advice.

Think about the price, the consequences that might be required. Think about how it will make you feel about yourself, or make others feel about you. Think about talking to God about it.

God made us thinking, feeling, loving beings. He wants what is best for us, and he wants us happy. He knows we're weak, and he expects us to need his guidance and help. Don't forget to ask for it.

Pray with me:
Lord, you know we need you, especially when it feels so right and we know it's wrong. Help us to depend on your strength. Amen

Clean Underwear, Wild Elephants and the Princess

December 17th

Holding The Keys

"Do not withhold good from those to whom it is due, when it is in the power of your hand to do so." Proverbs 3:27 (NKJ)

It's hard to do those things we aren't too crazy about doing, especially when it takes our valuable time to do them. It's even more difficult to do those things we aren't crazy about for someone we're not terribly crazy about.

I know you have had situations like this already, but let me assure you that you will have many more in your lifetime. You will also have those times when you hold the keys to someone else's happiness just by giving of your precious time, at a time when you would much prefer to be doing something else.

You have always been pretty good at doing those things you know you should do to make others happy. I know that it has often been at your own expense of giving up something, like time, or doing something you'd rather do. I am proud of you for that. I encourage you to continue, because I know you'll reap benefits from it that you may not be able to see immediately.

When giving of your time and yourself becomes difficult, try to think about the people who have done the same for you, and maybe it will make it a little easier.

Pray with me:
God, you did the ultimate for us. Help us to do at least a little for others. Amen

Patty B. Williams

December 18th

Disciplining Children

"He who spares his rod hates his son, but he who loves him disciplines him promptly." Proverbs 13:24 (NKJ)

You didn't get many spankings when you were little, though you did get some. Your brother, on the other hand, got as many as most little boys named Michael. As he got older he got in to more things than you did that got him in to trouble. Of course, you probably just hid it better or didn't talk about it as much as little blabbermouth did.

Neither of you ever believed that old saying that it hurt us more than it did you when you had to be disciplined. You will understand that one day, but it's still a few years away.

When you become a mom one day, I hope you and your children's father will not be afraid to discipline your children when they need it. I hope you work hard at teaching the values you and Michael have been taught. I hope you remember that children need and want to know who is in charge. They will need to know that you can be a friend to a certain extent, but your priority is to be a parent. God planned it that way and taught us accordingly through his word. Now, if I can just remember, when the time comes, that a Nanny has to discipline too!

Pray with me:
Father God, we thank you for parents who love us enough to "make us mind." Help us to appreciate the hard work. Amen

Clean Underwear, Wild Elephants and the Princess

December 19th

Getting Ready For Christmas

"So it was, when the angels had gone away from them into heaven, that the shepherds said to one another, Let us now go to Bethlehem and see this thing that has come to pass, which the Lord has made known to us." Luke 2:15 (NKJ)

Christmas is just around the corner, and you know me, I just love it. This year my shopping is finished a week before Christmas and I plan to enjoy what's left of the days leading up to Christmas. I am even taking some time off from work just so I can relax, enjoy your being home and do some of those things I never get to do.

Are you ready for the big day? Have you planned ahead so you can relax and get in the right spirit instead of a spirit of hurried-up-ness and last minute stress? I hope so. We need to have time to think about the true meaning of Christmas and to have time to enjoy friends and family.

I know you have taken time to think about the presents you've bought those people on your list. You have always been very thoughtful about that. I hope as you wrap them you will also be reflective about particular people and how important they are to you in your life. That in itself should be a good gift to you. You might also say a little prayer for them and ask God to watch over them and bless them with a peaceful and good New Year. What more could you want for those you love?

Pray with me:
For this special time of the year, Lord, we give you thanks. For the ultimate gift you gave on Christmas Day we are blessed. Keep us focused on what this time of year is all about. Amen

Patty B. Williams

December 20th

Different Kinds Of Families

"I will bless those that bless you, I will curse him that curses you; and in you all the families of the earth shall be blessed."
Genesis 12:3 (NKJ)

We had our office Christmas luncheon this week. As always, it was great! As I was walking back to my office and looking in the various offices of my peers, I thought about how different we all were. I walked by John's office, the serious one, the one who lets us know how the stocks are doing, the one who answers questions in minute detail, the one who has a kind heart. I walked by Colleen's office. She had just returned from being out on sick leave for six weeks after surgery. She lost her husband not too long ago to a long-term illness. I admired the way she handled it. Terry wasn't in the office, but if he had been, he would have been hard at work on some grievance problem or talking to one of the union members, and he would have been doing it with detailed professionalism—dotting his I's and crossing his T's. Then I thought about Doug, our great visionary person, the one who thinks so fast his words don't keep up and, therefore, talks in half sentences. Sometimes he drives us crazy trying to figure out what he wants, yet his visions keep us growing and learning. I could go on and on.

All of us have our own personalities, our own strengths and weaknesses. We sometimes get ticked at one another. Sometimes our different work styles cause problems, but we are still our own little family. We even act like a family. We fuss together; we laugh together. This year we have mourned together at the death of one of our co-workers and the sickness of our boss. Some of us are good friends. Some of us aren't such good friends, yet we still manage to get the job done.

Clean Underwear, Wild Elephants and the Princess

The point in the description of my office family is to remind you that you have many different kinds of families. You have your real blood family, your family of high school friends, and your sorority family, who each hold their special place in your life. Don't take any of them for granted because they each play a part in who you have become. I'm proud of all the families of which you have become a member. We are both blessed.

Pray with me:
Thank you, Lord, for those who are members of our family. Help us to remember the importance they play in our lives. Amen

Patty B. Williams

December 21st

Under The Circumstances

"Multitudes, multitudes in the valley of decision! For the day of the Lord is near in the valley of decision." Joel 3:14 (NKJ)

Today in his sermon Bob was illustrating a point when he made reference to the standard response some people give when they are asked the question, "How are you?" Some people respond by saying, "I'm fine, under the circumstances." Bob said he had a friend who would respond back and say, "well what are you doing under there?" I thought that was a clever come back.

Bob went on to say that if we are Christians, we don't have to live "under the circumstances." In other words, we can live well and happy in spite of the circumstances. I believe that. It's just a different attitude to maintain. There will always be times of bad, sad, hurtful circumstances. As I've told you many times before, the decision of how to handle them is left up to us.

You have already had some difficult circumstances that you've had to live under, and you've handled them well. I hope you continue to have a positive attitude about life and keep out from under the circumstances when it's necessary. I'll be praying for you.

Pray with me:
Lord, we live under many good circumstances that make our lives complete. Help us remember when difficult circumstances appear, that you are still with us. Amen

December 22nd
(Emily's and Ellen's birthday)

Emily And Ellen

" . . . .but I have called you friends, for all things that I heard from My Father I have made known to you." John 15:15 (NKJ)

I remember so vividly when Emily and Ellen became a part of our lives. I think they were six and you were four. I first met them at Jim's and Harriet's wedding and thought they were so cute.

Though I assumed those two little girls would become a part of our lives because of the special friendship we had with Jim, I never knew they would become such an important part of our family. Even when Harriet and I were still trying to determine our relationship with one another, you and the girls were fast becoming best friends. You played so hard and so well together. I loved having the three of you all to myself.

Then as you grew older and went to separate schools, I thought your friendships might wane, but they never did. You didn't have all the same friends, but you always loved each other. Then when the girls were about sixteen and you were about fourteen, you probably suffered some of your greatest hurt, anger and sadness when circumstances separated you for two years. That, too, could have destroyed your friendship, but it didn't. You are as close now as you always have been.

As the years go by, I think you will find that those friends who you have shared true heartache and joy with, spiritual growth (Methodist Youth Camp), and changes in maturity, will be those friends who will be lifelong friends. I hope that is the case with you, Emily and Ellen. It's such a blessing to have special people in your life who truly care about you and your wellbeing. You may not always be close socially as the years go by, but I hope you are close in heart and always there for one another if needed. I think God plans those friendships.

Pray with me:
Thank you God for lending us special friends that reflect your love and caring. Help us to take care of those friendships. Amen

Ellen, Emily and Brooke

December 23rd

The Perfect Son And Daughter

"Many daughters have done well, but you excel them all."
Proverbs 31:29 (NKJ)

While I've been home on vacation, I've been cleaning out files and trying to get parts of my life in order so I can function a little easier in my day-to-day activities. In one of my files I found a letter I wrote to you and Michael about three years ago before I left to go on one of my ski trips. It was a letter telling you some things I wanted you to know and things you needed to know in case something happened to me. Not a pleasant thought, I hope, but a necessary one.

That letter still exists with a few updates, and it is one I will continue to update as the years go by. The part I won't try to update is the part that says you and Michael have made my life complete. That will never change. You have been the perfect daughter and he has been the perfect son.

When you become a parent one day, you'll soon realize that there's no way to convey all your love to your children. They'll never understand until they have children themselves. God intended the relationship between parents and children to be very special. I hope we always please him in that regard. Sometimes it will be more difficult than others, but at all times I'm sure it will be worth the effort.

Pray with me:
Lord, you have blessed us with each other. Help us to take care of our relationships at all times, even when it takes effort. Amen

December 24th

The Night Before Christmas

"Now after Jesus was born in Bethlehem of Judea in the days of Herod the king, behold, wise men from the East came to Jerusalem, saying, 'Where is He who has been born King of the Jews? For we have seen His star in the East and have come to worship Him.'" Matthew 2:1-2 (NKJ)

'Tis the night before Christmas: the time for anticipation of what tomorrow will bring. I'm not sure you ever get too old to enjoy the anticipation. This year we are at Aunt Mary Jane's again. The only problem is we don't have all the little people to enjoy their excitement. Cassidy is the only little one, and she has her wish list memorized. She is so cute. She would be more excited about tomorrow if she weren't having such a good time tonight.

As you anticipate Santa's gifts and all the good food that will be waiting after the gift opening, I hope you take time to think about what Christmas meant so very long ago and the meaning it still has for us today. Also remember those less fortunate than us and say a special prayer.

Pray with me:
Thank you, Lord, for this special time, for the gifts we know will be forthcoming, and for the love that will be wrapped with each one. We ask your blessing on those who are less fortunate. Help us to do our part to change their situation. Amen

Clean Underwear, Wild Elephants and the Princess

December 25th

Christmas

"For there is born to you this day in the city of David a Savior, who is Christ the Lord." Luke 2:11 (NKJ)

The birth of a baby, there's not anything to compare with that experience. What a time of joy and excitement it can be, or what a time of sadness it can be if there are extenuating circumstances.

Can you imagine the thoughts that must have been going on in Mary's head when Jesus was born? She must have been excited, frightened, full of great expectations, nervous, exhausted—very similar to the thoughts of most mothers.

As we wait for the birth of the new baby in our family, I hope you will remember to keep Uncle Billy and Aunt Debbie in your prayers. Ask God for a healthy, happy baby; ask him for a special bond between the boys and the new baby and for wisdom, patience, and stamina for Uncle Billy and Aunt Debbie. Don't forget to also thank God for the wonderful extended family this baby will have to love and nurture it.

A baby born almost 2000 years ago and a baby to be born any day, both such an important part of our lives. We are truly blessed.

Pray with me:
Thank you, Lord, for the birth this day of your son that we may also rejoice in a new birth in our family. We ask your blessing on the new baby and on our family. Amen

Patty B. Williams

December 26th

Changes

"And He changes the times and the seasons; He removes kings and raises up kings; He gives wisdom to the wise and knowledge to those who have understanding." Daniel 2:21 (NKJ)

The gifts have been opened, a ton of food has been eaten, the paper and bows are picked up, and Christmas 1997, is over. What will we remember about it, and what will we take of it into 1998?

Well, it was rainy and warm; we didn't get up until 9:30, a record sleep-in time for us on Christmas Day. There were no little people to talk to about Santa Claus, no plate of cookie crumbs and milk left by Santa. There was no frenzy in opening gifts. It was a good Christmas but a different one. Times and circumstances change each Christmas, just like each day, just like relationships, just like us. We decide how we react to the changes and circumstances.

Did you like being with other family members on Christmas morning? Were you pleased with the gifts you bought and the gifts you received? Did you enjoy getting ready for Christmas? Do you think you spent enough time doing the things God would want you to do at Christmas—like doing things for those less fortunate, being involved in more than just the commercialism of Christmas? Did you use your time wisely so you could enjoy your holiday instead of being stressed? The point is, if you want things to be different next year, start working on those changes now. Take control of your circumstances as much as possible.

Christmas has always been a special time for our family. I look forward to the changes that will come in the future when I have grandchildren to enjoy it with, and maybe I'll even get a Christmas with snow one year. Changes are not always sad.

Pray with me:
Be with us, Lord, through the changing times of our life. Help us to cherish each stage. Amen

Patty B. Williams

December 27th

Tested Faith

"And the apostles said to the Lord, 'Increase our faith'."
Luke 17:5 (NKJ)

I saw my friend Bobbi today. My heart ached for her. She is experiencing what all mothers fear the most, the loss of a child. Her son is dying of cancer.

I was amazed at her faith but also at her integrity in questioning God's role in this circumstance. She said she was able to accept her son's death but that if he had to suffer, which is a strong possibility, she will have a difficult time with that. I can certainly understand her feelings. She knows God understands and knows God let his own son suffer, but she does not want that for her son and wants God to intervene. I wish I had the right words to comfort her, and I wish I could tell her that God will intervene and not let Alan Carl suffer, but I can't. All I can do is pray for strength for both of them to handle whatever may be in the future. It will not be easy even if there is no pain.

Keep them in your prayers, and remember every day to be thankful for your health and the health of those you love.

Pray with me:
Lord, be with Alan Carl and all his family and friends who love and care for him so very much. Give them strength and increased faith to handle whatever the future may hold. Amen

Clean Underwear, Wild Elephants and the Princess

December 28th

Making Transitions

"For lo, the winter is past, the rain is over and gone."
Song of Solomon 2:11 (KJV))

Even when we've made up our mind about something or think we have made up our mind, sometimes it is still difficult to get on with it, isn't it? It's hard to make transitions, especially if those transitions cause hurt, anger, or regret, or if they mean leaving some good times behind.

I know you are making some transitions in your relationship with Gabriel, and I know you have mixed emotions about it. I also know you haven't made your decision lightly. You need to remember and help him understand that if it didn't hurt, it would only indicate little substance was ever in the relationship.

The other thing you and he both need to remember is that if you spend your time being sorrowful about the yesterdays and worrying about the future, you won't be able to enjoy or be thankful for today. Be glad for all the good you both had in the past with one another, hope for each other's happiness in the future, and don't give up the joys that today may bring. God made you both too special for that. I will be praying for the two of you.

Pray with me:
Thank you, God, for love even when it hurts. This would be a very cold, lonely, dull world without it. Amen

Patty B. Williams

December 29th

Love

"Beloved, let us love one another, for love is of God; and everyone who loves is born of God and knows God." 1 John 4:7 (NKJ)

There have been many things written about love by many people—poets, songwriters, and prophets of old, and ordinary people. It is definitely a subject everyone is familiar with, but one that is expressed so differently from one person to another. Men and women in general speak and feel it so differently.

The Beetles said, "Love, love, love, all you need is love". Now we know that ain't true! There is an old Polish saying that says, "He who loves is a slave; he who is loved is master." For the most part, that is probably true. Shakespeare said that the course of true love never did run smooth. That is definitely true!

Ah, love, sometimes we hate it and sometimes we wish we didn't know it. Just remember, love comes in all kinds of packages. Sometimes it comes for a short time and leaves gently, sometimes it comes and leaves with sorrow, and sometimes it comes and leaves and we are forever touched. What I wish for you, in time, is that it will come and stay, be all you've hoped and prayed for, and will touch your heart and soul forever. I think that is what God has planned.

Pray with me:
Keep us open to love, God. Help us to look for it in all the right places. Keep us patient and alert to your guidance. Amen

Clean Underwear, Wild Elephants and the Princess

December 30th
(Stephen's Birthday)

God's Plans

"'I know the plans I have for you', declares the Lord, 'plans to prosper and not to harm you, plans to give you hope and a future.'"
Jeremiah 29:11 (NIV)

Don't you wish you knew what God has planned for you? It sure would make a lot of things easier, wouldn't it? It could save you some anguish and heartache. It could probably even help you get focused a little easier.

Well, as you know, we aren't going to know God's plans until they start to unfold. Even then, we may not be sure what the BIG plans look like. The date for the big sorority or fraternity weekend, a college major, a profession, a husband, a family, they are all part of the plans that are ahead. If you knew, would you work as hard at trying to make them all perfect? Would life be dull? Would you be as good an employee, as good a wife or mother if you didn't have to work at it instead of just sitting back and letting the plans fall in to place? Think about it. Isn't God giving us time to grow as the plans unfold? That's what I think.

I also think God has GREAT plans for you, Miss Brooke. I know you feel like you're floundering sometimes, but the plans are there. Be patient. Enjoy where you are now and the growth that is happening. God's timing is perfect. It's just hard for us to see that sometimes.

Pray with me:
Lord, help us to look for the plans you have for us, but help us to be patient as they unfold. Keep us excited about the prospects of the future and faithful to our commitment to you. Amen

Patty B. Williams

December 31ˢᵗ

New Beginnings

"Seek ye first His kingdom and His righteousness, and all these things will be added unto you." Matthew 6:33 (KJV)

Have you made out your list of New Year resolutions? My guess is, no, you haven't. Although you have probably made out a list of resolutions in your head, you most likely, like me, haven't committed them to writing. We both should, just because that's the way it's been proven to work the best. Make a commitment in writing to yourself and then put it somewhere that will keep it in your thoughts daily.

What do you want to accomplish this year? Losing weight is always on the list, right? How about developing good study habits, is that on your list? Do you want to be better about keeping in touch with friends? Do you want to improve your housekeeping or cooking skills? You know the sky is our limit. We have the ability to do most anything we want; discipline is the problem. That's what I plan to work on this year.

When you make your list, remember to ask God to help you with your commitment. Then ask a friend or relative to keep you accountable. We can all use a little help. My prayer tonight will be that we both work hard at making and keeping our resolutions so this time next year we can look back and say, yes, we did it!

Pray with me:
Lord, you know we need work on our discipline. Help us this New Year to be committed to our resolutions and to you. Amen

Clean Underwear, Wild Elephants and the Princess

January 1st

New Year's Resolutions

"Therefore, if anyone is in Christ, he is a new creation; old things have passed away; behold, all things have become new."
2 Corinthians 5:17 (NIV)

A new year, a new start, a new semester, a new opportunity to be all we want to be, are you ready? Are you excited? I hope so. Not everyone will have the same opportunities you and I will have, so doesn't that obligate us somewhat to do our best?

I hope you have some plans to work toward in this new year. Without some sort of plan, it's very easy to let all your goals slip by the wayside as you get involved in everyday living. You wouldn't start a trip to a new place without a plan. Your professors don't start a new class without a plan, and you don't normally start a new project without a plan. Surely a new year deserves as much consideration.

I admit I don't have my plans for the new year yet, but I will by the end of next week, and I ask you to be the one to hold me accountable, o.k.? Every now and then ask me how I'm doing with my plan; that's the accountability part. Now, let's get started. Welcome, New Year, we're ready for you!

Pray with me:
Thank you, God, for new years and new starts, for new opportunities to grow into the person you want us to be. We ask that you stay by our side and help us along the way. Amen

Patty B. Williams

January 2nd

A New Baby In The Family

"The Lord says that I will be God of all Israel's family groups, and they will be my people." Jeremiah 31:1 (NIV)

December 30th we received the call—A perfect, beautiful, new little boy; that's what Billy said we had in the family now. I can hardly wait to see him. I wonder if he knows how fortunate he is to be born into this family.

What could you tell him about your experiences in this family? Could you tell him he has wonderful parents and wonderful grandparents on both sides of his family? Could you tell him he'll have more than ample support in good times and bad? Could you tell him about the Nanny you and his brothers loved so much and who was such an important part of your lives? Could you tell him that he could be a Gator or a Seminole and he would still be loved?

Though we don't know his name yet, we know how much this little boy will be loved. We know as long as there is someone that is able to work in his extended family he will never go hungry or be without clothes unless he chooses to be that way. We know that the freedoms he will enjoy are because his Granddaddy and many other brave men fought for them in World War II, and we know that he'll be taught strong values by a Christian Mother and Daddy who want the best for all their boys. What a lucky, blessed little boy. We're so happy he has come into our lives.

Pray with me:
How blessed we are, Lord, with all our children, parents and grandparents in this family. Help us to never take each other, or all we have, for granted. Keep our love for one another and for you strong and steadfast. Amen

Clean Underwear, Wild Elephants and the Princess

January 3rd

Respect

"A good name is better than fine perfume . . ." Ecclesiastes 7:1 (NIV)

Respect is an attribute that is so important. It says a lot about your total character. It doesn't always come easy; you have to earn it, and you have to work at maintaining it. It's easy to lose with one careless act or one or two careless words. Once lost, it's hard to regain.

You earn it in your profession, you earn it as a parent, you earn it as a friend, you earn it as a student, or a child. How do you do it? I think you know the answer to that. You have earned respect from your friends, my friends, children, employers, I could go on and on. I hope you never take that for granted and are always careful to protect it. I think you know how to do that, too.

Keep aware of your actions and make sure they continue to deserve the respect that you've gained at such a young age. I'm proud of you.

Pray with me:
God, it's not always easy to maintain the respect we've had, nor is it easy to be respectful when we think others don't deserve it. Please help us in both cases to strive to do our best. Amen

Patty B. Williams

January 4th

One In A Million

The teacher says, "This is what I learned: I added all these things together to see if I could find some meaning for everything. I am still looking for it, but I have not found it. But I did discover that truly good people are hard to find. Such people are one in a million!" Ecclesiastes 7:27-28 (NCV)

Do you know someone who is "one in a million"? I think I have known two—Aunt Dolly and Jean Douglas, the mother of a friend of mind. You of course know Aunt Dolly and what she's meant to me over the years, but you never knew Jean. She lived in Brooker and died a number of years ago. She wasn't a big part of my life like Aunt Dolly has been, but she and her husband were friends of Nanny's and Granddaddy's and her children were friends of mine. I just remember thinking at her funeral that I had never heard anyone say anything bad about her as long as I knew her. Wouldn't you like that to be said about you one day? I sure would.

I know it's God's plan that we all be one in a million. We just manage to mess up those plans along the way, don't we? I think you are one in a million, but I guess Mommys all think that. I want you to work toward God's plan. I guess that's a Mommy thing, too.

Pray with me:
Thank you, Lord, for those special people whose lives you've shared with us. Help us to emulate them so that your plans are fulfilled. Amen

January 5th

Avoiding Sorrow And Sadness

"So avoid sorrow and sadness. Forget about all the bad things that happen to you. This is because the joys of youth pass quickly away." Ecclesiastes 11:10 (NCV)

Ah, youth—how I wish I still had it. It vanishes so quickly. It's not that I have many regrets from my youth; I would just like to have more time to enjoy life.

I hope you understand how valuable your youth is and how it won't last forever. Please don't waste it on being sorrowful or sad. If things happen, as they surely will, that make you sorrowful or sad, experience it. Know what it feels like so you can try and avoid it in the future; then get over it.

If you find you are experiencing sorrow and sadness more than you are enjoying life and being happy, think about what's going on and how you can change the picture. Don't wait too long either. Remember the youth thing and how fleeting it is. That's not just a cliché. It's so very true.

God wants us happy, even though he knows experiencing sorrow and sadness will help us grow. I want you happy too, and if you aren't, I need to know, so keep me on your call list along with God.

Pray with me:
Lord, help us remember how many things we have to make us happy. When the sorrowful and unhappy times appear, be with us as we go through it and help us not to get stuck. Amen

Patty B. Williams

January 6th

Finding The Right Guy

"Women of Jerusalem, promise me by the gazelles [an animal of the antelope family] and the deer. Promise not to wake love. Don't excite my feelings of love until I'm ready." Song of Solomon 3:5 (NCV)

I know you would like to have a boyfriend, and I understand why. I'm not sure if you want a serious boyfriend or not, but I guess I hope that you don't right now.

Love is serious business, as you have already learned to a certain extent. Though I don't think you have experienced the serious, marriage kind of love yet, I know that you will in the not too distant future. I just want you to be ready for it, and I don't want it to come before you are ready.

I think that's what happened to Bill, at least that's what he said. He thought he was ready, but obviously he wasn't. Moving too quickly caused a lot of pain and sadness. I don't want that to happen to you or your brother.

How do you get ready? Well, you date different guys, you use your head as well as your heart, you don't get in a hurry, you become confident enough in yourself and in God's guidance to make the tough decisions to walk away when you know it's not right. Examine your reasons for attraction and make sure they are ones that will last. Pray continuously for wisdom to make good choices.

Twice I made decisions too quickly. I may have made the same decisions if I had waited longer, but maybe not. I'll never know. I only know that you and Michael were a result of one of those decisions, and for that I am blessed. The lesson to be learned is obvious. Be patient. There is a plan. Don't try to figure it out on your own.

Pray with me:
Thank you, Lord, for choices. Make us wise and patient so those choices will be the right ones at the right time. Amen

Patty B. Williams

January 7th

Being Tired

"Come to me, all of you who are tired and have heavy loads. I will give you rest." Matthew 11:28 (NCV)

I heard you say how tired you were on numerous occasions while you were home on Christmas break. Part of the reason was the late hours you were keeping, part of the reason was having too much to do in a short period of time, and my guess is part of the reason was carrying a heavy emotional load about your boyfriend/girlfriend relationship.

Being tired physically is one problem. Being tired in spirit is another. They both can zap your energy completely and both need to be dealt with equally.

As you return to school and a new semester, you need to get your weariness in check. You need all your energy to start fresh, to concentrate, and to be able to make those early morning classes. I hope you are working on that.

Remember God's message above, too, if you get bogged down. Sometimes we find it pretty difficult to get things in check by ourselves. You don't have to do it alone.

Pray with me:
Renew us, Lord, physically and in spirit. Help us to take care of ourselves and remember to ask for help when we need it. Amen

Clean Underwear, Wild Elephants and the Princess

January 8th

Funerals And Parties

"It is better to go to a funeral than to a party. We all must die. Everyone living should think about this." Ecclesiastes 7: 2 (NCV)

My guess is you don't agree with the first part of the above scripture. I'm not sure I do either, at least not the literal meaning of it. I haven't been to any funerals that I enjoyed, and I have been to lots of parties I've enjoyed—some, a bunch!

I think the intent of the above scripture is that living with God is so much better than living on earth. We should be looking forward to heaven and not dreading it. Although we will most likely be very sad at a funeral, we should be looking beyond the death of the physical body and be thinking about how wonderful it will be for our soul when we are with God.

Grandma Green is not going to live much longer. Her heart is worn out. It will be very difficult for her children and just as difficult for Aunt Mary Jane. Grandma Green, though a mother-in-law, has been like Aunt Mary Jane's second mother. I have asked Aunt Mary Jane if she's prepared for what may happen soon. I think she is. She doesn't have regrets about her relationship with Grandma Green, and she knows Grandma Green will be in heaven with no more physical struggles. That at least is a comforting thought. She will be sad, but she won't be angry with God for taking Grandma Green home.

I hope you will be able to think about death in those terms when you have to face it one day with your family members and friends. Don't think of it as having to feel like the funeral is better than a party, but do think about it as a better place for all of us.

Patty B. Williams

Pray with me:
Lord, help us to face the death of our loved ones with the confidence that you will be with us to mend our hearts and help us understand the greatness of heaven. Amen.

January 9th

Stone Throwing

"A person without good sense finds fault with his neighbor. But a person with understanding keeps quiet." Proverbs 11:12 (NCV)

It's so easy to find faults in others and so difficult to realize them in ourselves, isn't it? Most everyone is guilty of it; some are just worse than others.

When discussing someone's demeanor or looks, or anything else about them, I think you have to use good sense to discern if the discussion is finding fault or is just simple discussion. Both your head and your heart know the difference. God knows the difference, too.

Sometimes it is awfully difficult to keep quiet when everyone else is finding fault with someone, especially if that someone has made you angry, hurt you, or just is not one of your favorite people. I think at those times we need to really think before we open our mouths. We need to remember that we will be judged by the same measure. I guess it's like the story in the Bible where Jesus says, "Let the one without sin be the first to cast a stone." That limits the stone throwing a little, don't you think?

Pray with me:
Lord, there are times we deserve to be talked about and criticized and times others deserve it too. Let us just remember that it's your job not ours. Amen

Patty B. Williams

January 10th

Homecomings

"Then all the people left, each for his own home, and David returned home to bless his family." 1 Chronicles 16:43 (NCV)

Homecomings are special, aren't they? I loved having you home for the holidays and being able to see some of your friends and our family. Having Don and Cindy home with the children and having a day with just Daddy and the children in the family was so special.

There are other special kinds of homecomings that you will enjoy as the years go by—high school homecomings, college homecomings, etc. They will be so much fun. I look forward to that for you. I'm glad you are close to your family and have so many friends because that is what will make it such a special time for you and them.

Your homecoming court ribbon hanging in your room at home is a reminder of a happy, sweet memory for both of us—for you, because it represents the feelings toward you by your peers, for me because it represents the fruition (fulfillment) of some of my hopes for you and your high school experiences.

We as Christians have another time of homecoming to look forward to, and even though it's not something we like to think about a lot, it should be comforting to know that we don't have to worry about it. We know where we will be, and that should make us at peace with the future.

Pray with me:
Keep us always mindful, Lord, of our ultimate homecoming so that we live our lives as you have planned. Amen

Clean Underwear, Wild Elephants and the Princess

January 11th

Ask Not What Your Country Can Do

"At the appointed time he shall return and go toward the South; but it shall not be like the former or the latter." Daniel 11:29 (NKJ)

There is a plaque in my office that is called the "We Made A Difference" award. It was given in recognition of the part I played in helping administer a successful HRD/Personnel Conference a year ago. It was really no big deal in some ways, but I guess if you stop and think about it, had our team not done a good job, the conference could have been a disaster.

The above scripture is in reference to the difference in the outcome of a war because of the leader and the circumstances involved. Making a difference, however, is important, regardless of wherever that is, or for whatever purpose. Just think how useless you would feel if you were working a job that you felt made no difference to anyone. What a waste that would be of time and effort! Life is much too short for that.

As you think about a profession, think about whether or not you want to make a difference in someone's life, the life of many people, or the life of the world. There are endless possibilities. Remember John Kennedy's famous line—"Ask not what your country can do for you, ask what you can do for your country." That may not be the exact words, but it's close enough. You get the picture.

Don't worry about your future, Brookie Bear, but do start thinking about it. You have all the qualities necessary to make a big difference somewhere for someone. I know you will.

Pray with me:
Lord, we know you put us here to make a difference. Show us the way. Amen

Patty B. Williams

January 12th

Timing Is Everything

"A son who gathers crops when they are ready is wise. But the son who sleeps through the harvest is a disgrace." Proverbs 10:5 (NCV)

Timing is everything! You've heard that all your life. Isn't it true in just about everything? Think about meeting that special guy. If you meet him right after coming out of a bad relationship with another guy, he might not even spark your interest. Think about friendships. If you can't be there for a friend when she needs you, what might happen to the friendship? If you don't study at the proper time, what happens when it's time to test your knowledge?

I remember when I wanted a car so badly and Daddy said he couldn't at the time because he owed his father-in-law some money. The timing was not right. He couldn't spend money on me for pleasure when he was in debt to someone else. It just wasn't the right thing to do.

I hope you will always stay mindful of your timing, regardless of what it's in relationship to. It will make a big difference in the way you feel about yourself and the way others feel about you. It is indeed important.

Pray with me:
Lord, keep us on our toes with our timing. Give us the fortitude (determination), the discipline, and the desire to want to do the right thing at the right time. Amen

January 13th

Peace And Harmony

"The Lord turn his face toward you and give you peace."
Numbers 6:26 (NCV)

There is a couple in my Disciple Group that have parents and siblings that are not Christians. You can imagine the difficulties that arise on occasion when they get together, especially at a time like Christmas.

This past Christmas there were some stressful periods of time and conflict when they were together. A question was asked of my friend, by the mother, if I remember correctly, as to when they were ever going to have a time together when it was peaceful. My friend's response was that she didn't think it would ever change unless the Lord became part of their lives.

That, of course, is not to say that all people who live without God in their lives are in conflict with others all the time, nor is it to say that all people who live with God in their lives live without conflict.

I think what we need to remember is that God teaches us in his word how to live in peace and harmony with others and with ourselves. As Christians, it's our responsibility to study those words and put them in action.

Three of my favorite books in the Bible for teaching every day living are Proverbs, Ecclesiastes, and Ruth. If we could follow those teachings, we would be in good shape in the peace and harmony arena.

You are going to continue to have conflict in your life, and hopefully you are learning with each occurrence, how to handle it better. You don't, however, have to be without peace in your heart. Regardless of the conflict, God can help with the peace to see you through it. Remember to ask.

Pray with me:
Thank you, God, for reassurance that you are with us always, whether it be in times of conflict or in times of peace. Help us to study your word to keep cognizant of what we must do to have peace and harmony in our lives. Amen

January 14th

Inside And Outside

"Therefore be imitators of God as dear children. And walk in love, as Christ also has loved us and given Himself for us, an offering and a sacrifice to God for a sweet-smelling aroma. " Ephesians 5:1-2 (KJV)

Jim Luther has been teaching our Sunday School class for several months now. He has such a gift for teaching. I wish you could take a class from him sometime. He really makes the Bible come alive and must have been a wonderful professor.

In our lesson this past week, we were talking about King Saul and what a driven man he was. We talked about how being driven can be good or bad, depending on your motivation. Saul's motivation was not good. His inward heart, compared to what he showed of himself outwardly, were not the same.

Jim asked a good question: "If we were to turn ourselves inside out, what would we see"? What would our inner self look like? Would we be filled with jealousy, greed, anger, hate, or would we be filled with love, kindness, joy, and gratitude? Would our insides look the same as the outsides?

Everyone knows people that are different on the outside from how they are on the inside. Sometimes the outside is better and sometimes it's worse. Our goal, of course, should be to be the person God wants us to be on the inside and the outside.

I think you're headed in the right direction, Brookie Bear, keep up the good work.

Patty B. Williams

Pray with me:
Lord, it is not easy to be the same inside and out, and it's even more difficult to be the person you want us to be all the time. We need your strength to help us. Amen

Clean Underwear, Wild Elephants and the Princess

January 15th

Being Loved

"So these three things continue forever: faith, hope and love. And the greatest of these is love." 1 Corinthians 13:13 (NCV)

I know we sometimes take lightly all the "I love yous" we say in our family. I suppose that's normal. Most everyone takes something for granted that they shouldn't. At least with all the I love yous we express openly now, we shouldn't get to the end of our days and wonder if we were loved.

I hope you never hesitate to express your feelings and words of love or caring to another person. Work toward never having any regrets about that.

Mary Jane told me tonight about she and Grandma Green telling each other how much they had always loved one another. I'm glad they had that time together, alone, to share their feelings with one another before Mrs. Green closes her eyes for that last time. I'm even happier that they both knew how one another felt long before they shared it at this difficult time. What a blessing that is for both of them.

And, aren't we both blessed? We've felt a lot of different feelings growing up in our family, but I don't think unloved was ever one of them, do you?

Pray with me:
Thank you, Lord, for life and love. Help us to always cherish both and to never hesitate to speak our love. Amen

Patty B. Williams

January 16th

Being True To Yourself

"Brothers, continue to think about the things that are good and worthy of praise. Think about the things that are true and honorable and right and pure and beautiful and respected. " Philippians 4:8 (NCV)

Today is Mark's birthday, one of my old boyfriends. He's the one that I told you I went to the prom party with after going to the prom with someone else. No, it wasn't the norm, but it was o.k. with my prom date and o.k. with Mark, and it really didn't matter what anyone else thought. It was a fun night for all of us.

Sometimes, in spite of what everyone else thinks, you have to make a decision if something is right or wrong. You may care enough about what others think or feel to go against what you want, and that, too, is a decision you will have to make. I just hope you will always look at your options and not always feel like you have to acquiesce (give in) to others. Weigh your decisions. Sometimes deciding against your personal feelings will be the right thing to do.

I'm not too worried about you in this area. You are a pleaser, but you are also true to yourself. Being true to yourself means you're o.k. inside with your decisions; in your heart of hearts, regardless of what others might say or think. It doesn't necessarily mean you won't agonize over the decisions. It just means that you can live with yourself long after the decision has been made.

Bottom line—if you have two dates in one night and you aren't hurting anyone, I say go for it!

Pray with me:
Thank you, God, for options and for good sense to make right decisions. When we start to falter, help us to get back on track. Amen

Patty B. Williams

January 17th

Understanding Your Parents' Desires

"This is my prayer for you: that your love will grow more and more; that you will have knowledge and understanding with your love; that you will see the difference between good and bad and choose the good; that you will be pure and without wrong for the coming of Christ; that you will do many good things with the help of Christ to bring glory and praise to God." Philippians 1:9-10 (NCV)

It's too bad that children can't comprehend the true desires of parents when they are growing up. I wish you could have truly understood at 14 why I didn't want you to drink, or to lie, or stay out too late, and why I hounded you to do things for others, be responsible, go to church and hang out with the right friends. Oh, you heard me and understood some of the reasons, but your knowledge base and deep understanding was limited, along with most of the other 14-year-olds I knew.

As you grow older and wiser you are beginning to understand more deeply, but it won't be until you have your own children or love someone else's that you will really begin to grasp the true understanding of your dad's and my desires for you and Michael both.

The above scripture pretty much tells it like it is. That's what most of us parents pray for routinely.

Keep growing, keep searching for that understanding even when it goes against what you may want for yourself at that moment. In the meantime, I'll keep praying!

Clean Underwear, Wild Elephants and the Princess

Pray with me:
Lord, help us as parents and children to work toward understanding each other's prayers and desires. Keep us mindful and sensitive of our different agendas. Amen

Patty B. Williams

January 18th

An Attitude Of Gratitude

"Although they knew God, they did not glorify Him as God, nor were thankful, but became futile in their thoughts, and their foolish hearts were darkened." Romans 1:21 (KJV)

An "attitude of gratitude", kind of catchy, isn't it? Wouldn't this be a happier, more peaceful place if everyone could adopt that thought? I'm reading a new daily devotional called *Simple Abundance*. It is a great book. It's more or less a teaching book on how to appreciate the things of life more and how to be more thankful.

Part of the learning process involves keeping a journal that lists, on a daily basis, five things that you are grateful for that day. In case you get stuck, it even has some suggestions of things we take for granted every day—like hot running water! I bet Nichole doesn't take that for granted any longer.

I was sorting through old pictures today trying to get some semblance of order to the thousands of pictures I have. Looking at them brought back some sweet memories, especially of you. Gosh, you were so cute! So—one of my things to be thankful for today will be motherhood. Another thing will be the memories of your childhood.

I hope you will always strive to have an "attitude of gratitude" and then pass it along to others.

Pray with me:
We have much to be thankful for, Lord. Sometimes we need a nudge to remember. Help us in that regard. Amen

Clean Underwear, Wild Elephants and the Princess

January 19th
(Aunt Mary Ella's and Terrie's birthday)

Aunt Mary Ella And Terrie

"Love is made complete among us so that we will have confidence on the day of judgment, because in this world we are like him."
1 John 4:17 (NIV)

Today is the birthday of two of my favorite people, Mary Ella and Terrie. I celebrate their lives and what they have both meant to me over the years. Les and Mary Ella helped raise me, as you know, and played such an important part in my life as a child and teenager. Mary Ella tried hard to make a sophisticated young lady out of me by sending me to finishing school in Atlanta. As you also know, it didn't work! Hopeless, you might say! Thank goodness she and Les continued to love me just the same.

Terrie, my friend who loves me too (somewhere amongst the love she has for all God's creatures, great and small—including spiders!), is my one in a million friend. We've been through times of happiness, sadness, laughter, and tears together. We've worked together, played together, shared secrets together and listened to one another at great lengths, yet we don't ask a lot of each other because it's not necessary. We've had separate lives, but have always been a part of each other's lives since becoming friends. I think we are both blessed.

The other thing that makes these two people so special is how they feel about you and Michael. They love you and have always been a part of your lives too. I guess you won't appreciate that entirely until you become a mother one day. I'm glad though that you hold them special in your heart too, and I know you celebrate today with me in wishing them a happy birthday.

Patty B. Williams

Pray with me:

Lord, for those we hold dear and whose lives have enriched ours, we give you thanks for lending them to us. Amen

January 20th

Prayer

"The Lord has heard my cry for mercy; the Lord accepts my prayer." Psalm 6:9 (NIV)

Even though yesterday was a holiday, I got up early to start on some projects I wanted to get finished. One project was painting the kitchen door and several of the cabinet doors; another was covering some chairs to be used in the kitchen.

Neither of these projects were tremendously difficult, just time consuming. I knew, however, if I didn't get up early, get busy and stay on task they wouldn't get done. Well, they did, but I think that little prayer I said this morning helped. I asked God to help me be motivated and organized and at the end of the day to feel like I had accomplished something, instead of spinning my wheels planning and thinking about all the things I needed to get done.

It's 10:30 P.M. now and not only do I feel I accomplished something, I still had time left over to have dinner with an old high school friend who's in town on business. It's amazing how much more God and I can do together rather than relying only on myself. Think about that.

Pray with me:
Lord, we know you are there when we need you for the big stuff, but help us to remember that you're there to help us with the everyday stuff too. Amen

Patty B. Williams

January 21st

Transcending Differences

"For there is no difference between Jew and Gentile—the same Lord is Lord of all and richly blesses all who call on him" Romans 10:12 (NIV)

Today is my Black friend Jackie's birthday. I say Black only to distinguish her from my other White friend, Jackie. I will call her to wish her a happy birthday, and we'll make plans to have lunch together. That ritual has become tradition with us. We always try to have lunch together to celebrate both of our January birthdays.

Jackie and I have been through a lot together since becoming friends. We've shared some real heartaches with one another and some real joys. We've seen each other grow in our professions and struggle with the politics of the working world. We've seen each other's children grow up and shared happiness and sadness during the teenage years and beyond.

Our friendship has transcended race differences. That never was an issue between us. We went to social events together and included one another in personal gatherings of friends and family. We've shared secrets, laughed, and seen each other cry. We care about each other, regardless of the time between our calls or visits. I guess you could say we're low maintenance friends. We know we can count on one another even if we haven't talked in months.

I know you have many different friends, not only black and white, but other nationalities too. I'm proud of that. I hope you continue to take care of those friendships so they can be as special as mine and Jackie's.

Clean Underwear, Wild Elephants and the Princess

Pray with me:
Thank you, God, for different friends and for making us all one in you. Help us to take care of each other as you have instructed us to do. Amen

Patty B. Williams

January 22nd

Breaking The Routine

"Yes, brother, let me have joy from you in the Lord; that I may have some benefit from you in the Lord; refresh my heart in the Lord."
Philemon 20 (NKJ)

It's nice to have a break from routine every now and then. It's good for the soul, good for the mind, and usually ends up being good for those around you. When something gets to be routine, it's time to try something different. You won't continue to do your best if your heart isn't in it.

Breaking the routine or trying something different doesn't mean you have to change completely. Sometimes that's not possible. What it does mean is that at least you should try and make a little change, even if the change is only in your attitude. You'll be amazed at what a difference that change will make.

So, when you find yourself studying the same way and learning less, going out with the same people and not having as much fun, or working harder at your job and getting little out of it, get busy trying to improve the situation. You have the brains, the skills, and the ability to do that. What you don't have is a good excuse not to.

Pray with me:
Help us, Lord, to work at keeping excited and motivated in all that we do. When we start to waiver, give us the boost needed to rejuvenate ourselves. Amen

January 23rd

Wild Elephants

"Therefore, get rid of all moral filth and the evil that is so prevalent, and humbly accept the word planted in you, which can save you."
James 1:21 (NIV)

Once again the moral character of our president is being questioned in great detail. The media is in a frenzy, and the important issues going on in the country are taking a back seat to sordid (shameful) tales of the president's sexual life outside his marriage. What a sad state of affairs he appears to have gotten himself, his family, and his country into. He definitely, as Granddaddy would say, "chose a wild elephant to ride," and unfortunately the ride may take him away from and out of the White House. What an awful shame that will be if it happens.

You have been taught from the time you were little to watch out for "wild elephants." We didn't call them wild elephants, but now that you understand the term, you know that's what they were. Lying, cheating, gossiping, drugs, alcohol, pre-marital sex—you understand all of them. Sometimes they are tempting. Sometimes they're easy to resist. The fact is they're always lurking somewhere. I pray that you will be fortunate enough to avoid many of them and wise and strong enough to resist the others.

Pray with me:
God, we pray for our president and our country and for an end to this sad experience. We pray for growth and learning through the heartache so that all our lives will be better lived. Amen

Patty B. Williams

January 24th

Study Habits, Discipline, And Balance

"David also said to Solomon his son, 'Be strong and courageous, and do the work. Do not be afraid or discouraged, for the Lord God, my God, is with you. He will not fail you or forsake you until all the work for the service of the temple of the Lord is finished."
1 Chronicles 28:20 (NIV)

I asked Michael to give me some ideas to write about, something that would have been helpful to him in school. Right away he suggested encouragement about study habits and discipline. He felt those were two of his greatest weaknesses. Another was his focus and forgetting the reason why he was in school. He said remembering the fact that a college education was a means to an end was important. He lost that for a while. He also said to tell you to have a balance of working hard and playing hard. I've tried to instill that advice.

Funny how years don't make a difference in some things. I had the same problems in school Michael did. Though we had some different paths, we had many of the same weaknesses to overcome. I know you have many of the same, too. Hopefully you'll be a faster learner than we were.

Remember there are other things that don't change over the years. Our source of strength for all our weaknesses remains the same from yesterday, to today, and for tomorrow. Don't forget to use it.

Pray with me:
Lord, we know we have many challenges to face in college life and life in general. Help us as we struggle to continue to get better. Amen

Clean Underwear, Wild Elephants and the Princess

January 25th

Karen

"First, I thank my God through Jesus Christ for all of you, because your faith is being reported all over the world." Romans 1:8 (NIV)

I couldn't let today go by without mentioning my college friend and sorority sister, Karen, who died today on her birthday some twenty plus years ago.

Karen and I quickly became friends. We had many of the same values, enjoyed the same things, and enjoyed each other's company. It's nice to find that quickly when you're in new surroundings as I was at FSU and in Delta Zeta.

Karen was so pretty, not just on the outside, but on the inside as well. She liked to have a good time, but she knew how to do it without alcohol, without pot, without putting others down, and without putting herself on a pedestal.

She had a tremendous faith, not only in God, but in people as well. It was that faith that sustained her while living with an alcoholic father, during her battle with cancer, in her loss of a leg, and through a divorce.

Her life, though short lived, was a blessing to many people who will be remembering her with love and fond memories on this, her birthday.

Pray with me:
Lord, you have blessed us with special friends that hold special places in our hearts. Thank you. Amen

Patty B. Williams

January 26th

Give Me A Sign

"Gideon replied, 'If now I have favor in your eyes, give me a sign that it is really you talking to me'." Judges 6:17 (NIV)

How many times do we wish that God would make our lives simpler by sending us a definitive sign that would answer our questions or our prayers. You know, just send us a little sign, on a string, dropped straight down from heaven in front of our faces.

Mary Jane asked me recently who the character was in the Bible that asked for such a sign from God so that he could be sure God was who he said he was. It was Gideon. God asked Gideon through an angel to fight for his people in Israel. Gideon wasn't sure it was the Lord asking him, and he knew he couldn't fight and win without God's help. Consequently, he asked God to prove it. When God proved it the first time by doing what Gideon requested, Gideon asked him to do something a second time as proof. He even asked a third time.

I think God often sends us signs, but we just don't recognize them or don't want to accept them. Red flags we call them, yet we choose to ignore them. Dumb sometimes, aren't we?

Be on the lookout for God's response to your prayers or request to see a sign. Look for it in something you read, in a friend's advice, in a sermon, in a daily devotional, or maybe in disrupted or failed plans. I know they're there. I've experienced them.

Pray with me:
Keep our eyes and minds alert, Lord, for whatever it is you would have us to know. Help us to respond appropriately. Amen

Clean Underwear, Wild Elephants and the Princess

January 27th
(Mommy's birthday)

Celebrating Life And Death

"Bring the fattened calf and kill it. Let's have a feast and celebrate." Luke 15:23 (NIV)

This year I shared my birthday with Grandma Green. The irony is I was celebrating life and she was celebrating death. You may think that being at a funeral home was not a very good way to spend a birthday, but think about it again.

We were both surrounded by mutual friends and family who loved us. Beautiful flowers adorned the room. We were both complimented for the way we looked and knew that we held special places in the hearts of most of the people who were there.

I was able to visit with friends I had not seen in many years and spend time with my nieces and nephew that I won't see again for a long time. We had a feast of homemade food made by some of the best cooks around. It was a very good birthday. I was blessed, and I'm sure Grandma Green was smiling from Heaven's golden gate.

Pray with me:
Thank you, Lord, for life and for death that can be entered into with anticipation. Thank you that we can celebrate both because we are your children. Amen

Patty B. Williams

January 28th

Afflictions

"It was good for me to be afflicted so that I may learn your decrees."
Psalm 119:71 (NIV)

It's so difficult to understand why things happen sometime, especially bad things like terrible accidents, cancer, broken bones, and broken hearts. We could speculate from now until a year from now and we still wouldn't have a definitive answer. We just won't know those answers until God explains it to us one day himself.

What we do know is that many times afflictions cause people to be greater than they may ever have been had the hardship not occurred. There are numerous examples in the lives of great artists, authors, and musicians. Even broken hearts have led to great love poems and novels—and even a devotional or two!

As you will realize one day, one of a mother's greatest fears is that something will happen to her child to rob her of a healthy, whole life. That's why we are so over protective sometime. We just can't help it! God forbid that anything bad ever happens to you or Michael or, for that matter, your dad or me. If it should, however, my immediate prayer will be that we use the affliction to make ourselves better rather than worse. Think about that in your everyday little misfortunes and see if you can turn them in to an advantage. It sure will make your life more interesting!

Pray with me:
Lord, help us to view adversities in a different light. Whether they are big or small, help us to work with them instead of letting them work against us. Amen

Clean Underwear, Wild Elephants and the Princess

January 29th

Jim And Jason

"Love must be sincere. Hate what is evil; cling to what is good. Be devoted to one another in brotherly love. Honor one another above yourselves." Romans 12:9-10 (NIV)

Today is Jim's birthday. You know we share a special friendship, much like you and Jason. Jim is the one that listened to me when I hurt and talked to me when he hurt. We counseled one another, took risk with honesty, respected each other's values, and truly cared about one another's happiness. We were intimate in hearts only, close in spirit, and comfortable being together and being apart. Sound familiar?

I know you feel much the same way about Jason, and I'm sure there are times when you miss him and what you shared together. I know though that you are happy he is with Jen and that Jen respects the special friendship that you have. You are fortunate.

As I think about Jim today on his birthday and thank God for the special friendship we've had and continue to have, I hope you will think about Jason too. Maybe he'd like a note to remind him you're thinking about him and that you appreciate the friendship you share.

Pray with me:
Thank you God for sending special people into our lives when we need them most. Keep us mindful and appreciative of all the blessings of friendship you bestow upon us. Amen

Patty B. Williams

Jason and Brooke

Clean Underwear, Wild Elephants and the Princess

January 30th

Church

"We must pay more careful attention, therefore, to what we have heard, so that we do not drift away." Hebrews 2:1 (NIV)

I have been so pleased when you have told me you've gone to church even without my hounding. I've been even more pleased to hear excitement in your voice when you've talked about going to FCA and finding new friends that were also interested in going to church.

I know it's hard to give up a few extra hours sometimes, especially when you've been up late the night before or have to go to work later in the day. It takes real discipline and commitment, just as studying does. I guess I can't tell you much more about how important I think that effort is than what I've already said over the years. It's not that I think you need to be there every Sunday. I don't think that. What I do think is that if we aren't reminded every now and then of what God's expectations are of us, we tend to forget, or at least not work as hard as we might if it's fresh in our minds

The other part of being at church, at least for me, is what it does to refresh my spirits, especially if I'm having a difficult time over an issue. It's amazing sometimes how the minister's message seems to speak right to my heart. I don't think that is a coincidence. It's nice also to feel like you're surrounded by others who love God and care about you even though they may not know you. I would be so happy to know that you had a Christian family that would help you if you needed it and I couldn't get to you immediately. Think about that and how important it could be. I hope you'll consider establishing a church home away from home. They would be so lucky to have you!!!!

Patty B. Williams

Pray with me:

Help us, Lord, to remember the commitment we made to you long ago. When we're tired, or hurt, or lonely, or when we're ecstatic with joy, help us to remember that your house is always open and we're never just guests. We're family. Amen

Clean Underwear, Wild Elephants and the Princess

January 31st

Getting Even

"Do not say, I'll pay you back for this wrong! Wait for the Lord, and he will deliver you." Proverbs 20:22 (NIV)

How many times have you been really angry with someone and vowed to get even? Did you? How did you feel about it? My guess is there were many more times that you spoke the "getting even" words than you actually followed through on your threat.

I think when we're really hurt, or angry, or embarrassed by something someone says or does, the initial reaction to want to get even is pretty normal, but not God-given.

We've talked about this before, probably in other devotionals, but I think it is something we need to think about periodically. That way we won't get caught off guard and try to follow through on our threats.

The scriptures teach us that it is not our job to get even, no more so than it is our job to judge others. Both are God's job, and he hasn't delegated that responsibility to us. My goodness, that's hard to remember sometimes, isn't it? It's even harder to actually leave the jobs to him, especially when we think we could handle them so well.

I encourage you to leave God's work with him and to encourage your friends to do the same. It won't always be easy, but it will always be right.

Pray with me:
Lord, you have given us plenty of work to do. Help us to stick to what our responsibilities are and leave yours to you. Amen

Patty B. Williams

February 1st

Swearing

"But I say to you, do not swear at all; neither by heaven, for it is God's throne, not by earth, for it is His footstool; not by Jerusalem, for it is the city of the great King. Nor shall you swear by your head, because you cannot make one hair white or black. But let your yes be yes and your no, no. For whatever is more than these is from the evil one."
Matthew 5:34-37 (NKJ)

Do you remember when you were little and saying "damn" made you feel really big? What about now? When you swear, how does it make you feel? My guess is sometimes you don't even think about it, sometimes you use it for emphasis, sometimes it's out of frustration, and other times you think it might make the person you're talking to perceive you in a different light—more like them, cool, not a goody two-shoes. The reason I know that is because those are still some of the same reasons I have for swearing.

Whatever your reasons for swearing or using ugly words, I hope you will think about it before using them the next time. Think about it, not because I ask you to, but because of the above scripture. Look at God's instructions. He tells us just to say what needs to be said and nothing more. It's not necessary. If you tell someone something and you're trustworthy, why do you need to say "I swear" or "I swear to God" to validate it? Why do we need other swear words? Is our vocabulary that limited? I don't think so.

We don't need to be someone we're not. If we're so frustrated we have to swear, we need to look at what's causing the frustration and "get a grip." If we're swearing and not really conscious of it, we have some work to do, and if we have to use swear words to try and make our statements more believable, we need to look at why. I really don't think this is a big issue, but it's just one of those things we need to think about.

Pray with me:
Lord, help us to stay in control of our thoughts and words, especially in those difficult times when swearing seems to be the answer to our frustrations. Amen

Patty B. Williams

February 2nd

Getting Started

"In the beginning God created the heavens and the earth."
Genesis 1:1 (NKJ)

Getting started is sometimes the hardest part! It is for me, at least, in almost anything I have to do. That's the way it's always been. Cleaning my room at home, washing the dishes when I was a child, writing a term paper in high school, starting a project at work, and even getting back to writing devotionals when I've taken a break, the most difficult part of the task is taking that first step.

I find myself making all kind of excuses for not getting started sooner or not getting started at all. I need to make a phone call, I have to have the right comfortable clothes on, the mood has to be right, all the housework has to be done, I have to be alone. I could go on and on. The problem, of course, is discipline, commitment, determination and attitude. You know, all those things that get in our way on a daily basis. The same things that get in the way of doing the things God has given us to do, like helping others, being kind to those not kind to us, tithing, of loving when we don't feel like loving.

I hope, when you have a difficult time getting started, you will think about what you're doing and ask for help from above. I've found that anytime I've remembered to ask for help, getting started is always easier. I know you will have the same experience.

Pray with me:
Help us, Father, to remember that you are the author of beginnings, of getting started and carrying through. Help us remember that you can push us beyond all our excuses. Amen

February 3rd

Not My Will

"And he was withdrawn from them about a stone's throw, and he knelt down and prayed, saying, Father, if it is your will, take this cup away from me; nevertheless not my will, but yours, be done." Luke 22:41-42 (NKJ)

The "cup" Jesus was talking about was his suffering and pending death. He was asking God to take it away, but he still said, "Not my will, but yours be done." In your worst situations have you found yourself asking God to make it go away? I have prayed that prayer many times. The hardest part, of course, is including the last part of that prayer.

What if God's will isn't ours? Many times it's not, you know. Sometimes we think we are so much smarter. We want to tell God what needs to be done, regardless of whether or not it's his will.

You're pretty normal if this is your reaction. The only problem is that the reaction isn't too well thought out if you ask God for help, trust that he can do something, and then tell him how to do it. Do you really think he is going to do the wrong thing? I don't think so.

God understands our anguish over bad situations and he knows our desires to rectify them. I think our conversation with God might also include, "God, if your will is different from mine, please help me to accept it, to grow, and to learn from it."

Pray with me:
Lord, help our prayers to always be those that ask for your will to be done. Keep us mindful of your greatness and wisdom beyond our comprehension. Amen

Patty B. Williams

February 4th

Tattle-tale, Tattle-tale

"Moreover, if your brother sins against you, go and tell him his fault between you and him alone. If he hears you, you have gained your brother." Matthew 18:15 (NKJ)

Tattle-tale, Tattle-tale, hang your britches on a nail! How long has it been since you have heard that? You and Michael used to tell on each other just like every other brother and sister. Well, you did until your early teen years when you started keeping secrets between each other so that your dad and I wouldn't find out something.

When your friends did something you didn't like, you usually told another friend and then stayed mad or hurt for a while. Unfortunately, when you get in the work world, you'll continue to have situations where your co-workers or a manager will say something or do something that will make you mad or hurt your feelings. What will you do about that?

There are several ways to handle it. You can ignore it. You can complain about it to the other staff members. You can go to that person's superior, or you can go directly to the person and discuss it with him. There are risks with each choice. My experience, however, has been that the best choice is the last one, and I think that's God's direction too. Sometimes that choice presents an uncomfortable or scary situation, but if you think your words through, speak with kindness and integrity, and ask God to help, then you will do the right thing.

Pray with me:
Help us to remember, God, that when someone wrongs us it's usually between us and them, not the rest of the world. Help us to treat it that way. Amen

Clean Underwear, Wild Elephants and the Princess

February 5th

Familiar Voices

"And when he brings out his own sheep, he goes before them; and the sheep follow him, for they know his voice." John 10:4 (NKJ)

I know you love babies as much as I do. I know you will be crazy about little Stephen when you see him. I also know by the next time I see him he will have changed so much. He will be much more attuned to his mom's and dad's and his brother's familiar voices and faces. He will look for them when he hears their voices and is with someone else.

I was amazed at how excited Emily became recently when she spied her mom out a window when she was in the church nursery. I could hardly contain her in my arms.

Familiar voices and familiar faces, they are comforting aren't they? They are especially nice at 2:00 A.M. when you can't sleep, aren't they? I know how much they meant to me when I was a little girl and had such bad dreams or was away from home and was sick or lonesome.

Don't forget that there is always another familiar person in your life who is more available than anyone else, 24 hours a day, 7 days a week, holidays, and especially Sundays! All you have to do is call. You can even do all the talking. He's a great listener!

Pray with me:
Help us listen, Lord, for your voice in our hearts. Help us to follow when we know you are talking to us. Amen

Patty B. Williams

February 6th

Destiny

"When I tried to understand all this, it was oppressive to me till I entered the sanctuary of God: then I understood their final destiny." Psalm 73:16-17 (NIV)

There is a quote on a daily calendar by William Jennings Bryan that says, "Destiny is not a matter of chance, it is a matter of choice." For the most part I agree. Our daily and long-term choices lead us in different directions, just as our personal interest do. Sometimes our choices are the right ones and lead us to better things. Sometimes, as we both know, our choices end up causing heartache, aggravation, or frustration.

It was hard for me to make a decision some years ago to leave state government when I had so many years invested toward retirement. My plan was to leave, gain management experience, and return one day to a state government management position. It turned out that I made a good choice. My plan worked. I don't think, however, that Human Resource Management was my destiny. I think a series of career choices set that destiny. When I was a little girl, I wanted to be a cowgirl. Do you think that might have been my true destiny?

I believe God has a plan for our lives and that's the destiny that should concern us. We need to seek his will for our lives. We should try and discover the gifts that will help point us toward that plan. I hope you will do that and will appreciate my encouraging you to pray and think about it. Had I been better at that, I might be in a different profession and feeling better about my contribution to society. When I retire in a few years, I may have another opportunity to discover God's plan. I hope so.

Pray with me:
Thank you, Lord, for choices. Help us to look to you to make the right ones. Amen

Patty B. Williams

February 7th

Do It Well

"Give her the reward she has earned, and let her works bring her praise at the city gate." Proverbs 31:31 (NIV)

I don't know who Howard W. Newton is, but he was quoted in a mini book on excellence. He said that people forget how fast you did a job, but they remember how well you did it. I agree with him wholeheartedly.

You have been a wonderful employee everywhere you have worked, and you continue to receive accolades months and months after having left the jobs. You should be really proud of yourself. I certainly am.

I hope you remember that the same principle applies to most anything in life. How well you do your college assignments, how well you take care of your friendships, how well you treat people, are the things that really matter and will be remembered. Keep up the good work, Bear; you will be remembered by many.

Pray with me:
God, we have many jobs to do and the ability to do them well or do them well enough to get by. Help us to care enough to do our best. Amen

February 8th

Greatness

"And they were all amazed at the greatness of God . . ."
Luke 9:43 (NIV)

Winston Churchill said, "The price of greatness is responsibility." Jesus, of course, sets the standard for greatness and responsibility. We will never measure up to him, but we should always be striving to emulate him.

When you become that great teacher, counselor, accountant, or princess one day, that greatness will come with expectations and responsibilities. People will look up to you, will want to be like you, will expect more from you, and will demand more than you will feel like giving at times. The greatness will have its rewards but it will also have its difficulties.

I think the clue to success before you get there is to practice now with being responsible in the little things of life—keeping the checkbook balanced, keeping your life in order so you don't get stressed out, doing your homework on time. You know, all those "fun" things that take up your valuable time. You know how to be a responsible person. My hope is that you'll stay in practice.

Pray with me:
Lord, if we're destined for greatness, prepare us so we'll know how to handle it in a manner that glorifies you. Help us in our daily lives to be responsible in all that we do. Amen

February 9th

Walk The Talk

"By their fruit you will recognize them." Matthew 7:16 (NIV)

Andrew Carnegie said that as he grew older, he paid less attention to what men said and instead just watched what they did.

I think Mr. Carnegie had the right idea. Talk is easy. Walk is a different story. It's easy to make promises, to agree to do a job, to make plans, or to offer to help. It's more difficult to follow through on what you've said you would do.

I hope that when people watch what you do that your actions match what you say and what you are inside. That doesn't mean that you have to be a total open book—especially with guys! (You have to keep them guessing, you know.) What it does mean is that you should think before you commit to anything so you don't say one thing and do another.

I really think you are pretty good about this. It's just something you need to keep in mind.

Pray with me:
Help us walk our talk, Lord, and to remember that if we can't, to keep quiet. Amen

Clean Underwear, Wild Elephants and the Princess

February 10th

Failures

"We who are strong ought to bear with the failings of the weak and not to please ourselves." Romans 15:1 (NIV)

Everyone fails at one time or another. Sometimes it's our fault and sometimes it's not. Regardless of where the fault lies, it usually doesn't make us feel too good. Sometimes the bad feelings are so strong they cause physical or mental problems.

You have had successes and failures. We both hurt terribly when you failed to make the cheerleading squad one year, and then we both rejoiced when you made it the next year. Fortunately, tears and a short period of disappointment that first year is all you experienced from that failure. I hope that will always be the extent of your bad feelings, that you will be able to pick yourself right up, remember what you learned from it, and get on with life.

Henry Ford said "Failure is the opportunity to begin again more intelligently." I think he was a wise man, don't you?

Pray with me:
Lord, give us enough failures to keep us learning and humble. Give us enough successes to make the failures easier to handle. Amen

Patty B. Williams

February 11th

Obstacles

"I urge you, brothers, to watch out for those who cause divisions and put obstacles in your way that are contrary to the teaching you have learned. Keep away from them." Romans 16:17 (NIV)

What are the things in your life that keep you from reaching your goals? Is it food, friends, ability, knowledge, lack of discipline? Is it maybe all of the above? Well, if you know, you're already on the road to improving.

I think this statement made by Henry Ford is pretty good: "Obstacles are those frightful things you see when you take your eyes off your goals." When you're studying really hard because you know you have to do well on an exam, and the phone rings with an invitation to go out, does that become an obstacle? My guess is at a minimum it becomes a temptation if not a full-blown obstacle. So what do you do? Obstacles are everywhere. Well, look at the scripture above; I think it's good advice. When you know something is an obstacle, do your best to avoid it. Try hard to keep your eyes on your goal.

I think I know some of your goals—at least a 2.7 overall GPA this year, staying within your budget, reading your devotionals, finding a special guy. Whatever they are, I hope you'll be tenacious in reaching them. The obstacles will be there, but I know you can handle those too. I'm counting on you.

Pray with me:
Lord, we are weak so often when obstacles are placed in our path. Keep us focused so our goals can be realized. Amen

Clean Underwear, Wild Elephants and the Princess

February 12th

The Aged

"Is not wisdom found among the aged? Does not long life bring understanding?" Job 12:12 (NIV)

I know you realize how fortunate you are to have Granddaddy in your life, not just to do things with but to learn from too. Grandparents have such a different perspective on things because of their vast amount of experience and the wisdom they've gained from it.

You can understand, too, how difficult it must be for them to see our world today in comparison to the world they lived in when they were younger. Values have changed, relationships have changed between parents and children, the economy has changed, our beliefs have changed. It's a very different world.

I hope as you go through life that you will continue to respect and seek out the wisdom of older people. They have so much to give and teach us—things that we know nothing about except what we have read in history books. Learn all you can from Granddaddy, Granny and PaPa. Listen to their thoughts about life and values and what they did. You will want to share it one day with your grandchildren.

Pray with me:
Lord, help us to cherish the opportunity to gain wisdom and understanding from our elders. Keep them close in heart and presence. Amen

Patty B. Williams

February 13th

Challenges

"O Lord, the king rejoices in your strength. How great is his joy in the victories you give!" Psalm 21:1 (NIV)

General George S. Patton said, "Accept the challenges, so that you may feel the exhilaration of victory." Have you accepted any challenges lately? Maybe accepted isn't the right word. Maybe the better question is, have you had a real challenge lately? Maybe it was a big term paper, a difficult situation with a friend, a relationship problem with a co-worker, whatever, I'm sure you probably have had one or two.

I hope when a challenge comes along you are willing to take it on, that you don't run from it, or hide, just because it's difficult or uncomfortable. Challenges, like adversities, are opportunities for growth. Go for as many of them as you are capable of handling.

I know you will be pleased with the results when you accept a challenge and then conquer it. The feeling will be wonderful. Remember the cheerleading victory, the homecoming court, the couple of guys that were a challenge? I remember well!

You have all the qualities necessary to seek, accept, and be successful in numerous challenges. I'll be waiting to hear about all of them.

Pray with me:
Challenges are scary sometimes, Lord, and sometimes they seem unattainable. Help us remember that we don't have to accept them alone. Amen

Clean Underwear, Wild Elephants and the Princess

February 14th

Valentine's Day

"And now these three remain: faith, hope and love. But the greatest of these is love." 1 Corinthians 13:13 (NIV)

"How do I love thee? Let me count the ways . . . ." Oh my goodness, it's that day again, and where is your sweetheart? You have been worrying about this day for how many days now? Surely you aren't worried that no one loves you. You are one of the most loved young ladies that I know.

You're feeling down though because you don't have that special guy that others may have today that will shower them with flowers, candy, or some other special surprise, right? Well, what can you do to make yourself feel better?

I had to figure that out myself this year or it could have been a really sad time for me. What I did was start to plan early about what I could do to make someone else's day special. I made and mailed cookies to all my college kids—you, Ellen, Mary, Amy, Christine, and Jen. I bought special little surprises for Michael, Mitch, Matt, and Shane, and I sent valentine cards to all the "little people" in our family. It was like having Christmas all over again. It was so much fun.

Always remember that when you're down, it always helps to make someone else happy. You're good at that, so get on with it, and have a happy Valentine's Day. I love you!

Pray with me:
Thank you, Lord, for all the love we are given and for all we have to give. We are truly blessed. Amen

Patty B. Williams

February 15th

A House Divided

"But He, knowing their thoughts, said to them: 'Every kingdom divided against itself is brought to desolation and a house divided against a house falls." Luke 11:17 (NKJ)

You know many of the frustrations I have had at work during the last year. They have been caused by numerous reasons, but one of the biggest reasons is because the management staff has been divided among themselves and the rest of the staff has been divided against them. It has not been a comfortable situation for anyone.

As you get further and further into college life, you will have many situations to be involved in with other students on class projects, with your Kappa Delta sisters, or with your roommates. There will also be many times you will disagree on the way things should be done when you're working together.

I hope as you work together you will remember that it takes teamwork, that all ideas are worth listening to, and discussion, good communication skills and compromise can usually solve most disagreements. Arguing, destructive criticism, demanding to have your own way, and pouting only drive you further apart. And, then what happens to the project? Be prepared to be your team's facilitator to help them get back on track. Remind them that a house divided falls.

Pray with me:
Help us, Lord, to recognize when our disagreements are becoming destructive. Help us to step back, regroup, and re-focus. Amen

February 16th

Humbleness

"Everyone who makes himself great will be made humble. But the person who makes himself humble will be made great." Luke 14:11 (NCV)

I think one of the most attractive attributes someone can have is humility. Think about those you know who are really smart, famous, or well known. What does their demeanor (behavior, attitude) tell you about them? Are they arrogant, snootie, have an air of superiority, or are they modest, unassuming, and have an air of thanksgiving for who they are?

I've known both types. There's no question, of course, whose company I preferred. The arrogant ones left me wanting to punch their lights out! The modest, unassuming ones, left me with a warm and fuzzy feeling.

Regardless of who we are, what we have, or what we've accomplished, we couldn't have done it without God's help. I'm not sure why we tend to forget that at times. God gives clear teachings on how he feels about the matter. I think we should all pay closer attention.

Pray with me:
Lord, help us to have things to be proud of about ourselves, but teach us to handle our pride in a way that is pleasing unto you. Amen

Patty B. Williams

February 17th

A Cute Message

"This is the message we have heard from him and declare to you: God is light; in Him there is no darkness at all." 1 John 1:5 (NIV)

May your heart be light, may friends hug you tight. May your day be terrific from morning til night." Isn't that a cute little message? With the exception of a word or two, it is the message on a card I read recently. I just loved it—so simple, yet packed with the well-wishes that really matter in life.

A heart that is light, not burdened with worry, anxiety, fear, anger or all those other negative things that bring us down; isn't that what we're looking for? Friends that aren't afraid of showing affection, who truly care for us; isn't that what makes us feel loved and appreciated? Then, along comes a terrific day, filled with positive thoughts, God's beauty, food to eat and freedom to enjoy it all. What more could we ask, except maybe for love, the final ingredient that makes it all even richer.

I send you this message today, and hope you will pass it along.

Pray with me:
Keep us light-hearted, Lord, and filled with love. Give us many friends to enjoy and beautiful days to share with them. Amen

February 18th

Gossips And Busy Bodies

"Besides, they get into the habit of being idle and going about from house to house. And not only do they become idlers, but also gossips and busy bodies, saying things they ought not to." 1 Timothy 5:13 (NIV)

As you meet and make new friends at college, you will eventually pick and choose those that will remain acquaintances and those that become close friends. It's for sure there will be all kinds. Some will be kind and loving towards others, and some will be gossips and busybodies with nothing better to do with their time. I suppose it goes without saying what the better choice would be in that last scenario. That doesn't mean, of course, that you shouldn't love and care about the gossip and busy body. It just means you need to consider where and with whom, your time would best be spent. Sometimes it might be with the gossips; for hopefully you would be a positive influence in their lives. Just be careful that you don't get caught in the web, and be bold enough to suggest more positive ways to spend time and energy. I know God would support those efforts.

Pray with me:
Lord, help us to avoid the temptations to be a gossip or busybody. Help us instead to be a positive influence, guided by your instructions and love. Amen

Patty B. Williams

February 19th
(Spencer's birthday)

Family

"But if a widow has children or grandchildren, these should learn first of all to put their religion into practice by caring for their own family and so repaying their parents and grandparents, for this is pleasing to God." 1 Timothy 5:4 (NIV)

Today, little Spencer Douglas Green made his debut in the world. Again, we were fortunate to have another healthy, beautiful baby to join our family.

Because Spencer was born on my friend Carol's birthday, she is certain he is destined for great things. I guess I'm more certain that he is destined for a life filled with people who love him and care about him and want him to have a happy, healthy, and successful life. I'm also certain those same people will be the ones holding him accountable when he does things he shouldn't, just like they held you and all the other, nieces, nephews, and grandchildren accountable. Even though you may not have appreciated that part at the time, look how well you've turned out. Hand you a tiara, and I think a princess is in the making!

Pray with me:
Thank you, Lord, for sweet, healthy babies and families who love and take care of them. Keep us mindful of these and all our many blessings. Amen

February 20th

The Greatest Of Life's Gifts

"You have made known to me the path of life; you will fill me with joy in your presence with eternal pleasures at your right hand."
Psalm 16:11 (NIV)

There is a wonderful little book entitled, *Tuesdays with Morrie,* by Mitch Albom, that I hope you will read one day. You will cry, but you will be touched by it forever. It is a true story about a rekindled relationship of a college student and his favorite professor who is dying from a debilitating disease.

In his dying, the professor teaches his student how to live. He talks about things such as the importance of family, emotions, money, marriage, forgiveness, regrets, and even about death and saying goodbye.

The underlying wisdom of the professor helps us understand that the greatest of life's gifts is found in the simplest of God's blessings. I won't tell you what those are. You need to find them out for yourself. I hope you will want to read the book.

Pray with me:
Lord, we ask that you give us the wisdom to seek and enjoy life as you intended. When we receive it, help us to share it daily. Amen

Patty B. Williams

February 21st

Belonging

"But you are a chosen people, a royal priesthood, a holy nation, a people belonging to God, that you may declare the praises of him who called you out of darkness into his wonderful light." 1 Peter 2:9 (NIV)

When you wanted to join a sorority your first semester at school, I wasn't sure that was the best idea. You, however, felt it would be the best way to meet new friends and quickly become a part of college life. You wanted to belong, to be a part of something bigger than yourself. That is certainly very normal and understandable, and now that you are a Sister in KD and have succeeded in all those initial things you were looking for your first semester at college, I feel different about it. I think you were right.

My only concerns, however, are that you remember the obligations that come with sorority life, like monetary expenses and time commitment, and that you remember it's a privilege that requires continued good grades and responsible behavior. You have handled it well, and I'm more proud than I might show at times.

Part of that pride is knowing that you belong to something even greater than your KD family; you belong to God and that is the most important decision you ever made. For that I am not only proud, I'm thankful.

Pray with me:
Help us, Lord, to always have that feeling of peace and happiness that comes from belonging, especially belonging to you. Amen

Clean Underwear, Wild Elephants and the Princess

February 22nd

Special Friends

"The sun has one kind of splendor, the moon another and the stars another; and star differs from star in splendor."
1 Corinthians 15:41 (NIV)

I don't remember exactly when Paula and I became such good friends; I guess it was sometime after becoming roommates at South Georgia Jr. College. Three of us roomed together, Paula, Sharon and I, only I was the outsider because Paula and Sharon had already been living together before I got there.

Paula and I were very different. She was shy and disciplined when it came to studying. I was anything but shy and had no discipline when it came to studying. She didn't date a lot of different guys and didn't talk about them all the time. Like you, I loved meeting new guys and talking about them all the time. Paula was competitive in almost everything, and though I liked to win, you couldn't call me competitive. I just liked to play. I know she tolerated a lot with me as a tennis partner in intramurals. She was so good, and I was so mediocre. We won though, thanks to her! We even have a trophy somewhere on campus.

It's interesting that as different as we were in many ways, our friendship continued to grow and become stronger. Our differences never hindered our relationship. The significant things we had in common like our values and spiritual beliefs made our friendship what it has become.

I hope as you choose friends that you look for the important things that really matter in your relationship instead of just whether or not you both enjoy the same past times, the same food, or the same guys.

Patty B. Williams

Those things may keep you together more often, but my guess is they won't keep you together as closely.

Say a prayer of thanksgiving today with me on Paula's birthday, thanking God for sending special friends to share our lives.

Pray with me:
Lord, thank you for the special friends you have sent to share our lives and our love for you. We are truly blessed. Amen

February 23rd

Saying You're Sorry

"Godly sorrow brings repentance that leads to salvation and leaves no regret, but worldly sorrow brings death." 2 Corinthians 7:10 (NIV)

I was in a restaurant the other day and witnessed a heartwarming scene. I wasn't privileged to hear the total conversation between the two individuals, but I heard enough and observed enough that I could pretty much put the story together. There was evidently a disagreement over some money, perhaps a tip, between a young waiter and a female who appeared to be either his counterpart or his supervisor. It wasn't a big scene, but the young man walked away from the conversation, obviously upset, and mumbled an obscenity as he left. I thought that his reaction was pretty immature and unprofessional. It wasn't long though before I saw the young man walk back up to the young lady, give her a big hug, and say he was sorry. The conversation that followed had something to do with the fact that he didn't understand whatever the situation was that caused the contention. They talked briefly and the incident appeared to be over.

The food that day at the restaurant was not too good, but I won't forget my experience there for a while and will probably return just because I have a good feeling about the staff. I think when I go back I will even tell them that.

My point in sharing this story is obvious. I want you to always be big enough to say you're sorry and big enough to accept another's apology. The other thing I want you to always think about is the quality of your apologies. The verse above indicates that there's a difference. I think it means that apologies that are sincere cleanse the soul and make you feel better, and apologies that aren't sincere do nothing.

I know you know how to say you're sorry. That will help you more in your relationships than almost anything. So will accepting apologies of others. I'll be counting on you to be good at both.

Pray with me:
Father, we can't always be right, neither can anyone else. Help us to remember that and respond accordingly. Amen

Clean Underwear, Wild Elephants and the Princess

February 24th

Encouragement

"Therefore encourage one another and build each other up, just as in fact you are doing." 1 Thessalonians 5:11 (NIV)

When you are working very hard at something and becoming tired, frustrated, or upset, it's nice to have someone close at hand to give you some encouragement to keep going and finish your task, isn't it? For me, that encouragement has often been what helped me not give up.

In the same manner, it's important that we remember that we have an obligation to encourage others too. Sometimes that task will be difficult because it will be with someone who is ornery, ready to give up, or just doesn't care. That will be some of our greatest challenges.

You have already had practice giving encouragement to little people as a baby sitter and to your grandparents just by being with them, doing things with them, and talking. Encouragement comes in many forms.

I'm encouraged by what you're doing in school, your job, and your social life. Thanks for that. It helps more than you know.

Pray with me:
Lord, thank you for the encouragement we get from you through answered prayer and life's gifts. Help us to remember to always do our part in encouraging others. Amen

Patty B. Williams

February 25th

Long Hair

"But wearing long hair is a woman's honor. Long hair is given to the woman to cover her head." 1 Corinthians 11:15 (NCV)

Did you know this was in the Bible? I should have kept it a secret and brought it out as ammunition if you ever decide to cut your long, pretty hair one day.

Just in case I have never told you explicitly, I do love your long hair. I always have. It's very pretty, healthy looking, and has helped identify you for eighteen years. Actually, eighteen years is stretching it. You didn't have a lot those first few years!

Of course, you have to remember what really identifies you is not what you look like on the outside, or what you wear; it's what's on the inside that really identifies who you are. I know you know that because I've only told you 1,436,922 times, right?

I hope you don't tire of your long hair anytime soon. I loved your short and long pigtails that are plainly etched in my mind. Though I've finally adjusted to your outgrowing them, I'm not sure I could adjust to no long hair at all. I think I might feel like my baby was being taken away.

Pray with me:
Thank you, Lord, for all you've given us to help enhance who we are. Just help us remember that the heart part is the most important part. Amen

Clean Underwear, Wild Elephants and the Princess

February 26th

Good Health

"Dear Friend, I pray that you may enjoy good health and that all may go well with you, even as your soul is getting along well." 3 John: 2 (NIV)

Tonight I'm sitting in the emergency room with Daddy while they are running various tests to see if the pain he is having is a result of a heart problem. It's scary, but it's also a good time to reflect on how fortunate our family has been so far in regard to overall health.

It's also a time to think about how fortunate we are to be able to come to a hospital, receive treatment, and be able to pay for the services. I know we all take these things for granted, but we shouldn't.

When you felt so bad yesterday and had to go to the doctor, I'm sure your first thoughts weren't how you were going to pay for it, if you had a way to get there, or whether or not someone would take care of you when you got there.

I hope you never forget that there are many people whose first thoughts are these things. Don't forget to count your blessings tonight.

Pray with me:
Thank you, God, for all the blessings we take for granted. Help us to take a moment now and then to reflect on all we have and to pray for those who have so much less. Amen

Patty B. Williams

February 27th

Discrimination

"If you show special attention to the man wearing fine clothes and say, 'here's a good seat for you,' but say to the poor man, 'you stand there' or 'sit on the floor by my feet,' have you not discriminated among yourselves and become judges with evil thoughts?" James 2:3-4 (NIV)

I'm sitting and watching a *20/20* segment on racial discrimination by department stores in targeting shoplifters. It's just amazing to me that in this day and age we still have such humiliating discrimination going on in our day-to- day living. I'm truly ashamed of us as a nation.

I'm glad that you are still innocent of much of this discrimination that still happens in our society, but this is the very thing I feared for you and Gabriel that I knew you couldn't truly understand at the time. Prejudice and discrimination, as you know, are not God's will. We are all equal in His eyes, and we should treat each other accordingly. We have come a long way in the last 40 years but we have so much further to go. Until that time, I hope you will continue to educate and sensitize those who are less sensitive and educated as you, or who have parents that raised them with prejudices against others. Pray, too, that we will continue to grow in our understanding and treatment of others and that we will learn from our mistakes.

Pray with me:
Help us, Lord, to love and treat others as you would, and forgive us where we have failed. Amen

February 28th

Intimidation

"Most assuredly, I say to you, a servant is not greater than his master; nor is he who is sent greater than he who sent him. If you know these things, blessed are you if you do them. John 13:16-17 (NKJ)

Nanny and Granddaddy raised us to believe and understand that everyone is equal. They taught that equality may not be in material or physical things, but that it was in the thing that mattered most. We were equal in God's eye's. We were taught that we were no better than anyone else and no one was any better than us.

That teaching has helped me over the years to be able to talk to all kinds of people, to not feel intimated by others regardless of their status, and to treat others like I expected to be treated by them.

My hope is that you will always remember that you are as valuable to God as the next person; that the President, the biggest star, the Queen, the Pope would be as fortunate to spend time with you as you would be to spend time with them.

Don't, however, confuse lack of intimidation with lack of respect. There is a big difference. No one deserves the right to be intimidated or to intimidate. Many deserve the right to be respected. I know you know the difference.

Pray with me:
Lord, you have made us who you want us to be and love us all. Help us to treat one another with respect and as equals. Amen

Patty B. Williams

February 29th

Innocence

"Lord, defend me. I have lived an innocent life. I trusted the Lord and never doubted." Psalm 26:1 (NCV)

It's a shame that in some ways we can't stay children forever, that we can't approach life with the innocence of a four-year-old.

One of my favorite stories about Michael was when he was about four or five years old. He stopped a jogger on the road in front of our house and talked him into reading him a book. In his innocence he saw nothing wrong with talking to a stranger, asking for what he wanted, or accepting the graciousness of the young man.

Isn't it sad that our society has robbed us of the innocence of trusting strangers, the fearlessness of asking for what we want in plain English, or the innocence of being able to accept the good will of others without being suspicious.

As you approach life and others, I hope you can maintain some form of innocence that will allow you to see others as God sees them, to give people and situations the benefit of the doubt. I don't ever want you to be careless or put yourself in an unsafe situation. I just want you to use your head, your good judgement, and your heart. Don't stop the jogger on the street and ask him to read you a book, but you can smile and say hello.

Pray with me:
Oh, Lord, give us discernment and wisdom when it comes to dealing with others. Keep us safe, caring, and innocent enough to keep trying to make our world better. Amen

Clean Underwear, Wild Elephants and the Princess

March 1st
(Don's and Doug's Birthday)

The Twins

"When the time came for her to give birth, there were twin boys in her womb." Genesis 25:24 (NIV)

I remember the scene when I got the news that the boys were born. I was in the phone booth in my college dorm at South Georgia. I was so excited. They were to be called Don and Doug, the same names as two of my good friends at high school who just knew they must be named after them.

The boys were the exciting news around the big town of Brooker. Twins weren't too common, and since every one knew everyone in town, they shared in the family's joy and excitement.

Don and Doug grew up fast it seemed. They were working on the farm when they were just little fellas. They were fortunate to have grandparents and great grandparents to help raise them, and they enjoyed the same kind of life you, Weston and Justin enjoyed in Brooker and at Fantasy Island.

Very different to be twins, each was his own person. They didn't look alike or act alike, yet they basically had the same friends and had fun together.

Don, as you know, is the one that was always in trouble as a teenager. Doug probably did just as much bad stuff; he just didn't get caught. Having had you and Michael six years apart and remembering some of our experiences when you were each teenagers, I can't imagine having two teens at one time.

Patty B. Williams

Now the boys are grown with families of their own, with children who will give them the same headaches, heartaches, and joys as they gave their Mom and Dad—and, time marches on. We learn from each experience and each child, each headache and each heartache. God planned it that way. I just don't think he expected us to all be quite so hardheaded at times, do you?

Pray with me:
Keep us growing, Lord, in all our experiences. Thank you for the blessings we receive with every new birth in our family. Amen

March 2nd

Planning

"If you wanted to build a tower, you would first sit down and decide how much it cost. You must see if you have enough money to finish the job." Luke 14:28 (NCV)

I love the Bible. It's a book with so much everyday wisdom. We could be so smart if we would study it more.

The above scripture indicates to us how important planning is. I don't think it is talking about planning for just financial reasons but for any reason. It's important to plan so you'll have some goals, to know when you get there.

It's hard to do the planning part sometimes; at least it always has been for me. Planning often indicates that you need to delay gratification, to put off something until you have the money, or the time, or the right conditions. That can be the pits when you want to do something or have something right now.

Being on a budget, being in a sorority, working a job, all require planning, especially with your time. I hope you will work real hard at becoming a good planner because I assure you that you will reap the benefits as you get older and have other responsibilities. I'm counting on you to be better than I am at it. Your life will be so much easier.

Pray with me:
God, you are the great planner. Help us to follow in you footsteps. Give us determination and wisdom to do what we need to do. Amen

Patty B. Williams

March 3rd

Over-commitment

"Be very careful, then, how you live—not as unwise but as wise"
Ephesians 5:15 (NIV)

I am really proud of the responsibility you have taken on with a new job. I know it must be difficult at times when you have a lot of homework, sorority projects, and friends and family that demand your time too. That's why I didn't want you to work your first semester. I thought it would be too much all at once.

I know you think you manage your time better when you don't have a lot of extra time to spare. I guess it makes you plan better, avoid procrastination, and prioritize your task. At least that's what I'm hoping for daily.

Just be careful that you don't leave out time with God and that you don't over commit yourself. If you do you will end up being stressed, sick, grumpy, and tired—and I've seen you that way! It ain't a pretty sight!

I know you can do it all and do it well, but only if you are determined to do so. If you are successful, you will be so far ahead of many adults. I'll be checking on you and asking God to check on you too, so keep your guard up!

Pray with me:
Help us, Lord, to know where to draw the line before we over-commit. Keep us focused on those things we've set out to do, and help us to have the good sense to step back when it's necessary. Amen

Clean Underwear, Wild Elephants and the Princess

March 4th

Communication

"Don't let anyone look down on you because you are young, but set an example for the believers in speech, in life, in love, in faith and in purity." 1 Timothy 4:12 (NIV)

I can hardly believe six months of writing has gone by and I haven't had communication as a topic! Actually, I'm sure communication fits in to many of the devotionals in one way or the other, but it's certainly important enough to deserve it's own page.

Good communication, as we have sometimes learned the hard way, is the key to any good relationship. Whether it's between friends, boyfriends and girlfriends, husbands and wives, parents and children, employers and employees, it's critical to making and maintaining a relationship. If you can't communicate with someone, how can you ever get to really know him or her? If you can't know them, how can you really love them with any depth?

You have learned a lot about communication for an eighteen-year-old. You've witnessed the pain that is caused by poor communication and the joy that comes from good communication. You and Michael both have good communication skills. He is more seasoned for several reasons. He's had more experience, he's been forced to use his skills more, and he has a job that demands it. He's better than I am, too, so don't feel bad. Besides, we're better than he is in other things.

The point is, you should learn as much as you can about good communication. Practice what you learn, and teach others. It is so critical for everyone.

Patty B. Williams

Pray with me:
Lord, help us to be good communicators, not only with other people but with you also. Amen

Clean Underwear, Wild Elephants and the Princess

March 5th

Do Unto Others

"Do for other people the same things you want them to do for you. This is the meaning of the Law of Moses and the teaching of the prophets." Matthew 7:12 (NCV)

Over the past few days I've had the opportunity to observe two very busy medical facilities that had they been receiving marks for customer service, would have received two very different marks.

One facility had staff that was attentive, appeared sensitive, happy, and practiced good communication skills. The other was just the opposite. What made the difference? Was it training? Was it the management staff? Was it the amount of staffing on call, or was it just the individuals themselves? My guess is it was a little of all of the above.

It's too bad people can't sit back and observe themselves in action. They might make some changes. It really doesn't take a tremendous effort to be nice, and just being nice would improve any business's customer service.

God told us how to do it in the golden rule. Maybe we all need to read it a little more often. I have no concerns with your customer service. I know you care about others, are sensitive, happy, and have good communication skills. I'm sure your bosses appreciate you. Keep up the good work.

Pray with me:
Lord, keep us mindful of your instructions. Help us when we start to falter. Amen

Patty B. Williams

March 6th
(Nanny's and Emily Brooke's birthday)

Nanny

"Her children bless her. Her husband also praises her."
Proverbs 31:28 (NCV)

I miss Nanny and I know you do too. Sometimes I think about her at the most insignificant times like walking in the woods the other day and seeing African violets. She always loved them, and any time we used to see them, we'd pick them for her. Last night we were eating barbecued ribs that Daddy made that tasted like the ones Mama used to cook. We talked about her. It's funny how even the little things she did touched us, isn't it?

I think every one of the children and grandchildren thought they were Nanny's favorite at one time or the other, don't you? I think that's how special she made us all feel. I hope you and Michael and my grandchildren feel that same way about me one day.

I hope, too, that when you get married your husband will tell you, like Granddaddy told Nanny, that there is no one but you he would ever want to be the mother of his children or to share his life with than you. What a wonderful praise to give and a wonderful feeling to have after fifty years of marriage.

I am happy, too, that little Emily Brooke shares Nanny's birthday. Nothing could have made her any happier. Emily will be proud of that one day, too, when she is told all about her Nanny that loves her from above.

Pray with me:
Lord, you blessed our family when you sent Nanny. Help us to honor her by remembering all she taught us and all she meant to us individually. Amen

Nanny

Patty B. Williams

March 7th

The Devil

"Control yourselves and be careful! The devil is your enemy, and he goes around like a roaring lion looking for someone to eat."
1 Peter 5:8 (NCV)

Just about the time you think you have everything under control, things are going well, life is good, that ugly fella starts lurking around trying to change all that.

You know the one I mean, the one that whispers. "It's okay, Brooke, you can shave your legs; so what if Mom said, no; they're your legs." I know you remember that incident vividly, don't you?

Remember, the devil comes in all kinds of disguises. Sometimes he even comes in jeans, blue eyes, and blonde hair! Man, that can be tough. He is such a conniver. He even hides in potato chips and beer. You know what I mean?

Be ready for him, Bear; make a plan. When it's all out war, don't go in to battle by yourself. Remember you always have a source of power greater than he does.

Pray with me:
Lord, help us to be careful as you have warned us. When we fail, pick us back up and help us to be better prepared the next time. Remind us that you are there to give us strength we don't have alone. Amen

Clean Underwear, Wild Elephants and the Princess

March 8th

Think Upon This

"Brothers, continue to think about the things that are good and worthy of praise. Think about the things that are true and honorable and right and pure and beautiful and respected." Philippians 4:8 (NCV)

You can have a lot of things taken away from you. Many people can have authority and power over you, but unless you are mentally ill, you have control over your thoughts.

When you start to study more about the Holocaust you will be amazed at the people that were able to survive such horrendous conditions and abuse. Many books are written about the things they thought about and the things they did to live. Corrie Ten Boom was amazing in her struggle to survive. I hope you will read about her one day.

The point is, you control your thoughts. You decide if you want to think about things that bring you down or things that build you up. Understand though, that there are a lot of things working against you sometimes. Bad situations, hurt, anger, frustration, illness, attitude, and exhaustion can all be difficult to push aside to think about your blessings, or a beautiful sunset, or a sweet baby. Just be aware that you have the power, and sometimes you have to work harder at using it.

Pray with me:
Lord, help us to work on keeping positive thoughts and attitudes, even when the circumstances around us work against it. Amen

Patty B. Williams

March 9th

Self-centeredness

"Christ died for all so that those who live would not continue to live for themselves. He died for them and was raised from death so that they would live for him." 2 Corinthians 5:15 (NCV)

You've been around small children enough to witness their self-centeredness with their parents and especially with other children. It's pretty normal around the ages of 2 to 4. When children need or want a parent, they really don't care what their parent has going on at the time. They want their attention and they want it right then! They are relentless.

My guess is you've probably known some teenagers and adults that fit that basic pattern, too. I know I have.

Self-centeredness is not a pretty sight. It's not something we want in our repertoire of personality traits. Unfortunately, most of us have it to a certain degree. The challenge is learning how to use what we have constructively. For example, if I were to use my self-centeredness to protect myself from persons who tried to hurt me physically or emotionally, I think God would commend that. If I used it to hurt others, He would not be happy.

The bottom line is to be aware of self-centeredness. Know that you are going to encounter it in others and in yourself. Prepare for it so you'll know how to handle it in both instances.

Pray with me
Lord, help keep us Christ-centered instead of self-centered. Amen

Clean Underwear, Wild Elephants and the Princess

March 10th

At Peace With Who You Are

"And let the peace of God rule in your hearts, to which you were called in one body; and be thankful." Colossians 3:15 (NKJ)

I recently read a quote by Doris Mortman that said, "Until you make peace with who you are, you'll never be content with what you have." I think that's pretty accurate, don't you?

Are you at peace with who you are? Have you finally accepted the fact that you are too tall to ever be petite, that unless you buy contacts your eyes are always going to be brown, and that you're always going to wear an 8 or 9 size shoe? If you are at peace with that, you might begin to see the beautiful, stately young lady with radiant brown eyes, a pretty smile, and a nicely proportioned body that many envy. You might also see the spirit we all enjoy and be thankful for just who you are.

I know competition is tough out there. You should try it at 51! My hope is that you will strive to be the best you are, not what you wish you were. Accept what you aren't and celebrate what you are.

Pray with me:
Lord, you have made us who we are. Help us to recognize our beauty and learn to accept who we are even when it is less than we wish. Amen

Patty B. Williams

March 11th

Heart Conversations

"Commune with your own heart upon your bed and be still."
Psalm 4:4 (KJV)

You know how difficult it is to struggle with an issue when you don't know what to do. Do you remember how defeated, grumpy, and exhausted it makes you feel? Can you remember the times when you've called your best friend for comfort when you've been agonizing over a decision?

Sometimes when we don't know what to do in a situation, maybe we should try God's message and lie in our bed, be still and listen to our heart. Maybe that's some form of meditation, or maybe it's a way for God to speak to us in a whisper.

The next time you have an agonizing situation, I hope you will follow the scripture above. It is from a pretty reliable source.

Pray with me:
Lord, teach us to take time to listen, not only to others, but also to our own hearts. Amen

Clean Underwear, Wild Elephants and the Princess

March 12th

What Makes You Beautiful

"It is not fancy hair, gold jewelry, or fine clothes that should make you beautiful. No, your beauty should come from within you—the beauty of a gentle and quiet spirit. This beauty will never disappear, and it is worth very much to God." 1 Peter 3:3-4 (NCV)

When you were a little girl, I thought I would never get you in a pair of jeans. When you first became a teenager, I thought I'd never get you out of jeans and into a dress again! Funny how time changes so many things. One thing it hasn't changed, of course, is how much you care about what you wear. You've been concerned about that since you were a toddler. You were so different from Michael who, as a child, never cared whether or not he even wore clothes! For the most part, he would wear anything I put out, until he was a teenager.

I know you never have a thing to wear. Poor child! I know, too, that if you did think you had something to wear, it wouldn't be the perfect thing. You would still feel like you needed something else, something different, something that made you look thinner, or older, or sexier, or yada, yada, yada. I suppose you're pretty normal. At least I hope so, because it sounds like me, too,—except for the older part. Switch that to younger!

I know I don't have to tell you that your attire, whether it be jeans or a fancy dress, is not the most important part of your appearance. You can be beautiful on the outside, but if the spirit doesn't match, all the time and effort you put in to finding the perfect outfit won't matter. I think you know this. I just wanted to remind you.

Patty B. Williams

Pray with me:
Help us remember, Father, that you and others care much more about the inside of us than you do the outside. Amen

Clean Underwear, Wild Elephants and the Princess

March 13th
(Austin's birthday)

Arguments

"Stay away from foolish and stupid arguments. You know that such arguments grow into bigger arguments." 2 Timothy 2:23 (NCV)

Don't you hate arguing? I do. It's such a downer, and think of all the valuable time that is wasted when you could be doing something fun or worthwhile.

That doesn't mean you can't enjoy some lively discussions nor have a disagreement every now and then. Life would be pretty boring if you agreed with everyone all the time or never had to stand up for what you believed. Sometimes that builds character.

It's the arguments that are silly, or stupid, or destructive that you need to avoid. What's the point? Is someone really going to win? Is a silly, or stupid, or destructive argument worth causing someone or yourself anguish? Is it worth risking a relationship over? My guess is the answer is, "no".

So, the next time you find yourself in an argument that is dumb, stop and think about it, and you be the bigger person and take the initiative to end it. I think you'll feel better about it.

Pray with me:
We are certainly hardheaded sometimes, Lord. Help us to be wiser and willing to walk away from unproductive arguments. Amen

Patty B. Williams

March 14th

Bragging

"If I must brag, I will brag about the things that show I am weak."
2 Corinthians 11:30 (NCV)

One of the things I have always admired about Bob when he gives his sermons is that he always admits his faults and weaknesses. He's not afraid of using himself as an example of one who has not always done the will of God, or that has been tempted, or struggles with doing what he knows is the right thing to do.

I turned down the opportunity to compete for a new position this week because I knew the responsibilities of the job were in an area in which I was weak. The extra money would have been nice, and I could have just admitted my weaknesses to myself and to my superiors and hoped they would have placed me in the job based on my strengths, but I knew I wasn't the best person for the job.

I think you are pretty much aware of your strengths and weaknesses. I've never heard you brag about yourself, so I don't worry about your being a braggart. Just remember that people can identify with weaknesses much quicker than they can with strengths, so if you ever need to get a message across that points weaknesses of another, you might try explaining first how you can identify with those weaknesses.

Pray with me
Help us remember, Lord, that because we are weak and can admit it, others may be able to gain strength. Amen

Clean Underwear, Wild Elephants and the Princess

March 15th

Welcoming Strangers

"Keep on loving each other as brothers in Christ. Remember to welcome strangers into your homes. Some people have done this and have welcomed angels without knowing it." Hebrews 13: 1-2 (NCV)

From the time you were a little girl, you have been taught not to talk to strangers. I think children were taught that much more in the past decades than we were.

Remember the "what if" drills I used to play with you when you were little? Do you remember the secret code we had if someone ever came to get you and you didn't know if you should go? I remember; but since it's our secret, I won't put it in writing.

Even at eighteen, you have to be careful of strangers these days. That's sad, but it's unfortunately reality. I think, however, that this scripture is talking more about that person we make judgments about that we don't really know. It's about that clique we belong to that doesn't welcome outsiders, or that kid that wears the earring and has long hair. We don't know what angels lurk in any of them unless we get beyond our self-imposed barriers and welcome them.

Pray with me
Lord, protect us from strangers that might hurt us, but when we're in a safe environment, don't let us make someone feel like a stranger. Amen

Patty B. Williams

March 16th

When You Become Weak

"You have become weak, so make yourselves strong again."
Hebrews 12:12 (NCV)

Do you remember experiencing temptation, giving in to it, and then feeling really rotten about it later? I don't know many of us who haven't. It's not a great feeling.

Sometimes the temptation is minor in the realm of all the things it could be. Maybe the temptation is to eat a cookie when you're on a diet or to watch a favorite t.v. program when you should be studying. Maybe the temptation is something big like betraying a friend and going out with her boyfriend or copying someone's homework instead of doing it yourself. You get the idea.

Everyone has times of weakness. Thank goodness God gives us a chance to ask for forgiveness and start over. With that chance I think he expects us to try and do better, to do what we need to do to be stronger the next time the same temptation shows its ugly head.

I will pray that you will always be strong, knowing that at times you will still fail.

Pray with me:
Lead us not into temptation, Lord. Help to keep us strong. But when we fail, help us to know we are still loved. Amen

Clean Underwear, Wild Elephants and the Princess

March 17th
(Aunt Debbie's Birthday)

Aunt Debbie

"But you should continue following the teachings that you learned. You know that these teachings are true. And you know you can trust those who taught you." 2 Timothy 3:14 (NCV)

You have been so fortunate to have such wonderful aunts who have played an important part in your life. Today, on her birthday, I think about your Aunt Debbie.

I will never forget the look on Debbie's face the night you were born. As a matter of fact, it is one of the most vivid things I remember. She was in such awe. She and Uncle Billy had come up to Atlanta to a baby shower Nancy and Mark Vepraskas were giving your dad and me. She didn't expect to be able to see you. You were about a month early and made us all a little nervous.

Debbie loved you so much. I could see that look on her face each time she was with you. Then, when Weston came along, the two of you became best friends. Debbie spent hours playing with you both and trying to teach as she played. She, like Aunt Mary Jane, was a big part of your childhood and childhood memories.

I know when you become an aunt one day you will be a good one because you have had such good role models. I know, too, that you will join me today in saying a special prayer of thanksgiving for Aunt Debbie on her special day.

Pray with me
Thank you, Lord, for those people who have played special roles in our lives, who have taught us and loved us, as you would have them to do. Amen

Patty B. Williams

March 18th

Knowing The Right Thing To Do

"And when a person knows the right thing to do, but does not do it, then he is sinning." James 4:17 (NCV)

When we think about sin, we normally think about doing something bad, or doing something we know we shouldn't have done. We forget that often it's those things we don't do, that we should have done, that are the greatest sins.

Helping the homeless, feeding the hungry, clothing the poor, taking care of the sick are all things that we can each have some small part in making better. If we don't do our part, what message do you think that sends to God?

We don't all have the same financial ability to do for others, but we all have the ability to do something. We can donate our time or talents in other ways. That's one of the things I'm glad they teach and require in sororities. Community service is so important. I'm glad you have the opportunity to volunteer your time to be a part of those projects. I know it must make you feel good to be doing something for someone less fortunate than you. You make me very proud.

Pray with me:
Lord, help us to remember all the different ways we can be the people you want us to be, doing the things you would have us to do for others. Amen

Clean Underwear, Wild Elephants and the Princess

March 19th
(Papa's Birthday)

Contentment

"Now godliness with contentment is great gain. For we brought nothing into this world, and it is certain we can carry nothing out. And having food and clothing, with these we shall be content."
1 Timothy 6: 6-8 (NKJ)

Today is Papa's birthday. If my memory serves me right, he will be 87. I can assure you his age is only chronological. He's not 87 in appearance or spirit. I only hope I can be as fortunate as he if I make it to 87.

I was always puzzled why Papa was so content to be in Lulu all the time, never really caring about traveling to other states or vacationing away from home. He never came to Atlanta when we lived there, and if he ever came to Tallahassee, it was only once or twice.

As I've gotten older and hopefully a little wiser, there is a part of me that envies the contentment that Papa could have with a simple life, filled primarily with his immediate family, his church family, and his work. He didn't need the excitement of city life, the luxuries of a fancy house, or a big bank account to love and enjoy life. Wouldn't that change the world if we could all be more like that?

I truly believe that is the way God intended it. Even though some of God's people had to want and do more to make the advances we have in the world and to take care of the huge social problems we've created, I still think God planned for us to be more simple with our personal desires when we are looking for fulfillment. Maybe Papa figured that out a long time ago.

Pray with me:
Thank you, God, for Papa and for what he has meant to us in our lives. When we think about what it takes to make us happy, help us to be more like him. Amen

Granny and PaPa

Clean Underwear, Wild Elephants and the Princess

March 20th

That Thorn In Your Side

"The soldiers used some thorny branches to make a crown. They put this crown on Jesus' head and put a purple robe around him."
John 19:2 (NCV)

Has anyone or anything been a particular thorn in your side lately? You know what I mean, that person or thing that's been bugging you or, at minimum, been causing you some discomfort or anguish. I could name several of mine—the delay in completing the house addition, computer problems with trying to file my taxes, tensions at work, should I go on?

Have you ever thought about the possibility that even thorns have their purpose? If nothing else, they usually require some action from us. We finally do something to change the situation, we grow through it and get over it, we drive ourselves nuts or we turn it over to God. Hopefully we choose one of the more positive actions.

Bob said in his sermon last Sunday that God is not so much concerned about our temporary comfort. He's more concerned about our Christian maturity. In other words, if the thorns help us to become better individuals and to depend more on God than our own human strength, then maybe they've served their purpose.

As a mother, my hope, of course, is that you don't have many thorns to contend with, but when you do, I hope you might look at them with a little different perspective.

Pray with me:
Lord, help us to put thorns in their proper place—with you. Keep us mindful of your strength compared to ours. Amen

Patty B. Williams

March 21st

God Knows

"Lord, who may enter your Holy Tent? Who may live on your holy mountain? Only a person who is innocent and who does what is right. He must speak the truth from his heart." Psalm 15:1-2 (NCV)

If you've been paying attention to the news at all lately you know the accusations that have been made against the President and against the highest-ranking enlisted man in the army. The accusations seem very plausible, but of course both men are adamant that the things they were accused of never happened. The army guy, was acquitted of the charges against him. The women who brought sexual harassment charges against him still swear that what was charged was factual. We may never know the real truth. God, of course, does.

In situations like this, I always wonder if the person(s) lying really think they are getting away with something. I wonder how they look themselves in the mirror every day and not feel sick inside, especially when they know they are hurting someone else.

I guess they do it just like we commit our share of sins. How sad that we have created such a broken world. We are so blessed that God didn't give up on us long ago, aren't we?

Remember to pray for our leaders and to ask forgiveness for all those things that have made them and us less than what God intended.

Pray with me
Lord, help us each day to strive to be the individuals and leaders you planned for us to be. When we fail, help us to not compound it by losing our integrity. Forgive us our trespasses as we forgive others. Amen

Clean Underwear, Wild Elephants and the Princess

March 22nd
(Kelly's birthday, Nanny's death, 1994)

Keeping Things Inside

"When I kept things to myself, I felt weak deep inside me. I moaned all day long." Psalm 32:3 (NCV)

I have a difficult time understanding how people can be so private and keep things to themselves, especially things that are emotionally draining, hurtful, or sometimes even joyful. I truly do struggle with it because I am so open.

I don't think one way is right and one way is wrong, but I do think that those people who are more open with sharing their feelings make life less stressful for themselves. Burdens are so much lighter when you have someone to share the load with, and happiness is multiplied when there's someone to share it with.

If something is bothering you, it helps sometimes to have another person to just listen, to help you think it through, or to offer a solution. Often if you've been mulling over something a long time, you lose your ability to be objective, to think clearly. Another person can offer a different perspective.

I know you are pretty open most of the time and are willing to talk about your problems, concerns, or issues. I'm happy about that. Don't ever lose that ability.

Pray with me
Lord, we know you are always there for us when we need you, but when we need a person we can hear or see or touch, we ask that you lend us one of your children. Amen

Patty B. Williams

March 23rd

The Bad Apple

"Be careful that no one fails to get God's grace. Be careful that no one becomes like a bitter weed growing among you. A person like that can ruin all of you." Hebrews 12:15 (NCV)

You've heard me say a million times to choose your friends wisely because they can make or break you. They can cause you to grow or they can cause you great heartache. You have had both kinds.

I know it was, and maybe still is to a lesser degree, difficult for you to understand that being with the wrong person at the wrong time can cause you a lot of trouble, even if you're not doing anything wrong.

Another kind of person that can hurt you, though not intentionally, is that person who is always negative, always complaining, always down instead of up. You have to be careful that he or she doesn't drag you down, too. If you know someone like that and ever get that feeling, distance yourself from him or her for a while. Regain yourself. Then when you're sure you're strong, you can try to help them. It'll be a challenge.

Pray with me
Lord, help us to keep alert to potential pitfalls with others. Use us to be helpful, but give us wisdom when it's time to remove ourselves from a harmful situation. Amen

March 24th

Love Your Enemies

"But I tell you: Love your enemies and pray for those who persecute you." Matthew 5:44 (NKJ)

Do you remember those times when you were so angry with some of your friends that they made you cry? I remember. I could have shaken every one of them till they were starry-eyed. I also remember your anger when you felt betrayed by one of your best friends. It was a difficult time for you. It was difficult for me, too, having to watch you hurt. I don't remember all my thought processes at that time, but I wonder how much we prayed about it or prayed for the friends. Thinking about it now, I'm sure I prayed some, but I'm not sure I prayed the right prayer or prayed enough.

I know how difficult it is to think about doing anything positive for someone who has hurt you or made you angry. However, had God not wanted us to handle it in a certain way, he wouldn't have given us such good instructions.

I think when we pray for those who have hurt or angered us it does as much for us as it does for the other people. It makes us think about them in a little different light when we're praying for them. We usually are, in the same breath, also praying for ourselves, too, and asking God to help us handle the situation appropriately. If, after praying, we're listening and looking for his guidance, we don't have as much time to be concentrating on our hurt or anger.

So—the next time someone really makes you mad or hurts your feelings, try praying for them. See if it makes a difference.

Patty B. Williams

Pray with me:

You know, God, how hard it is to pray for those who we feel don't deserve our prayers at the moment. Help us to think about how you would handle the situation, Lord, and remind us to ask for your guidance. Amen

March 25th

Cleaning Out Your Heart

"Create in me a clean heart, O God; and renew a right spirit within me." Psalm 51:10 (NCV)

We spend a lot of time cleaning out things in our life—we clean out the refrigerator, the garage, the closets. Sometimes we even clean out our bedrooms—well, some of us do! You and Deborah just don't do it as often as you should maybe.

Have you ever thought about cleaning out your head or your heart? There sure is a lot of garbage that accumulates there sometimes, things like resentment, anger, envy, hurt, stress. They sure take up a lot of space that could be used in better ways, don't you think?

Perhaps we should just set aside a day a month to ask God to help us with our personal cleaning. I think that might help us feel better than seeing the refrigerator or closet clean. It's certainly worth a try. Just think what might be accomplished with a clean head and a clean heart. Boy, talk about new beginnings!

Pray with me:
Lord, the heart and head cleaning is not a job to tackle alone. Help us to remember to ask for your help. Amen

Patty B. Williams

March 26th

The Christian Scientist

"Go up to Gilead and take balm, O virgin, the daughter of Egypt; In vain you will use many medicines; You shall not be cured."
Jeremiah 46:11 (NKJ)

I don't know a lot about the beliefs of Christian Scientist, but I dated a guy in college one time who belonged to this religious group, and now I have a friend at work who is a Christian Scientist. One thing I know they practice is healing by prayer rather than by medicines. I remember the guy I dated having a bad cold and not taking anything for it. It didn't make sense to me at all at the time. I still have difficulty with it, but I respect their beliefs and practices much more than I did when I was younger.

Though I do believe in medicine, I'm not sure that it is always the best immediate approach. Sometimes I think we may look to medicine to solve physical problems that might really be a disguise for a head or heart problem that could be helped by prayer and/or a counselor rather than a $40 prescription.

You know how we often cause our physical problems just because we don't take care of ourselves. We don't get enough rest; we don't eat right; we get ourselves in stressful situations or don't remove ourselves from them. Sound familiar? We all do it. I don't think we need a bottle of medicine to cure those ills. We need discipline. What do you think?

Pray with me:
Help us, Lord, to use medicines when it's necessary, but help us to use discipline and prayer to keep us on a healthy track. Amen

Clean Underwear, Wild Elephants and the Princess

March 27th

Guilt

"My guilt has overwhelmed me. Like a load it weighs me down."
Psalm 38:4 (NCV)

Guilt, my what a powerful punch it carries! It can really knock you flat, can't it? It can also make you do all kind of crazy things that you wouldn't ordinarily do. It can make you shy away from friends and loved ones or make you grumpy and depressed. It can also cost years of happiness. What a waste, especially when there's such an easy way to relieve oneself of the burden.

Guilt, of course, isn't always bad. Sometimes it makes us do things that we would ordinarily procrastinate in doing or not do at all. Sometimes it makes us a better person because of something we accomplish along the way while we were called to action out of guilt. Maybe laying that guilt trip every now and then isn't all bad.

There's lots of good reasons I'd rather you be called to action than out of guilt, but I can't promise I won't use guilt every now and then if it works. I'll try to use it sparingly though if you'll try not to tempt me. Deal?

Pray with me
Lord you have taught us how to pray for forgiveness when we feel, or are, guilty. Help us to heed your words and then get on with life. Time is much too precious to waste on guilt. Amen

Patty B. Williams

March 28th

Crying

"And God will wipe away every tear from their eyes; there shall be no more death, nor sorrow, not crying. There shall be no more pain, for the former things have passed away." Revelation 21:4 (NKJ)

Well, I had one of those teary times the other night and for no apparent reason. I was watching the academy awards, laughing and enjoying them, and all of a sudden there was a mention of a particular movie and then a touching song, and that's all it took. All the sweet memories came flashing back and all the bad memories were buried somewhere among the ruins of the Titanic. It's funny how that can happen, isn't it? I know you understand.

Actually, I guess crying every now and then isn't so bad. It cleans out the cobwebs so to speak. It makes you realize you can still feel, and it makes you think instead of pushing all your thoughts away. I guess if you have the right attitude it also makes you thankful for what you once had even if it didn't last.

I hope the tears you and Michael experience, for whatever reason, are limited. Mothers have such a difficult time with their children's tears! But when they come, as I know they will, I hope you know you don't have to shed them alone—unless that is your choice.

Pray with me
God, we know you are always close at hand during times of sadness and times of joy. Remind us to ask you to join us. Amen

Clean Underwear, Wild Elephants and the Princess

March 29th

Do These Things

"Remind the believers to do these things: to be under the authority of rulers and government leaders, to obey them and be ready to do good, to speak no evil about anyone, to live in peace with all, to be gentle and polite to all people." Titus 3:1-2 (NCV)

The above scripture sounds like *All I Need To Know I Learned In Kindergarten*, doesn't it? It's too bad that more people don't know that all they need to know for the right kind of living is in the Bible. Wouldn't it be a changed world if people just followed the simple scripture above?

I'm glad you don't appear to have a problem with submitting to authority when you should. In the same vein, I'm also glad that you appear to have the confidence in yourself to challenge authority if that authority is being abusive. You don't try to hurt others in speaking about them, to my knowledge, and I know you are a peace lover. I get accolades on your behalf all the time about your politeness and your sweetness and concern for others so I know you are doing well in that area too.

Today is a day then to tell you once again how proud I am of you, for what you stand for, for how you treat others, for what you have been to your grandparents and other family members, and for what your are becoming. Don't stop. You're on a roll!

Pray with me
Thank you, God, for the instructions you give us for the right kind of living. Keep us focused on those instructions and protect us from the temptations to do otherwise. Amen

Patty B. Williams

March 30th
(Aunt Dolly's birthday)

Work Your Best

"In all the work you are doing, work the best you can. Work as if you were working for the Lord, not for men. Colossians 3:23 (NCV)

I know you must have some of the same type of days at work as I do. You don't want to be there, your supervisor and your customers are being pains in the neck, you don't feel like you're getting paid enough for what you're doing, and you feel totally unappreciated. Sound familiar?

Those are the days you have to pull deep from within to continue to do a good job in spite of everything that is falling down around you—including your attitude!

One way you might accomplish that in your work situation is to think about that next customer being an angel sent from God to audit your performance. Boy, that would change your attitude in a hurry, wouldn't it? Well, that next customer might not be an angel, but he might need an angel to brighten his day. That is a job I know you can do well when you want to. I hope that desire finds its way to you more often than not.

Pray with me
Lord, you know some days are just better than others. On those not so good days, please be near to lift our spirits and improve our attitudes regardless of what's going on around us. Amen

Clean Underwear, Wild Elephants and the Princess

March 31st

Who's Responsible?

"While he is a child, he must obey those who are chosen to care for him. But when the child reaches the age set by his father, he is free." Galatians 4:2 (NCV)

There was some tragic news a few days ago that involved an eleven-year-old and a thirteen-year-old boy who opened fire at an elementary school and killed several students and adults. Then on the radio the next morning a question was asked of listeners as to who was responsible for the actions of the boys. Was it the parents, the school, society, t.v. programming, or the boys themselves? The radio announcers asked for people to call in and give their opinions. I guess if I had called, I would have said it was all of the above. We have all failed. As Bob would say, "We live in a broken world." I would add "that we have created." I would also have added that, yes, even the announcers had a part in it! The things people say on the air for young people to hear are often times way out of line with what God would approve if he were doing the programming. Many of their comments are not wholesome, positive, or a good influence on others, especially not on children.

Whatever possessed those two young boys to do what they did is beyond imagination. Is it their parent's fault? What a question! Can you imagine what those poor parents must be going through? If there is blame to be laid, my guess is it is shared by many. What a very sad situation. What a terrible waste of so many lives.

Pray with me
Oh, Lord, for these children and for all who share in the guilt of a broken world, we ask your forgiveness. For the lives that must continue in the midst of this tragedy we ask for your peace and love that passes understanding. Amen

Patty B. Williams

April 1ˢᵗ
(Mom Bigham's birthday)

Mom Bigham

"As the Father loved Me, I also have loved you, abide in My love."
John 15:9 (NKJ)

I am so sorry that you never got to know your great-grandmother, Mom Bigham. You would have loved her. Some of my best childhood memories were times Mary Jane and I spent with her and Pop Bigham. I spent hours playing beauty shop with her like you did with Granddaddy, and my most favorite Christmas memories were of Mom and Pop driving up in the yard with their car loaded with presents.

Mom also made the best pancakes in the world, and she was crazy about Granddaddy. Uncle Teddy and Uncle Robert used to tease her about your granddaddy being her favorite. Of course, we thought that was true, too.

Every year we went to the state fair in Tampa and spent the night in Lakeland with Mom and Pop. I guess you would call it tradition. It was sad when those times ended.

I guess the reason Nanny and Granddaddy were such perfect grandparents is because they had such good role models. Hopefully you and my grandchildren will feel the same way about me one day. I sure hope so.

God has certainly blessed our family with a long line of love, hasn't he? I hope we always appreciate that as much as we should. Today, on Mom's birthday, I will say a special prayer of thanksgiving for all she meant in my life and for how her life continues to touch us all.

Pray with me:

Thank you, God, for all those who loved us and for those who we loved. We have been blessed beyond measure. Amen

Patty B. Williams

April 2nd

Fooled Again

"Be very careful, then, how you live—not as unwise but as wise, making the most of every opportunity, because the days are evil. Therefore do not be foolish, but understand what the Lord's will is." Ephesians 5: 15-16 (NIV)

Yesterday was April Fool's Day and you fell for a trick again. You're too easy, Brookie Bear! At least this time it wasn't your mom fooling you.

I know your sorority sisters were having a lot of fun teasing you, but as you go through life you will be in a lot of different situations that can fool you, and, unfortunately, those doing the fooling will not always be doing it for fun. There are unscrupulous business people out to make money, so-called friends who will take advantage of you, and guys who will be who you want them to be so they can try to convince you to do what they want you to do. Sometimes it won't take a rocket scientist to see through the facade, but other times motives will be well hidden, so be aware.

Have a good sense of humor—even at 3:00 in the morning if the teasing is in good, clean fun, but the minute you detect someone trying to fool you for the wrong reasons, remove yourself from the situation as soon as possible. Use that pretty head God gave you, wisely!

Pray with me:
Keep us alert, Lord, to anything that might be harmful or hurtful to us, and forgive those who wrongly use others to their advantage. Amen

April 3rd

A Mother's Joy

"It always gives me the greatest joy when I hear that my children are following the way of truth." 3 John 1:4 (NCV)

Some of my greatest times of joy were when you and Michael came back from Mountain Top and told me about your experiences and how your lives were touched spiritually by things you saw and did. It always made me feel like some of the hopes I had for each of you were realized.

You know it pleases me to hear that you go to church on your own without me there to nag or make you feel guilty. I'm glad church has a place in your life, even if it's not every Sunday. I guess you're going to have to help me with your brother.

As a mother, I want so much for you and Michael to have the peace I know you can have in your lives if you are grounded spiritually. I know that if the grounding is there, you'll be able to face all the trials and tribulations life will bring. Not only will you be able to face them, you will be able to grow through them and help others.

I know how you were raised. I guess at some point you each have to decide what part it plays in your lives. I think you're headed in the right direction, and my heart is full!

Pray with me:
Thank you, Lord, for those little glimpses of success we see as our children grow and mature and make choices that not only please us but please you, too. Amen

Patty B. Williams

April 4th

Assumptions

"Behold, You desire truth in the inward parts, And in the hidden part You will make me to know wisdom." Psalm 51:6 (NKJ)

I'm thinking about Ramona today because it's her birthday. I don't know if you remember that it was she and Harold who got your dad and me together for our first date. Your dad and Harold were roommates at the time, living in Jacksonville, and Ramona and I were roommates living in Tallahassee. Actually I don't think your dad was too keen on the idea of having a date with me at the time. Without knowing me, he made some wrong assumptions about what I was like and whether or not he would like me. Well, I guess he did like me, considering we were married 6 months later!

I suppose had it been left up to your dad, we would never have dated, just because he assumed some things instead of checking them out first before making a decision. I wonder how many things in life we miss out on because we do the same thing. We don't make an effort to meet someone because we assume something negative about him or her from their appearance or from something we've heard. We don't make a phone call to someone because we assume their reaction to the call will be something less than what we want, or we don't try something we really want to do because we assume we can't succeed at it. Now think about it. Is that too smart? I don't think so.

God gave us brains and he expects us to use them. I think he expects us to seek the truth in everything, and I'm not sure making rash assumptions fits in to that plan. I hope you will be aware of those times when you start to make an assumption about something before checking it out first. It just may be to your detriment.

Pray with me:
Lord, sometimes assuming things without spending the effort to check them out is a lazy cop-out. Help us to be smart enough to figure that out and act accordingly. Amen

Patty B. Williams

April 5th

Mistreatment

"I have hated the assembly of evildoers, and will not sit with the wicked." Psalm 26:5 (NIV)

I have been amazed over the years to know some of my friends who lived in physically and mentally abusive situations with their spouses, or worse yet, young girls or women who continued to date abusive guys. I'm sure part of my amazement comes from a naïve background of what all is involved but also a strong support from family members who would never have allowed that to happen.

I know you know there are a lot of crazy people out there in the world. What you are probably still too innocent to know at this point is how to discern those that are hiding in sheep's clothing. That's even difficult for those of us who are older and not quite so innocent.

I'm sure you know this, but just because it's the Mommy thing to do, let me remind you that there is no reason you should ever be mistreated abusively by anyone. You don't deserve it and never will. There is always a way out, and life is much too short to live five minutes in such a situation. The minute you suspect anyone might have a tendency to be abusive, distance yourself from them and tell someone about your suspicions.

I'm not telling you to be afraid or suspicious of everyone, I just want you to always be aware and cautious.

Pray with me:
Lord, keep us aware of and safe from those who act outside your will. Give us wisdom, strength and courage to distance ourselves when we should. Amen

April 6th
(Shanise's birthday)

The Heart Part

"But the Lord said to Samuel, Do not look at his appearance or at his physical stature, because I have refused him. For the Lord does not see as man sees, for man looks at the outward appearance, but the Lord looks at the heart." 1 Samuel 16:7 (NKJ)

One of my favorite *Flavia* cards says, "'And what is as important as knowledge?' asked the mind—'Caring, and seeing with the heart,' answered the soul."

For the next four years you will hopefully be increasing your knowledge tremendously. You will learn things that will help you in daily life, help you make a living on your own, and help you understand things and people better. As I have said many times, I envy this opportunity you have. I would love to have the time and money to do it over again the right way.

With all the knowledge I know you will gain, I hope you will remember that there are other things just as important as knowing a lot of "book stuff." I call it the "heart part," that part of your education that begins as a child and continues until old age. It's that part that makes you the person God intended. It's the education of your heart towards others.

Unfortunately, the heart part is sometimes the most difficult part of your education to master, primarily because there are so many temptations and distractions to do otherwise. I don't think you'll have any problem with it, though. You started with good marks a long time ago.

Patty B. Williams

Pray with me:

Thank you, Lord, for the opportunity for education in all realms of our life. Help us to do our best to master them all. Amen

Clean Underwear, Wild Elephants and the Princess

April 7th

Time

"Blessed is he who reads and those who hear the words of this prophecy, and keep those things which are written in it; for the time is near." Revelation 1:3 (NKJ)

Time—we each have the same amount, but it certainly doesn't feel like it, and we sure use it differently, don't we? I never seem to have enough of it. Because of that, it frustrates me to waste it. I guess that's why I'm late to meetings and events. They seldom start on time, so my philosophy is, why get there on time and have to wait!

Time is funny. It's always slow when we're waiting and fast when we don't want something to end. Go figure!

My advice on time is, treat it as precious because it is! We only have so long on this old earth, and if we want to use what time we have, we need to get on with it. Maybe every six months we should stop and ask ourselves what we would do differently if we knew our time on earth was limited to only two more months. The scary thought is, it could be. We never know.

I know you have a busy schedule with classes, work, sorority life and family; I hope you are using your time wisely. Rest when you need to. It's okay. Just don't waste time. It's too precious of a resource.

Pray with me:
Keep us focused enough, Lord, that we don't waste the precious time you give us. Keep us mindful of its importance. Amen

Patty B. Williams

April 8th

Shredded Wheat

"Be patient, then, brothers, until the Lord's coming. See how the farmer waits for the land to yield its valuable crop and how patient he is for the autumn and spring rains." James 5:7 (NIV)

The glances over cocktails that seemed to be so sweet, don't seem quite so amorous over shredded wheat! That's a little ditty by Benny Fields that most certainly is true! Unfortunately, romance between most couples doesn't last as long as it should. Reality sets in much too fast. That's why you need to be very careful before you go making long-term commitments. You need to be pretty sure that you can be as happy with him across the table eating that bowl of shredded wheat, tired and stressed from a busy day at the office, as you can with him in that fancy restaurant with stars in his eyes and a glass of wine!

I know what you've always said you wanted to find in a boyfriend or a husband one day. Don't give up looking for the right one too quickly. You have plenty of time. Life is too short not to enjoy where you are right now. God has a plan; don't try to rush it. If you get impatient, ask him for a little clue every now and then; you might be surprised at the response you get.

Pray with me:
Lord, help us to seek your will for our lives and not our own, even when we think we know best. Grant us patience and peace while we look forward to your plans unfolding. Amen

Clean Underwear, Wild Elephants and the Princess

April 9th

Spiritual Maturity

"Perseverance must finish its work so that you may be mature and complete, not lacking anything." James 1:4 (NIV)

Remember a time when you were hurt badly? No, not the time Michael broke your arm or I spilled coffee on you. I mean an emotional hurt, not a physical one. I suppose you didn't think at the time that it could be a wonderful lesson to learn young so you could use the experience to help yourself and others to grow spiritually and emotionally. I know that sounds a little weird, but that's exactly what happens if you approach the hurt in the right way.

Think about that person who hurt you. Are you an enemy of hers or his? If you are, I don't know about it. Maybe you aren't as friendly with them as you once were, but do you wish them harm? Would you like to see them hurt more than you did? I don't think so. My guess is you would be kind to anyone even if they didn't deserve it. I said, kind, not overly friendly! That's because you have grown spiritually. You are a lover of persons, not a judge. You feel for others as much as you feel for yourself. Those are good traits to have on your journey to spiritual maturity.

God knows we are far from perfect in both our actions and our thoughts. That's why he's still around to finish what he started. I hope you want forget to stay in touch with him.

Pray with me:
Lord, we know spiritual and emotional maturity is a daily process. We need your help always to keep us headed in the right direction. Amen

Patty B. Williams

April 10th

Those Who Help Shape Us

"And again, I will put my trust in him. And again he says, Here am I, and the children God has given me." Hebrews 2:13 (NIV)

As you grow up, you will look back and remember fondly special people that played memorable roles in your life. About this time 25 years ago, I was thinking about one of my special folks, the first little boy I ever baby sat, Jimmy Temple. I was in labor with Michael. I knew it was Jimmy's birthday, and if my baby would hurry and come, it would share his birthday. Well, that didn't happen; Michael was born the next day, but each year on this day, I think about Jimmy.

About six years later, you were born 5 days before the birthday of the first little girl I baby-sat, Jimmy's sister, Larie. I always loved that coincidence. Jimmy and Larie were my first children to be responsible for. They helped me prepare for my real ones. Didn't they do a good job?

You'll be surprised at the things that will help you along the way to become a better mother, wife, sister, daughter, and granddaughter. That's why you should approach all things in life with a positive attitude. Those baby sitting nights with Amanda, those days working at the baby store, the times behind the cash register at the restaurant, they're all helping prepare you for great things! When you think about it that way, you might approach each differently.

Pray with me:
Thank you, Lord, for memorable people and experiences that help shape who we are. We pray that we are headed in the right direction for becoming who you have designed. Amen

Clean Underwear, Wild Elephants and the Princess

April 11th
(Michael's Birthday)

Pookie Bear

"And he has given us this command; Whoever loves God must also love his brother." 1 John 4:21 (NIV)

Your brother, that fella you love and could sometimes strangle at the same time, loves you and is more proud of you than he'll ever say or let you see. He's the one that adored you when you were little, more than you did him. He's also the one that years later aggravated you to death and had little time to show you any attention, much less affection. He's the one that you wrote poems and speeches about. Do you remember? I remember vividly. I also remember another time, a time when Michael won something at school and you ran out on the basketball court to congratulate him. You were so proud that he was your brother, and he was so proud that you came running out on that court. I, the Mommy, was just heart-struck. I loved that moment.

Aren't we blessed that on that day he was born so early and had such a small chance of living that he had such a will to live. Today, on his birthday, I know you join me in thanking God for loaning him to us—dimples, good looks, charisma, and all—well, maybe not all, but mostly all!

Pray with me:
God, thank you for that little life that almost didn't make it 25 years ago. Our lives have been richer and blessed because it did. Amen

Patty B. Williams

Pookie Bear

April 12th

Grief

"But you, O God, do see trouble and grief; you consider it to take it in hand. The victim commits himself to you; you are the helper of the fatherless." Psalm 10:14 (NIV)

You remember my talking about Richard, my first love. You also remember my telling you that he committed suicide last year shortly after I had written a devotional about him that he never got to see. You can imagine how devastated I and other friends and family were who loved him. We were grieved so greatly because we didn't know he was having such a difficult time or that we didn't have an opportunity to try and help him. What a terrible waste of God's greatest gift.

What do you think could have been so terrible in his world that would make him feel like he no longer wanted to be a part of it? Why do you think he didn't call some of us to let us know he was so depressed? How could he second-guess God and make the decision to take his own life? So many of us wish we had those answers.

Life can get pretty ugly at times, and a devastating situation one day can make you wish you were somewhere other than where you are at that moment. A heartache can rip you apart, and poor health can wear you down. What I think we have to try and remember is that regardless of the circumstances, God is still in control. With his help and the help of others, we can make it through anything. Grief, depression, heartache, poor health, whatever the problem is, it can be handled. Don't ever think there is no way out of a situation. Remember todays aren't always perfect, that's why God made tomorrows.

Patty B. Williams

Pray with me:

Oh, Lord, sometimes life is a real struggle. Be with us during those times, comfort us, and make us know that you are near and can help us through any situation. Amen

Clean Underwear, Wild Elephants and the Princess

April 13th

Money

"Do not wear yourself out to get rich; have the wisdom to show restraint. Cast but a glance at riches, and they are gone, for they will surely sprout wings and fly off to the sky like an eagle."
Proverbs 23:4-5 (NIV)

I worry about Michael's working the long hard hours he does, six days a week, with only one day off a week. He says the money is good and if he manages it wisely, he won't have to work after he's forty. I suppose that is a lofty goal, but I'm not sure the juice is worth the squeeze. What happens if you're burned out at forty? Can all that money buy back the time lost?

I know if he's going to work those hours, now is the time to do it while he's young and still doesn't have a family that needs his time and presence. I guess my wish is that he would find a job that paid him as well and gave him a little more freedom.

For similar reasons I worry about your working too much while trying to keep up your grades. I'm glad you feel obligated to help out with your expenses, but I don't want you to wear yourself out for the wrong reasons. I don't want you working too many hours just because you want extra money to buy things because you can't delay gratification when that is what you should consider. Delayed gratification and living within a budget are two lessons that are as important as any others you will learn in college. Don't blow them off. I know you can do well in both areas if you try; I'm counting on you to bring home A's in both subjects!

Patty B. Williams

Pray with me:
Lord, spending money and spending it when we want to are terrible temptations. Help us to discipline ourselves so we don't get worn out trying to satisfy our wants instead of our needs. Amen

Clean Underwear, Wild Elephants and the Princess

April 14th

Are You Bored?

"Our people must learn to devote themselves to doing what is good, in order that they may provide for daily necessities and not live unproductive lives." Titus 3:14 (NIV)

When you were a little girl, you could play for hours in your own little world. You could entertain yourself with a group of your dolls and stuffed animals, with your kitchen appliances, or with pulling books down from a shelf. It didn't have to be anything elaborate, just a few groceries in boxes to play store, pine straw to build rooms in a make-believe house, blocks of scrap wood to build a cash register. I don't ever remember your complaining of being bored, and I hope you never do.

There are so many worthwhile volunteer programs you can get involved in with just a phone call, and I'm sure your church has some opportunities for you to become involved with agencies or people who could use a helping hand. You've already participated in some of your sorority philanthropy projects.

Actually, I don't think boredom is a problem for you at this stage in life any more than it was when you were little, but when your life slows down a little, remember that all those opportunities that are out there now will still be there then. They are there for your friends, too, so don't hesitate to encourage any of them who might be bored.

Pray with me:
Lord, help us to stay busy enough to avoid boredom and wise enough to stay involved where we're needed. Amen

Patty B. Williams

April 15th

It's The Pits

"And whatever things you ask in prayer, believing, you will receive." Matthew 21:22 (NKJ)

There is a line in a country song by Don Gibson that asks, "Is this the best I'm gonna feel?" Some days I ask myself that question, knowing the answer, but feeling just as lousy anyway. Sometimes life is just the pits, isn't it?

I have a friend at work going through a romantic break-up. She is really hurting. I want her to be convinced that things will get better, that there is happiness after heartache, but right now I know she doesn't feel that way. It's difficult to feel whole when you're alone and used to being with someone, and it's easy to remember the reasons why you were together, instead of the reasons why you are now apart.

What is possible at such a difficult time is to let go and let God take care of the parts you can't handle at the moment. I hope my friend can do that. It won't be easy, I know, because I struggle with it myself. That will be my prayer for both of us tonight and a thought I hope you won't forget.

Pray with me:
We know, Lord, that you never promised us a rose garden; you just promised you would always be there for us among the roses or among the thorns. We are blessed. Amen

Clean Underwear, Wild Elephants and the Princess

April 16th
(Mary's birthday)

Conformity

"And do not be conformed to this world, but be transformed by the renewing of your mind, that you may prove what is that good and acceptable and perfect will of God." Romans 12:2 (NKJ)

"Everyone does it," you would say. I must have heard that a thousand times as an excuse for doing something. The fact, of course, was that some had done it, but just as many had not. The other kids were telling their parents the same thing you were telling me and hoping that it would be their ticket to freedom to do whatever it was they wanted to do.

Conformity, doing what everyone else does, why is that so important? Why can't we be more original, be the leaders instead of the followers? How will progress ever be made if we continue to conform to the way things are and don't try something different? Are we afraid of not being accepted if we don't do what everyone else does? Have you ever considered that non-conformity may be the thing that sets one apart and makes them an example others want to follow?

There are proper places for conformity. Being a non-conformist just for the sake of setting yourself apart may not be good in some circumstances. When, however, being a non-conformist is the position God would want you to take, then think twice and ask for the wisdom and strength to set yourself apart. I know you've had some practice in doing this. I'll always pray that you'll make the right choice.

Pray with me:
Lord, it's difficult to be a non-conformist at times, especially when it involves things we want to do. Give us wisdom and courage to make the right choices. Amen

Patty B. Williams

April 17th

Do Your Best

"Peace I leave with you, My peace I give to you; not as the world gives do I give to you. Let not your heart be troubled, neither let it be afraid." John 14:27 (NKJ)

I don't know who J. Lubbock is, but a quote of his says, "When we have done our best, we should wait the result in peace." That's a good philosophy, don't you think? The problem is we too often don't do our best and, therefore, we aren't at peace; we're in turmoil. Can you relate that to test taking?

I certainly would be delighted if you made the dean's list every semester, but I will never ask that of you. I only ask that you do your best. If you do your best, then I know you're being disciplined with studying and participating in extra-curricular activities. I know that if you do your best you will be more confident in yourself at test time and won't be consumed by stress and guilt for not trying harder.

Being at peace where most anything is concerned is a blessing. Life is too short to live without it for too long, so try hard to pursue it, not only in your academic world but also in your life in general.

Pray with me:
Thank you, Lord, for brains to know how to obtain peace. Help us to use them. Amen

April 18th

Looking For Mr. Perfect

"For the law appoints as high priests men who have weakness, but the word of the oath, which came after the law, appoints the Son who has been perfected forever." Hebrews 7:28 (NKJ)

I know you are always on the outlook for Mr. Right. That makes you a pretty normal 18-year-old, female, college student. I know, because I was there once—a long, long time ago! My guess is you're also looking for about the same thing I was—someone who is handsome, smart, sexy, conversant, a Christian from a good family, sweet, and well-off. You know, Mr. Perfect!

I hate to burst your bubble, but if you're looking for the guy with no imperfections, you'll never find him! That doesn't mean you won't find someone who you think is perfect. It just means that you'll eventually find out he's not, just like he'll find out you're not.

I hope that doesn't keep you from looking hard to find the one you think is perfect, the one you think you can live with together in harmony and happiness. You should strive for that. Just know that imperfections are going to be part of the package, whether you see them at first or not. Remember, only Jesus was perfect. The rest of us have a long way to go!

Pray with me:
Lord, forgive our imperfections, and help us as we strive daily to be the people you would have us to be. Amen

Patty B. Williams

April 19th

Acceptance

" . . . I pray that God, through Christ, will do in us what pleases him. And to Jesus Christ be glory forever and ever." Hebrews 13:21 (NCV)

For the most part, you have always been a pleaser. You try to do those things which make others happy.

Do you remember times when you've done things to make others happy even when those things were not things you should have done? Do you think if you were to go back to that same place and time with the maturity and confidence you have in who you are now, that you would make the same choices

I would like to think that I've matured spiritually and personally enough that I would make better choices, but I know at times I am still weak, still give in to temptations, and continue to do things just to be accepted or to please others.

Remember, God never put us in charge of happiness and pleasing everyone. He put us in charge of loving one another.

Pray with me:
Lord, when we're faced with a situation that calls for a choice between pleasing you or pleasing someone else, give us the strength and courage to always choose you. Amen

April 20th

Opportunity

"Therefore, as we have opportunity, let us do good to all people, especially to those who belong to the family of believers."
Galations 6:10 (NIV)

What opportunity are you looking for at the moment? Is it the opportunity to meet the right guy, the opportunity to change jobs, the opportunity to get rich, the opportunity to make a difference in someone's life? Where are you looking? Are you going to the right places, meeting the right people, or doing the right things to help those opportunities appear?

Have you thought that perhaps where you are right now, doing what you're doing, going to the places you're going, talking to people you know may provide the opportunity to reach your goals in the future? Don't give up that possibility. Look around you, think, be creative. Be open.

Often times we create the atmosphere for the doors of opportunity to be open. We can also stifle the atmosphere. Keep that in mind. My hope is that you will always be alert to possibilities and opportunities to grow and do things for yourself and others. You have so much to offer. I know you will have many opportunities to shine.

Pray with me:
Thank you, God, for opportunities to serve others and to serve you. Keep us alert, willing, and able to seize opportunities whenever and wherever they arise. Amen

Patty B. Williams

April 21st

The Company You Keep

"Do not be deceived: Evil company corrupts good habits."
1 Corinthians 15:33 (NKJ)

Do you have some friends that could be better friends if it were not for their demeanor? Have you known some friends, or acquaintances, that talked a good game and appeared to be nice, but you just didn't trust them? Have you found yourself and your demeanor changing when you were around them too long?

I have to admit that I have. I've been around negative people or people who talked about others and have found myself falling to that level rather than lifting myself above it. Instead of refusing to be part of the discussion or the situation, or trying to turn it around, I took the easy way out and joined in. I am not proud of that.

As Christians we have a responsibility to strive toward perfect love toward one another. I don't think that perfect love has a space for gossip, complaining, or putting others down. We have much more productive work to do than that.

I know your heart, and I know you care for others and would not do anything intentionally to hurt anyone. Be careful, however, to avoid company that may influence you to be someone you aren't.

Pray with me:
Lord, keep us strong in our convictions, especially when the temptation is great to be otherwise. Amen

Clean Underwear, Wild Elephants and the Princess

April 22nd

Disputes

"But avoid foolish and ignorant disputes, knowing that they generate strife." 2 Timothy 2:23 (NKJ)

Having roommates and boyfriends you will have many opportunities for disputes. Being in a sorority with girls from different backgrounds, with different ideas will also give opportunity for disputes.

Having differing opinions is o.k.; as a matter of fact, that's what makes life interesting. That's one way we learn to do things differently and to grow. What you want to avoid is arguing about those differences that lead nowhere, don't matter anyway, and just end up making you angry or stressed out. Life is much too short for that.

When you find yourself entering that realm, try to find a graceful way out. Make an excuse. Ask yourself and the other person or persons what is going to be accomplished by the dispute. Will winning the dispute be worth the end result of possible anger, hurt, or stress of all concerned, especially if the dispute is over something that is stupid?

It's something to think about. Keep alert.

Pray with me:
As we interrelate with one another, Lord, help it to be for positive reasons, not for reasons that set up opportunities for negative results. Amen

Patty B. Williams

April 23rd

Instructions To The Rich

"Command those who are rich in this present age not be haughty, nor to trust in uncertain riches but in the living God, who gives us richly all things to enjoy. Let them do good, that they be rich in good works, ready to give, willing to share, storing up for themselves a good foundation for the time to come, that they may lay hold on eternal life."
1 Timothy 6:17-19 (NKJ)

One of these days you may be among the rich and famous. You're only eighteen years old, have plenty of time before you, and all the ingredients to be whatever you want to be. If you want to be a doctor bad enough, you can be a doctor. You just have to want it enough. Whatever you decide one of these days, I know you'll be successful. If you end up being rich along with your success, I'll be happy for you. I just hope if that happens that you will give a lot of thought to how you'll handle that wealth.

Will you be overwhelmed by wealth? Will you throw it away on things that won't last? Will you use it to have fun on a continuous basis? I would hope that you would do with it just as I think you would. I think you would be wise with it. I think you would invest wisely, plan for the future, and do things that would benefit others less fortunate than you. I think you would ask God for guidance and do just as he would expect.

It's not too early to plan your actions for that fortune when you make it, nor is it too early to be wise in the use of small riches so you know how to handle the big ones when they get here. I'll be counting on you.

Clean Underwear, Wild Elephants and the Princess

Pray with me:
Lord, you have taught us about many things, riches are no exception, whether they are great or small, help us to handle them as you would have us to do. Amen

Patty B. Williams

April 24th

Remember Me

"To the One who remembered us in our low estate His love endures forever." Psalm 136:23 (NIV)

You've heard me say before that one of my greatest fears when you and Michael were little was that something would happen to me and you wouldn't remember all the things we had done together, or talked about, or worse, that you wouldn't remember much about me at all. Well, I guess that fear is no longer valid. You would remember me and would remember the bad stuff along with the good stuff. It's funny, but I still think a lot about how much I know you will forget about you and me, about the things we've done together during your teen years, and it makes me sad. I guess the sadness is because I have forgotten so much about Mother when I was young, and I so much want to remember.

I don't remember Mother and I being as close as I think you and I are. I suppose one reason for that is that she would never dream of talking to me about some of the things you and I have talked about. I remember when I asked her if you could get pregnant from kissing, she responded by asking me if I thought kitty cats got pregnant from kissing. To my knowledge, that's the only answer I got. I remember her taking Mary Jane and me to dance class and recitals, and I remember one night that she made soup and we ate it at Mary Jane's little table Daddy made, in front of a big fire, in our living room. I remember crawling in bed with her and daddy at night when I would get scared, and I remember she and daddy taking us cheerleaders to away games. I don't ever remember us going through a mother/daughter difficult time like you and I had. Maybe that was because of the goodie-two-shoes thing!

Clean Underwear, Wild Elephants and the Princess

Maybe the letters I've written you and Michael over the years and have stashed away will help you remember some of those uneventful things you will tend to forget. I hope so. In the mean time, let's just keep making those memories, and I'll keep telling you to remember them.

Pray with me:
Lord, help us to remember that in everything we do we are building memories. Help the good ones to far outweigh the bad ones. Amen

Patty B. Williams

April 25th
(Brittany's Birthday)

The Right Equipment

"All Scripture is given by inspiration of God, and is profitable for doctrine, for reproof, for correction, for instruction in righteousness, that the man of God may be complete, thoroughly equipped for every good work." 2 Timothy 3:16-17 (NKJ)

Are you struggling with a situation you don't know how to handle? How have you been trying to solve it? Have you talked to a friend about it? Did you think about calling your dad or me? Have you been thinking about past experiences that were similar and how you handle them? What about the Bible? Have you thought about looking there?

If the situation deals with temptation, you might look at Proverbs 1:10. If someone has hurt your feelings, you might look at Colossians 3:1. If someone has made you really angry, you might look at Proverbs 30:33. You get the drift. The Bible is such a wonderful resource that we seldom use. It has so many instructions to tell us the right way to do things. We should think about consulting it more often.

I hope you will get an interesting, easy to understand version of the Bible soon and start reading it through. You will just be amazed at the things it has to say and how it will benefit you in your thinking about some things. When you're ready, tell me, and I'll search for the best version for you.

Pray with me:
Your book of instructions, Lord, is the best textbook we'll ever purchase in or out of college. Help us to not lose sight of its benefit to us in our daily lives. Amen

April 26th

Brittany's Horse

"Hope deferred makes the heart sick, but a longing fulfilled is a tree of life." Proverbs 13:12 (NKJ)

Finally, for her eighth birthday, Brittany got the horse she'd been promised for years—"five years to be exact", she said! Can't you just imagine her excitement? I wish I could have been there, not only to witness her excitement, but also to witness the excitement of her parents and grandparents.

You know, as much as kids find it hard to believe sometimes, parents really love making and seeing their children happy. It's just that they also have the responsibility of their welfare in addition to their happiness, so sometimes they have to make them unhappy too.

I'm glad Brittany didn't give up on her hope of having a horse one day, although I know at times she got discouraged. I also trust that you won't give up on some of your hopes and dreams that you may have had for a number of years. Do what you can to bring them to fruition (success), and then be patient. Ask Brittany; I bet she'll tell you it will be worth the wait.

Pray with me:
Help us, Lord, to be patient, to keep hope alive, and to encourage others who may be discouraged. Amen

Patty B. Williams

April 27th

It Gets Easier

"For my yoke is easy and my burden is light." Matthew 11:30 (NKJ)

A quote by a man named John Norley says, "All things are difficult before they are easy." If you think about that, you should know from your own experience that he is right. Remember how you felt your first week at your new job? You were a little surprised that it was as difficult as it was, weren't you? Now, don't you feel pretty confident each time you go to work? What about math or any other subject that you are starting for the first time. Remember how you feel at the beginning of a semester? You feel pretty overwhelmed at first, don't you?

It's not just work or college coursework that are difficult before they are easy. That applies to a lot of things. An exercise program is really hard in the beginning after you get over the initial enthusiasm of getting started. When you find out how much discipline and effort it takes to keep up the program, it becomes more and more difficult. Then after a while it becomes second nature, a habit, and it becomes easier. The same thing is true about Bible study, going to church, eating right, or budgeting. Staying focused is difficult until it becomes part of your nature.

The point in this message is, don't get discouraged too quickly when something seems difficult or overwhelming at first. Accept that as normal and "keep on trucking," knowing that it will become easier with time and experience.

Pray with me:
Lord, help us with our frustrations, fears, and patience when at first a task seems so difficult. Give us perseverance to continue so that we can enjoy the rewards. Amen

April 28th

Think Before You Speak

"But I tell you that men will have to give account on the day of judgment for every careless word they have spoken." Matthew 12:36 (NIV)

We both know people who have hurt our feelings by saying something thoughtlessly or by saying something intentionally without thinking before they spoke. We both have done it to others, too. Hopefully things were never said with malice, they were just said with carelessness.

We have a God-given responsibility to avoid careless words that hurt or harm others. We also have a responsibility to forgive those that speak hurtful or harmful words to, or about, us. Both are tough at times. I think one way to remember the first responsibility is to think often about that old adage (saying) that goes, *if you can't say something nice, don't say anything at all!* The way to remember the second responsibility of forgiving is to remember all the things that we have done that have been forgiven. That kind of puts things in perspective, doesn't it?

I know you are a kind, loving and thoughtful young lady, and I don't think you would ever say or do anything to make someone feel bad intentionally. I do know, however, that you are very human and will make mistakes. This is just a reminder to think before you speak and to think about the forgiveness of others who don't think before they speak.

Pray with me:
Lord, help us to use our brains as much as our mouth and our hearts as much as our heads. Amen

Patty B. Williams

April 29th

What Happened To Yesterday?

"Jesus Christ is the same yesterday, today, and forever."
Hebrews 13:8 (NIV)

It seems like the minute I learn one new computer program, another one comes along I need to learn. I finally get to a point that I'm comfortable with the direction we're going at work, and a new boss comes along and changes direction. I liked being married and the changes that brought in my life; now I'm having to adjust to the changes of a single life again and all the positives and negatives that brings. Sometimes I just want everything to stay still for a while, to let me catch my breath and regroup. Do you think age has anything to do with that?

Even the familiar words in the Bible have changed for me over the past six months while I've been in the Disciple class. We have several different Bible translations that class members have, and it's been interesting to see the differences in the way passages are written.

It's comforting to know, however, that in the midst of change all around me, I can count on God being the same. I may change because circumstances cause me to change. My attitude toward God may change, but his attitude toward me won't. How scholars and writers translate the message about God may continue to change, but the basic message has not changed.

I have loved watching you change over the years, even though those changes meant leaving sweet memories behind. As you continue to change and watch change all around you, I hope your faith and trust in God will never change. It will give you the strength and courage to face any changes that come before you.

Pray with me:
Help us to know, Lord, your sameness and your nearness always. Amen

Patty B. Williams

April 30th

Seeking God's Will

"He withdrew about a stone's throw beyond them, knelt down and prayed, Father, if you are willing, take this cup from Me; yet not my will, but yours, be done." Luke 22:42 (NIV)

How many important decisions have you had to make lately? How many situations have you had that you wished you knew what to do? How many times have you wanted something to happen so badly that you prayed for it and gave God no options?

Praying earnestly for God's will in everything is very difficult, especially when we think in our infinite wisdom that we know what is best for us and everyone else. It takes great courage and faith to be able to trust God and ask that his will be done instead of ours.

I can't imagine going through a tragedy involving a child and having the courage, when it comes to the child's life, or quality of life, to be able to say, not my will, Lord, but yours. My guess is that it's the hardest thing anyone has or ever will have to do. The consequences of situations like losing a child require prayerful seeking of God's perfect wisdom and well-grounded faith.

One way to be ready for facing tragedy is to face everyday life with an attitude of seeking God's will in little situations and decisions, keeping an ongoing relationship with Him, and studying His word. Of course, I hope you never have a tragedy to face, but if you ever do, I want you as prepared as you can be.

Pray with me
Help us to seek and accept your will in all things, Lord. Amen

Clean Underwear, Wild Elephants and the Princess

May 1st
(Stacey's birthday)

Just Having Fun

"Having lost all sensitivity, they have given themselves over to sensuality so as to indulge in every kind of impurity, with a continual lust for more." Ephesians 4:19 (NIV)

May Day, this is a day that brings back memories of fun times with good friends. It's a day when the guys, adult guys, I might add, would all dress up as women and have a beauty pageant. It was hysterical. They went all out and really hammed it up. Of course, the beer made them a little less reserved, so they were a bit out of character—thank goodness! I know it doesn't sound too adult, does it? How about fun? Surely it sounds a little entertaining.

I suppose some people might have frowned and suggested that we were making fun of others with different lifestyles than ours, but that was not the intent. Of course, at a different time and a different place, it may have been very inappropriate behavior. It may have shown insensitivity to others' feelings, but that was not the case. The people who were there knew what was going to happen. They came to have a good time, with good friends, to laugh, and be funny. That is a huge difference from things some people do, intentionally, to put others down.

The point in this is to remind you that there is a time and place for everything. There is a time to tell a joke and a time not to tell one if it hurts someone's feelings or makes him or her feel uncomfortable. There's a time when behavior is appropriate and times when it's not. I know you know the difference. I hope you will continue to have appropriate behavior always and to have the courage to lead others in the right direction at the right time.

Patty B. Williams

Pray with me:

Lord, teach us to be sensitive to others always, using the actions of Jesus as our example. Amen

Clean Underwear, Wild Elephants and the Princess

May 2nd
(Uncle Stanley's Birthday)

What Do I Say?

"May the words of my mouth and the meditation of my heart be pleasing in Thy sight, O Lord, my Rock and my Redeemer."
Psalms 19:14 (NIV)

There are so many situations that call for us to communicate to others when we feel like we don't know what to say. Situations where someone has really hurt us, really made us mad, when we have to face someone who has lost a loved one are all difficult times. What is your first inclination in how to handle them? I hope your first inclination is to know that you *can* handle them. Second, I hope you know that in at least these particular situations, probably the less you say the better it will be.

In most cases, if someone has hurt you, he or she most likely knows it, and unless they are just a jerk, they are already dealing with it themselves. You don't need to say a lot. If someone has made you mad, he or she may, or may not, know it (by the way, a lot of guys fall in this category). You don't have to dwell on it, but let them know how you feel, and then move on. If someone has lost a loved one, it only takes a hug and three words, "I am sorry." That's usually all he or she needs at the time to know you really care. Again, as I've said a million times before, just use your heart, use God's help, and the words will come easy.

Pray with me:
Father, God, help us as we communicate to others, to do so in love that is pleasing to you. Amen

Patty B. Williams

May 3rd

The Need To Know

"Bear with each other and forgive whatever grievances you may have against one another. Forgive as the Lord forgave you."
Colossians 3:13 (NIV)

We've talked about forgiveness before, but I heard something recently in a Sunday school lesson that made me think about it in a little different light.

The statement was made that true forgiveness is not curious. What do you think that means? I had to think about it for a few minutes myself. What it means is, if you truly forgive someone, what happened, or the reasons for why something happened to warrant forgiveness, doesn't matter. What matters is it is forgiven.

Does that mean the person being forgiven gets off scot free, that there's no consequence to their actions? I don't think so. The husband or wife that is unfaithful, the teenager that is untruthful with their parents, or the alcoholic that is abusive to his children will all suffer losses, even if the loss is only one of innocence or peace of mind.

So, the next time you tell someone you forgive them, think about the sincerity of your forgiveness. If you truly want to forgive, have said that you do, but are still having a difficult time letting go of it, ask God to help you get past the curiosity and hurt. Ask for peace about the situation. He can help us when we can't help ourselves.

Pray with me:
Thank you, Lord, for giving us the capacity to love and forgive. Help us to strive to be as good at it as you are. Amen

Clean Underwear, Wild Elephants and the Princess

May 4th

Stained Glass Windows

"You, O Lord, keep my lamp burning; my God turns my darkness into light." Psalm 18:28 (NIV)

Elizabeth Kubler-Ross said, "People are like stained glass windows; they sparkle and shine when the sun is out, but when the darkness sets in their true beauty is revealed only if there is a light within."

I think Ms. Kubler-Ross is right. It's easy to wear a smile to be cheerful, to be thoughtful of others, to have a sense of humor, to trust when things are going well. It's much more difficult to be the same when things are going all wrong.

Do others see the Brooke I see most of the time, the Brooke I see some of the time, or the Brooke I see little of the time? Sounds like a test question, doesn't it? Well, maybe it is. It's a test of that light within you that I know can burn so brightly at times. It's a test of how you feel about yourself, how you acknowledge your blessings, and how strong your family and faith roots are. For if you pass that test, it won't matter if the sun is out or the darkness falls; that light within, even if temporarily dimmed a little, will still shine through. I know it's there, I hope you make a habit of letting the world see it, too.

Pray with me:
Lord, let your light shine brightly through us in good times and bad. If it starts to dim, touch us quickly and gently to remind us that you are near. Amen

Patty B. Williams

May 5th

Sean

"If one falls down, his friend can help him up. But pity the man who falls and has no one to help him up!" Ecclesiastes 4:10 (NIV)

I remember a time twenty-six years ago today when your dad and I shared one of God's greatest miracles with our best friends, Jim and Glenda. We were with them during the birth of their son, Sean. Helping Glenda through labor, waiting outside during the actual birth, and then seeing the baby right after he was born was something I'll never forget. It was an awesome experience.

A lot has changed since that day of Glenda's pain and all our great excitement and happiness. We have been through many more painful experiences together and apart as friends. We have shared in one another's successes and times of happiness, even when miles apart and with different spouses after divorce. Life certainly weaves its changes, good and bad, into our lives, doesn't it?

It won't be long before you are sharing these kinds of experiences with your best friends. I know you look forward to that in many ways, although the pain I'm sure you would like to skip! Unfortunately, it doesn't usually work that way. You will most likely share lots of heart pain and some physical pain along the path of life. Look for good friends to share the load. They really do help.

Pray with me:
Lord, thank you for special friends that have shared our lives. Keep us mindful of the blessings those friendships bring, and help us to remember that you are the greatest friend of all. Amen

May 6th

Do What You Can

"I am telling you this, but it is not because I need anything. I have learned to be satisfied with the things I have and with everything that happens." Philippians 4:11 (NCV)

Do you have times when you get frustrated because you can't do something just like you want to and so you give up? Are there times when you feel so inadequate, especially considering others you're around, so you make excuses not to try? Actually, that is a rhetorical question. I know you have felt that way before because you have expressed it to me in regard to some of your straight "A" friends.

Remember, you don't have to be the best or do the best, you only need to do *your* best with what *you* have, whether that is in regard to intelligence, talent, money, looks or a host of other things.

God didn't make us all the same on purpose. You have strengths where others have weaknesses. Others have strengths where you have weaknesses. The point is, do whatever with what you have. Don't use what you don't have as an excuse not to do anything, regardless of what the anything is. Got it? I thought so. Now . . . ..

Pray with me:
Thank you, God, for who we are. Help us to use our strengths and grow through our weaknesses. Amen

Patty B. Williams

May 7th

Home Cooking

"But food does not bring us near to God; we are no worse if we do not eat, and no better if we do." 1 Corinthians 8:8 (NIV)

I heard a joke about a school cafeteria that lost its power right before lunch and the cooks were unable to prepare the normal hot meal for the elementary school children. They didn't know what they were going to do, when all of a sudden, one of the cooks decided she would make a bunch of peanut butter and jelly sandwiches. When the first little boy came in the cafeteria, he loaded up his plate with sandwiches, looked up and said, "Well, finally, a home-cooked meal!"

I guess you and Michael can identify with that little boy somewhat. You didn't get many peanut butter and jelly sandwiches over the years, but you didn't get a lot of creative, home-cooked meals either. Maybe that's how you both turned out so well. You weren't spoiled in the kitchen!

Actually, I guess all mothers feel like they either failed or performed poorly in some areas of motherhood. I know I do. What we hope is that some other areas we did well in made up for our weaknesses in others. I guess you and Michael will have to decide that one day.

In the meantime, I will keep looking at both of you and thinking that your Dad and I must have done some things right among all the things we botched up. I truly thank God for his mercy!

Pray with me:
Lord, help us to remember that it takes more than peanut butter and jelly sandwiches or full course, home-cooked meals to make us healthy overall. Amen

May 8th

Working Where It Counts

"For we are God's fellow workers; you are God's field, God's building." 1 Corinthians 3:9 (NIV)

While you're thinking about what type work you want to do after you graduate, you might think about what George Macdonald said. He said, "If I could put one touch of rosy sunset into the life of any man or woman, I would feel that I had worked with God." Now I don't know who George Macdonald is, but I would like to know him. He has the right idea about a profession.

Can you just imagine having God working right beside you in the classroom, next to you while you're balancing business accounts, or between you and a child learning about good nutrition and healthy bodies?

There are lots of ways to put rosy sunsets in the lives of others. You don't have to wait until graduation. You can befriend a lonely, elder person, calm a small child's fears, help mend a broken heart, or buy food for a homeless person. I have no doubts that you will find many ways to continue the rosy sunsets you have already begun to put in the lives of others. I am proud of you.

Pray with me:
Lord, help us to seek your will in our work and in our daily walks of life. As we touch others, may they see your hand. Amen

May 9th

Life Puzzles

"I tell you the truth, you will weep and mourn while the world rejoices. You will grieve, but your grief will turn to joy." John 16:20 (NIV)

I heard the most beautiful message at the funeral of a young person named Roxanne the other day. She was the daughter of a life-long friend of mine. The minister, Terry, talked about our lives being a puzzle and how all the people that touch our lives are the pieces that make up the puzzle. It was sad that this one precious person who touched so many lives was called home at such a young age. Yet she had already become such an important piece of so many life puzzles. To some, as Terry explained so eloquently, she was an integral part of their puzzle, and to others she was a piece that formed only a small part of the border. Yet, no one will take her place.

I cannot fathom the loss of you or Michael. I'm sure it would be an emptiness that would never be filled, only made more bearable with the God-given peace that passes understanding.

I suppose the message in telling you this is to help you remember that every life you touch and every life that touches you, regardless of the circumstances, will make up yours or someone else's life puzzle. That's something to think about.

Pray with me:
Lord, help us to touch other's lives in the same manner that we want others to touch ours. Keep us connected to you daily, so that task will be easier. Amen

Clean Underwear, Wild Elephants and the Princess

May 10th

The Present

"You have made my days a mere handbreadth; the span of my years is as nothing before you. Each man's life is but a breath." Psalm 39:5 (NIV)

"Yesterday is history. Tomorrow is a mystery. Today is a Gift. That's why they call it the PRESENT."

I don't know who said the above, but I sure like the thought behind it. It's so true. Today is a gift. We are so blessed. We forget how fragile life is until it is taken away from someone we know. An accident can happen as quickly as it takes to look at the good-looking guy passing by in a jeep. You look at the guy at the same time the lady in front of you slams on brakes when a dog crosses in front of her. You run off the road to avoid hitting her, your car flips, and the friend sitting next to you is thrown from the car. A gruesome thought I know, but a realistic one.

The message in this is twofold. First, don't concentrate so much on past regrets, especially those you can do nothing about; they are history. Tomorrow is a mystery. We don't know what it holds; so don't worry so much about it that you rob yourself of today's blessing of life. Second, remember how fragile life is and be careful that in your day-to-day living that you don't put yourself in harmful situations. In other words, think! Keep your brain turned on all the time, and keep your eyes on the road, not on the jeep!

Pray with me:
You know we need your help, Lord, to appreciate the gift of life as you intended. Keep us safe, alert and thoughtful in counting our blessings. Amen

Patty B. Williams

May 11th

Our Partnership

"Because of your partnership in the gospel from the first day until now, being confident of this, that he who began a good work in you will carry it on to completion until the day of Christ Jesus." Philippians 1:5 (NIV)

When I look at your college expenses, I think back to the years I was in college and wonder how Mother and Daddy did it, especially when they still had Billy at home. You are much more conscientious about what's going on with expenses than I ever was, and I'm proud of you for that. I don't want you to have to worry about money all the time, but I do want you to worry enough so that you will be wise in watching where your money goes.

When you were a little girl you were so theatrical in your demeanor most of the time that we thought you might be an actress one day. Then as you got a little older, you were sure you wanted to be a geologist. Granddaddy may have thought you would be a hairdresser! Michael just thought you were going to continue to be a pain—the same as you thought about him at the time. Well, I guess the door is wide open, so to speak. You still have time to decide what you want to be when you grow up. I know God has a special plan for you. I hope you are prayerfully asking him to guide you in the right direction. In the meantime, we will continue to do our financial part as best we can, and you keep up the accountability part of doing your best. It's a partnership!

Pray with me:
Lord, you know that finances are a struggle at times just as decisions about career choices are. Help us to remember to seek your guidance in both. Amen

Brooke, the performer

Patty B. Williams

May 12th

My Prayer

"Therefore, my dear friends, as you have always obeyed—not only in my presence, but now much more in my absence—continue to work out your salvation with fear and trembling, for it is God who works in you to will and to act according to his good purpose."
Philippians 2:12-13 (NIV)

My prayer for you and Michael has often been that if you start to do something you know is not right, God will tug at your heart so much that you won't be able to ignore Him. I know that has happened at times because you both have told me so on different occasions.

As you know, there is just so much that parents can say and do, especially if their children are 300 miles away. At some point we have to let go and let you live your lives according to your own values. We have to let you make mistakes and live with the consequences. We have to trust your judgment and accept that you won't always do things the same way we do or think the same way we do about something. That's more difficult at times than you can imagine, so please be patient with us as we try to be patient with you. And don't forget when you're having a struggle with a decision, wrestling with whether to do or not do something, stop long enough to check for any tugs. I'll keep praying!

Pray with me:
Thank you, Lord, for your guidance and for the brains and hearts you gave us to make good decisions. Help us to always remember to use them both. Amen

May 13th

No Place Like Home

"My people will live in peaceful dwelling places, in secure homes, in undisturbed places of rest." Isaiah 32:18 (NIV)

I know you have had moments of homesickness and will continue to have them every now and then, even though you are happy at school. I think that is normal. As a matter of fact, I think I would be a little hurt if you didn't have that feeling, to some extent, on occasion.

I'm convinced that you can travel all over the world and do all kinds of exciting things, but there's still no place like home. At least for me, that was the feeling I always had and hope you will always have. Home always offered a feeling of security, a place of peace and rest, a place I could go and know love was waiting. It was a "Fantasy Island." How blessed we are considering how others have had just the opposite experiences, suffering abuse, conditional love, no love, or trauma. We need never take our experiences for granted.

While you are thinking about career choices or volunteer opportunities, you may want to think about how you may use your good experiences to help others who haven't been as fortunate. Ask God to help you. You have so much to offer others in so many different areas.

Pray with me:
Use us, Lord, where we can serve you and others the best. Help us recognize signs you send along the way to guide us. Amen

Patty B. Williams

May 14th

Calling the Guys

"But let patience have its perfect work, that you may be perfect and complete, lacking nothing." James 1:4 (NKJ)

It has been fun for me to watch your interest in boys grow over the years. When you were little, the first boy in your heart was Casey who lived down the street. You were great playmates even though your personalities were very different. He was quiet and shy and you, for the most part, were anything but! Then as the years went by you had others of interest, but it wasn't until later in high school and now in college that you seem to be more interested in finding the "right" one than in just having dates. That's good and is a sign of maturity. I hope you see it as that.

Don't ever compromise your values or the standards that you have set for yourself just to have a date. If it's important to you that boys call you first, be patient. Let them call. Don't, however, be so ridiculous about an arbitrary rule that you've imposed on yourself that you end up "shooting yourself in the foot." You have pretty good instincts, a pretty head, and a good brain. You should use all three to your advantage, whether it pertains to boys or anything else. God wants us to be in control with his help and guidance. Just remember not to leave him out of the decision-making process.

Pray with me:
Lord, we need your help in defining our values and standards for relationships with the opposite sex and with others, please keep us attuned to your will. Amen

Clean Underwear, Wild Elephants and the Princess

May 15th
(Bill's Birthday)

Confronting Others

"Be strong and courageous, because you will lead these people to inherit the land I swore to their forefathers to give them."
Joshua 1:6 (NIV)

If you don't know who Nathan is in the Bible, you may want to look him up. He was a courageous young advisor to King David who took his life in his hands when he confronted David about something terrible he had done. He confronted David because he cared about him. He knew the great things David had done, the relationship he had had with God and to the people he ruled. Nathan also knew his own relationship to God and his responsibility because of that relationship.

There will most likely be times during your college life and life after college that you will have a responsibility to confront others because of things they are doing that are dishonest, hurtful, unkind, or against the law. I know you have already had this experience to some degree, and I know it took courage not only to confront the person, but also to take it a step further and notify others that needed to know. I am so proud of you for that. I hope those type instances don't happen too often, and I certainly hope that your decision to do the right thing and confront someone is not a threat to your life as Nathan's was. My prayer will always be that you are courageous enough, wise enough, and confident enough to do what your heart of hearts and your brain tell you to do.

Pray with me:
Lord when we have to make a decision to confront or not confront people because of their behavior, help us to make the decision prayerfully, cautiously and with all the skills, knowledge, and abilities you have given us. Amen

Patty B. Williams

May 16th
(Cassidy's Birthday)

Think About Rabbits

"Brothers, continue to think about the things that are good and worthy of praise. Think about the things that are true and honorable and right and pure and beautiful and respected. "Philippians 4:8 (NCV)

Remember those times when you were hurting, frightened, or in an uncomfortable situation when you were little and your dad would tell you to think about rabbits? I'm not sure I ever knew the meaning behind that or how it originated, but I know I used it with you sometimes, too. It seemed to help.

I think the purpose of "think about rabbits" was to help you fix your thoughts on something other than what was causing you the pain at the moment, whether it was physical or mental. You know, as silly as it may seem now that you're all grown up, this advice really has a lot of merit. There will certainly be times ahead of you that if you can fix your thoughts on something more pleasant, or get involved in something more productive than negative thoughts, you will be able to avoid a lot of unnecessary stress, hurt, and depression. You have a lot of positive things in your life to focus on and be thankful for; I know you know that. Sometimes you just need a reminder to focus on those. Consider yourself reminded!

Pray with me:
When life brings its down times as it surely will, help us, Lord, not to stay there in thought and make it worse. Lift us up quickly and help us to fix our thoughts on things that are good and pleasing to you. Amen

Clean Underwear, Wild Elephants and the Princess

May 17th

Those Who Inspire Us

"Join with others in following my example, brothers, and take note of those who live according to the pattern we gave you." Philippians 3:17 (NIV)

Remember Nanny and Granddaddy's friends, Peggy and Del? It was such a treat for Mother and Daddy when they came to visit, and now it continues to be special for Daddy and me when they come to visit us. I guess they are our oldest and two of our dearest friends. They are amazing at 83 and 85 years old. They are still traveling in their RV across country, going on cruises, staying in touch with family and friends, and enjoying life in general.

What is the secret to their longevity, their mental and physical stamina, and their drive to keep going? I think it has to do with their positive attitude, their continued quest for positive experiences, their love of life, love of God, and love of people. Sounds like a good plan for college students, too, don't you think?

I hope as you experience college life that you will always approach it positively, that you look for new experiences that will help you grow intellectually and emotionally, that you will continue the love of God and people (all kinds of people) that you have always had, and that you will love and enjoy life to the fullest. You are on the right track. Don't get sidetracked.

Pray with me:
Lord, thank you for people who inspire us. Keep us mindful of their positive influence and help us to emulate them for the benefit of others and ourselves. Amen

Patty B. Williams

May 18th

Show Your Appreciation

"Give thanks to the Lord, for he is good. His love endures forever." Psalm 136:1 (NIV)

When someone gives you good service or does something nice for you, are you grateful enough to take the time to tell them they are appreciated? I hope so; such a small gesture can be such an uplifting experience for both of you.

If you think about relationships in general and about your own experiences in terms of feeling appreciated, you will quickly realize how important a small gesture of appreciation can be. Think especially about husbands and wives, boyfriends and girlfriends and how often they take each other for granted.

When you sit down at a table with enough food to eat, surrounded by people who care about you, or when you crawl in bed at night and have enough cover to keep you warm or an air conditioner to keep you cool, do you think about telling God how much you appreciate all those things? I hope so. It's so easy to take them for granted.

I hope that you also know how much I appreciate all you do as a daughter, a sister, a granddaughter, a friend, a niece, a cousin, and a child of God. I know you work hard at being the best you can be in all your relationships. You have blessed many. I can hardly wait to see you appreciated as an aunt, a special girlfriend, a wife, and a mother! Whew, that's a lot of relationships and a lot of appreciation! I'll count on you to handle both well.

Pray with me:
Lord, help us to remember how important taking time to show or

speak our appreciation is, even for the little things in life. Keep us forever mindful of all our blessings and to whom we owe the greatest appreciation. Amen

Patty B. Williams

May 19th

Are The Differences Important?

"Multitudes, multitudes in the valley of decision! For the day of the Lord is near in the valley of decision." Joel 3:14 (NIV)

I know I don't need to tell you how blessed we are to be part of such a caring, loving, family, who, for the most part, share the same values in life. It's easy to love those who think like us, appreciate the same things we appreciate, care about who we care about, or enjoy what we enjoy. It was difficult for me in years past to understand why others, if exposed to our family, our values, and our life in general, would not embrace it as much as we did.

You may have the same difficulty if you aren't careful. People are different. They have different natures, different upbringing, different likes and dislikes, and different values. As wonderful as we think our family is, as much as we share in each other's lives, and as much fun as we have together, it is not what all others think is wonderful. For some we have too much togetherness, too much sharing, too little diversity, too much diversity, more than we need in some areas, less than we need in others. You get the picture. My point is, don't sell others short just because they don't embrace what we embrace. Remember that others, most likely, give as much credit to their way of thinking as we do ours. Is either right or wrong? I don't think so.

Your responsibility in having relationships that don't think or feel the same way you do about things is to determine if the relationships are still important to you and important enough to either work through the differences or accept them. If you can't do that, then be honest enough to admit you can't and move forward from there. It won't always be easy, especially when the decision involves moving forward and away from someone you really care about. It will, however, be better in the long run.

Pray with me:
Relationship decisions are not always easy, Lord. We need all the help we can get. Please be near when we need you most, and guide our thoughts and actions. Amen

Patty B. Williams

May 20th
(Obie's birthday)

A Greater Plan

"To You, O Lord, I lift up my soul: in you I trust, O my God."
Psalm 25: 1-2 (NIV)

I often think of all you have experienced in terms of relationships at such a relatively young age. Some things, like divorce, death, broken friendships, and disappointments by people you loved, I wish you had not had to experience. Unfortunately, they have been part of your life.

Have you ever considered that maybe it has been those very things that have helped make you the wonderful young lady that you are? Have you thought that maybe the divorces you went through with your Dad and me may make you more careful in choosing a mate and more determined to make your marriage work? Has Nanny's death made you more sensitive to others' losses? Have the shallow friendships you've experienced with some made you look for real friendships with others? Have the disappointments with those you loved made you more careful in becoming the person you want to be? My guess is that all those questions can be answered with a "yes."

Isn't it comforting to know that there is a greater plan than we can fathom that can take all the bad stuff we experience, along with the good, can take our mistakes and our weaknesses and can make something good happen? You and Michael are certainly examples of good things that happened in spite of a divorce. Your dad and I are blessed beyond measure because of you both.

Pray with me:
Lord, in spite of us, you still do great things. Help us to trust you without reservation. Amen

Patty B. Williams

May 21st

Great Communicators

"If I speak in the tongues of men and of angels, but have not love, I am only a resounding gong or a clanging cymbal." 1 Corinthians 13:1 (NIV)

I know you have heard eloquent speakers in classes, church, or some other gathering. Aren't you just amazed at what some people can do in terms of motivating and inspiring people when they speak?

Your dad and your brother are both skilled in the art of communication, at least the "talking" part. Your dad has always been good in carrying on conversations regardless of whom he was talking to. Michael, even at his younger age, is just as good. They are both in the right professional field to use the talents God has given them.

You are right behind them. You are just as skilled and talented and will continue to improve even more with time and experience. I see it happening right before my eyes, and I hear the compliments from my friends and yours.

The thing I want you to remember as you continue to grow in your communication skills is the scripture above. What it means, in essence, is that you can be eloquent in speech and be a great motivator. You can sell the moon and sell yourself. You can be the envy of your friends with the gift of gab, and take home tons of money using your skill, but if you aren't true to yourself and true to your fellow man, if you don't have or can't back up your gift of communication with love for your fellowman, then you'll be less than God intended. I certainly don't fear that from you. I just wanted to give you a little Mommy reminder!

Pray with me:
God, thank you for the gifts you have given us. Help us to use them in a way that glorifies you. Amen

Patty B. Williams

May 22nd

Angel Kisses

"Are not all angels ministering spirits sent to serve those who will inherit salvation?" Hebrews 1:14 (NIV)

I wrote Nanny a little story one time for Mother's Day. It was about dimples and where they came from. If I remember correctly, the story tells about angels coming down and kissing you and Michael and leaving dimples that were from Nanny.

I love dimples. I think most people do. They are cute, sexy, or at minimum, a lead into conversation. I remember when Michael was first born. He was so tiny, yet his dimples were shining through. I knew Nanny would be tickled. Then you came along and had a little dimple, too. Yours wasn't as prominent as Michael's, a fact you've bemoaned over the years. Even when I explained that, in reality, dimples were deformities, it didn't help your feelings.

I'm not really sure why we get dimples. Nanny had such pretty ones. I guess I like to think that an angel kissed her, too. Whatever the reason, I hope when you and Michael catch a glimpse of yourselves in a mirror that your dimples will remind you how blessed you are to have a little part of Nanny in your everyday smile.

Pray with me:
Lord, thank you for the little things in life that remind us of those we love. Amen

May 23rd

Stepping Up

"When Jesus landed and saw a large crowd, he had compassion on them, because they were like sheep without a shepherd. So he began teaching them many things." Mark 6:34 (NIV)

Have you gotten really aggravated or angry with someone and then at a later time realized he or she was acting the way they were because they knew no better? Maybe it was something they said. Maybe it was something they should have done but didn't. Maybe they acted like jerks because they didn't know how to handle a situation appropriately so they handled it inappropriately. Unfortunately, that happens all too often.

When those kinds of situations occur, you might want to think about it a little longer before you get all bent out of shape. Try the ole count to ten trick. Try to figure out if there are any underlying reasons that might be causing the inappropriate behavior. Maybe you are being offered an opportunity to help someone, to teach them what they might need to know so the same thing doesn't happen again.

You are pretty perceptive about people, and I think you believe that people are basically good and want to do good, in spite of what their actions show at times. I think that is what God wants us to believe, but I also think that he wants us to do our part in helping those on the wrong path to get back on the right track.

If you see your sorority sisters or other friends floundering in a situation because of a lack of leadership, then step up and lead if you think you can, even if for that particular situation only. That's what Jesus did when he saw his people acting like sheep without a shepherd.

Patty B. Williams

You are much more mature in your thinking than many your age. I know you try to give people the benefit of the doubt when they act or talk inappropriately. I'm proud of you for that. You will have the opportunity to "teach" others as much as you will have the opportunity to learn from others. My prayer will be that you do both well.

Pray with me:
Lord, when you can use us to benefit others in their learning processes, help us to be ready. When others can teach us, help us to be ready for that also. Amen

Clean Underwear, Wild Elephants and the Princess

May 24th

Whose Interest Is It?

"Each of you should look not only to your own interests, but also to the interests of others." Philippians 2:4 (NIV)

I wonder if it would make any difference in how politicians do their work and how they vote on issues if they were required to read this scripture daily. I wonder if they would study issues more before they cast that ballot.

I have never been a staunch Democrat or a Republican. I don't vote by party. I vote for the candidate and what I think they believe in and will work toward. I hope you will do the same.

I think, however, that the above scripture speaks of arenas other than politics. I think it is good advice for college officials, professors, officers in sororities and fraternities, and for us as individuals. Just think what a much better place our world would be if we thought as much about others' interest as we do our own and then acted accordingly. The results would be incredible.

I am proud that you think about others before you act, that your interests include the interests of others. That is a mark of Christian maturity. God and I are smiling!

Pray with me:
Lord, it is sometimes difficult to put our own desires aside when another path will serve the greater needs of others. When we should do that, give us the right attitude and strength to do it. Amen

Patty B. Williams

May 25th

Healthy Bodies

"Or do you not know that your body is the temple of the Holy Spirit who is in you, whom you have from God, and you are not your own? For you were bought at a price; therefore glorify God in your body and in your spirit, which are God's." 1 Corinthians 6:19 (NKJ)

The "freshman 15." It's a real bummer, isn't it? I guess now you know it wasn't a myth. I agonize with you over it, because I know how much gaining weight has always depressed you, even when you gained a pound!

So, what do you do about it? I think you know the answer to that, but doing what needs to be done is not easy. I know, because I've tried too. I think we both need a new approach, because obviously we aren't doing too well with whatever we've been trying. Truthfully, I haven't even been trying lately, and that's awful!

God gave us good, healthy bodies. They may not be proportioned exactly the way we want, but they are strong and free from disease. We are fortunate. We also are responsible for keeping them that way. That's what we need to think about.

I'm going to start working on that next week, and I'm not going to try to do it myself, because I fail every time. I'm going to ask God to help me with my discipline, my appetite, and my energy level so I will start exercising again. As soon as you ask, I'll pray for you, too, and also hold you accountable; so don't ask until you're ready.

Pray with me:
Lord, you know how weak we are, and we know our responsibility to take care of the body you gave us. Help us as we try to meet that responsibility. Amen

Patty B. Williams

May 26th

Set The Path

"Do you see a man skilled in his work? That man will work for kings. He won't have to work for ordinary people." Proverbs 22:29 (NCV)

Once you decide on a profession or happen to fall into one, you will immediately begin to set the path on how good you will be. When you are given an assignment, you will decide how well you will do it. You will decide if you want to learn from it, if you want to do more than is expected, if you want to use it as a stepping stone to become better at the task or assignment, or if you want to do just enough to get by and get the job done.

I suppose you know what path I hope you take. Regardless of whether or not the assignment is in your profession or it's in the assignment you're doing for a class now, I hope that when you complete it you'll feel that you know more than you did, that your skills in that area are better than when you began. If they aren't, do you think you might be wasting time and money?

It's important to have good self-esteem. Being and feeling skilled in various areas can help toward that end. Just remember that becoming really skilled in something is not always easy. It's certainly not the path of the lazy person. It does, however, have its benefits.

When job cutbacks are made, do you think it would be a good management decision to let the most skilled employees go? When decisions are made for choice assignments, do you think they will be given to those with fewer skills or more skills? When promotions are being considered, do you think the employee who does just enough to get by will be the one promoted? Well, you get the picture.

Clean Underwear, Wild Elephants and the Princess

Make yourself valuable as a student or as an employee. Become skillful in what you learn in class or learn on the job. That way you'll put yourself in a position of making choices rather than having choices made for you. If a king offers you a job one day, be confident enough in your skills and abilities to accept it or decline it. When the curve is set in class, you set it instead of having someone set it for you.

Pray with me:
Lord, help us to become the best we can be by doing the best we can do every day. Amen

Patty B. Williams

May 27th

When We're Apart

"... Let the Lord watch over us while we are separated from each other." Genesis 31:49(NCV)

You'll never fully understand the concern I have when you are away from me and I don't know if you are safe or not. I guess you have to be a parent to get the full impact of how it feels.

When I know you are at the library, on a date, at a party, walking to your car at night, driving to the sorority house, or doing any one of those million and one things you do on a routine basis, I worry. Fortunately I seem to be able to control that worry enough to keep from having you call me on an hourly basis for a safety check!

I always wonder if you'll remember all those safety things you've been taught over the years, if you'll use that pretty little head for something more than thinking about the cute guys, the paper you have to write, the class you're running late for, or the upcoming social event of the year.

Please remember the importance of everyday safety and common sense. It can literally save your life. Don't take shortcuts where it is concerned. It could be a tragic mistake.

I, on the other hand, will try to keep a grip! I will continue to pray for your safety and well being when we're apart and when we're together.

Pray with me:
Lord, watch over us continuously, but help us to be responsible in doing our part. Amen.

Clean Underwear, Wild Elephants and the Princess

May 28th
(Melissa's Birthday)

Thank Goodness

"And above all things have fervent love for one another, for love will cover a multitude of sins." 1 Peter 4:8 (NKJ)

Thank goodness for that little four-letter word, love. What would we do without it? Can you imagine a parent trying to raise teenagers without it, marriage partners trying to live together without it, abused children without it, friends and families of addicts without it? It does, indeed, make a multitude of sins bearable, doesn't it?

You have seen a number of wrongdoings during your teenage years; you've been the victim of deep hurt by close friends, and we shared some trying moments as mother and daughter during your early teen years. Love played an important role during all those times, don't you think? I can assure you, also, that it will play a major role with your marriage partner in the future.

Don't ever lose that deep love that I know you have for others. Let it always be the factor that makes the difference in how you handle bad situations and people who act unlovable. Let love define who you are rather than a situation or another person defining you. It won't always be easy, but it will always be right.

Pray with me:
Lord, we surely can't love all people, at all times, in all situations without a lot of help from you. Help us to get there, even if we're slower than we should be. Amen

Patty B. Williams

May 29th

What Keeps Us Sane

"Those who respect the Lord will live and be content, unbothered by trouble." Proverbs 19:23 (NCV)

I read a little message on a daily calendar that said we need to pay special attention to whatever keeps us sane. This may be listening to a favorite CD, going to a movie, taking a long walk, running, or picking up the phone and calling home or calling a friend. Whatever the activities are, I think paying attention to them is good advice.

I'm not sure what it is that keeps me sane, but it's probably talking to close friends or family members that truly listen, or making sure I get those frequent hugs from my three-year-old Sunday Schoolers or my nieces and nephews.

If you don't know what it is that keeps you sane, you could get into deep trouble very quickly, so try to figure it out. Pay attention to what seems to make you relax in a stressful situation, what turns a bad mood into a happier spirit, or a tear into a smile. When you figure it out, cultivate it so it can genuinely help you at those times when you need it most. Just be careful if what keeps you sane are a bag of skittles, a box of sugar cookies, or a Big Mac!

Pray with me:
Help us, Father, to learn how to relax when we need to and to keep life stresses, in general, in their proper place of importance. Amen

Clean Underwear, Wild Elephants and the Princess

May 30th

A Desire To Know The Future

"God has also given us a desire to know the future. God certainly does everything at just the right time. But we can never completely understand what he is doing." Ecclesiastes 3:11 (NCV)

How many times in the last week have you wished you knew what the future held for you? My guess is that you have wished no less than a dozen times in no less than a half-dozen realms of your life. What does the future hold in terms of grade-point average this semester? What kind of professional future is in store? Is there a future with that cute guy at the Sweet Shoppe?

I wonder if we knew what the future held we would work hard trying to change it or improve it? I wonder if we would recognize the merits of God's choices in the future over what we think is best for us at the moment? My guess is, we wouldn't. There are, however, many things that we do know about the future, have the opportunity to work at, and yet fail to do anything about. That's pretty silly, don't you think? We know Christmas is coming every year at the same time. We know, unless there are some unforeseen circumstances that prevent it, you will graduate in the near future. We also know the future holds old age and a time we won't be able to work. We know one day the future holds unexpected bills we'll have to pay and know that most likely a wedding is going to be in yours and Michael's future. I could go on and on, but you get the drift.

My point, of course, is that the future is in good hands, don't worry too much about the part you can't control. Do instead something about the part you can control, or at least influence. That is your responsibility. I'll try to work on my part, too, but please give me some time on the future wedding part!

Patty B. Williams

Pray with me:
Lord, we ask your blessing on our future. Keep us mindful of our responsibility in making it better. Amen

Clean Underwear, Wild Elephants and the Princess

May 31st

Silence

"When he opened the seventh seal, there was silence in heaven for about half an hour." Revelation 8:1 (NIV)

A man named George Eliot said that silence is the only thing that cannot be misquoted. Think about that. It's a good quote to remember.

Silence is often times the best course of action, especially if you don't know what to say, how to say it, or how it will be interpreted. I know that in the case of gossip that the best course of action is silence, at least it is if you don't have the courage to challenge the gossiper(s).

Silence is also a good course of action when it is evident that another person needs you to listen. Many times you will have friends and acquaintances that will ask advice about a situation or concern when all they really want is a listening ear.

A good listener whose silences make the other person think can help that person grow. Think about what your silence may say in a time of anger or hurt. Think what it may mean in the heat of an argument or when someone has asked you to think about his or her opinions in a debate.

Don't get me wrong; you know I am a great advocate of communication. I think it is the crux of any relationship, but remember that silence is a form of communication. It very often speaks much more and much louder than your words ever could.

Pray with me:
Lord, help us to know when silence is golden, and when it is time to speak, give us the words you would have us to say. Amen

Patty B. Williams

June 1st

Hansel And Gretal

"You have made known to me the path of life; you will fill me with joy in your presence, with eternal pleasures at your right hand."
Psalm 16:11 (NIV)

Like Hansel and Gretal, you often leave a trail of where you've been. On the bedroom floor there are a pair of jeans and a tee shirt; the bathroom has two brushes, a comb, six Kleenexes beside the wastebasket, not in it, of course, and 10 strands of hair in the sink. The kitchen has two asthma puffers, dirty dishes, and an open bag of chips. No doubt, you've been somewhere around the neighborhood. Hansel and Gretal would be proud!

From stories I hear from other parents, I suppose you are pretty normal. I suppose, too, that I'll miss all the "trails" one of these days when you're living in your own home and keeping it clean and tidy—a picture that I admit is a little hard to envision as I pick up the kleenexes, wash away the hair, and close the bag of chips.

I want you to know, however, that I recognize that all the trails you're leaving are not made of jeans, tee shirts and dirty dishes. With every choice you make to give up your personal time to spend with granddaddy, your dad, your cousins, aunts, uncles, or me, you are leaving a trail of happiness for us. With your smiles and laughter you leave a trail of spirit lifting, and with your respect and kindness for others you leave a trail of gratitude and respect. For these trails you should be proud.

I know as time goes by you will have greater and greater opportunities to leave trails that epitomize the young lady you have become. The world is in for a treat.

Pray with me:

Lord, you are our guiding light on any path, road, or trail we decide to take. Help us remember to seek the direction you would have us take and the trail you would have us leave. Amen

Patty B. Williams

June 2nd

Dad's Birthday

"He will turn the hearts of the fathers to their children, and the hearts of the children to their fathers; or else I will come and strike the land with a curse." Malachi 4:6 (NIV)

I know you will be thinking about your dad today, not that that is so different from any other day, but you'll be thinking about how you can make it special for him in some way. What you don't realize is that just having you is special enough for him. Aren't you a lucky little girl?

It's hard to imagine now that at three weeks old he didn't think he wanted to be with you. Of course, it wasn't you; it was life with me that was in question, and that life happened to include you. Isn't it ironic that now his life would be devastated without you? Life certainly changes things, doesn't it?

You are without doubt your dad's princess. I know you have no questions about that. I hope you will always be close and share the same feelings that your Granddaddy and I have shared over the years as father and daughter. I hope you will always have a sense of security in knowing that no matter how bad you may botch something up, how disappointed you may become with others, how difficult life may become or how far away you may go, you can always depend on your dad to be there for you with open arms and an open heart. How truly blessed you are and how truly blessed he and I are to have you—not a bad ending for a poor start, is it?

Pray with me:
Lord, thank you for loving fathers and princesses. Help us to never take either for granted. Amen

Clean Underwear, Wild Elephants and the Princess

Brooke and Dad

Patty B. Williams

June 3rd
(Charlie's birthday)

Old Baggage

"If you hide your sins, you will not succeed. If you confess and reject them, you will receive mercy." Proverbs 28:13 (NCV)

You know there are all kinds of rehabilitation organizations and establishments to work with addicts. One that has had great success is Alcoholics Anonymous. I think one of the first things they encourage is acceptance of who you are, truthfulness to yourself and to others. It's just too hard to change your life and move forward if you can't admit and accept where you've been. Once you've done that, you can begin to heal and move forward.

I think that is true in most aspects of life. You can't move forward and make necessary changes if you have old baggage hanging around that you need to take care of. The load just becomes too heavy.

If you have apologies you need to make for past mistakes, make them. If you have old debts to pay, pay them. If you need to mend a relationship, mend it. If you need to clarify a misunderstanding with someone, clarify it. If you need to admit a wrongdoing, admit it. Don't let excess baggage that needs to be cleaned up lie around and prevent you from the joy moving forward brings. Life is much too short.

You're a bright young lady. I know you don't need a counselor to tell you these things. Just keep them in mind. Then, if your load seems unusually heavy one day, you might examine what it is you're carrying around.

Clean Underwear, Wild Elephants and the Princess

Pray with me:
Help us remember, Lord, that we can't appreciate forgiveness if we aren't willing to admit what needs to be forgiven. Amen

Patty B. Williams

June 4th

Don't Break 'Um

"You have heard that it was said to our people long ago, when you make a promise, don't break your promise. Keep the promises that you make to the Lord." Matthew 5:33 (NCV)

Florida is planning to have a new law in statute soon that will require those seeking to be married in the state to either have a three-day waiting period or attend pre-marital counseling. I support the efforts to pass the new law.

Those entering marriage need all the help they can get to think about the promise they are going to make to one another and the promise many of them will make in God's house. I wonder if Jesus were standing beside us in person, at the alter, if it would make it easier to continue our commitment and keep the promises we make. That's the way we should be thinking, you know. God is there, even when we can't see him. He will hold us accountable.

The Bible says we have a responsibility to keep a promise when we make one, whether it's in relation to marriage, to a brother, to a sister, or to a friend. The message is simple. Don't make promises that you aren't willing to do everything in your power to keep. If you've made a promise and need help in your commitment to keep it, ask for help. Ask God and ask those God has equipped to help, like a counselor, a minister, or a trusted friend. Unfortunately, you have experiences to draw from that show you the results of broken promises. Use those experiences to learn and grow and to not make the same mistakes. Make your promises the forever kind.

Pray with me:

Forgive us, Father, when we have failed to keep promises made in your presence. Teach us to think before we commit. Amen

Patty B. Williams

June 5th

Make Me Strong

"And the God of all grace, who called you to his eternal glory in Christ, after you have suffered a little while, will himself restore you and make you strong, firm and steadfast." 1Peter 5:10 (NIV)

Robert Nivelle is someone you may study about in a philosophy class one day. He is known as one of our great thinkers. One of his quotes I like is, "Whatever does not destroy me makes me stronger." I guess I like it because I believe it.

Think about some of your most difficult times, times that you were distraught, heartbroken, angry, or depressed about a situation. As you look back on it now, do you think you are wiser and stronger because of it? Did you learn anything through your tears, your frustration, or your hurt? My guess is that you did.

It's too bad that we have to go through some of the things we do. It would be nice if life was always a bed of roses, but you know it is far from that.

You will have opportunities while at school to pass along Nivelle's quote. It may be a good lead-in to a conversation with a friend who is hurting. Think about it so you will be prepared.

I hope those things that happen that tend to crush the hearts of young people don't happen to you, but if they do, I hope one of your first thoughts will be Nivelle's quote.

Pray with me:
Lord, we know that with you we can bear anything. Help us to remember you as our greatest path to growth. Amen

June 6th

Don't Break A Shin

"The righteous cry out, and the Lord hears them; he delivers them from all their troubles. Psalm 34:17 (NIV)

There is an Irish proverb that says, "Do not be breakin' a shin on a stool that's not in your way." Can you guess what that means? I had to think about it a minute. It means don't go looking for something that's not there.

That something might be trouble, or a particular reaction, or a negative attitude you think someone has. It's something that you anticipate being there when, in fact, it isn't.

If you ever catch yourself starting to "break a shin", stop for a few minutes and evaluate what's going on with you. Consider that whatever it is, it might be influencing what you think about others or what you think is going on around you. Maybe your being worn out makes everyone else's normal chatter and noise magnified. Maybe someone else's bad attitude is your inability to consider another's opinion. Maybe your guilt about not doing something you should have done makes someone's comment about your not doing it a mountain rather than a molehill.

There's enough real trouble that comes along in our lives. We don't need to go looking for trouble that's not really there.

Pray with me:
We do stumble over a lot of things, Lord, and we often need your help to get up. Please help us not to hesitate to ask. Amen

Patty B. Williams

June 7th

Don't Miss The Message

"Now the Bereans were of more noble character than the Thessalonians, for they received the message with great eagerness and examined the Scriptures every day to see if what Paul said was true." Acts 17:11 (NIV)

I hope you remember the two primary reasons I started writing these daily devotionals for you. One was to get you in the habit of reading your Bible daily (if only a verse at the time). The other was to have a way to stay in daily contact with you.

I'm not sure either purpose has been accomplished well, but maybe we've accomplished something better along the way. I guess only time will tell that.

I do hope, however, that you will one day have a desire to read the Bible on a daily basis and to understand what it has to say to you personally. There are many different paraphrases that make it so much easier to read. I have many times gone from one version to another while doing this work.

Remember though, when you start reading different versions that our language changes through the years, but the basic teachings of God, don't. Make sure you don't get hung up on words and translations you may not specifically agree with and miss the overall message. We have so much to learn, and God's inspired message has so much to teach us.

Pray with me:
Give us the desire, Lord, to want to read and understand your word. Let us get your basic message even if the language is not perfect. Amen

Clean Underwear, Wild Elephants and the Princess

June 8th

A Tear Floating Down The River

"To you, O Lord, I lift up my soul; in you I trust, O my God."
Psalm 25:1-2 (NIV)

One of the little ditties I have saved over the years says, "One tear met another tear floating down the river. The first tear said, 'I am the tear of one who lost her love.' The other tear said, 'and I am the tear of the one who found him'." Remember Garth's song, "Thank God For Unanswered Prayer?" I suppose the first tear might have appreciated this song more after talking to the second tear; what do you think?

If you fall into the norm, you will have a few lost loves along the way and a lot of tears. I won't waste my time or yours trying to tell you to prepare for it, because I don't think you can. I guess the only advice I can give is to trust God. He certainly can see a lot clearer than we can, especially when we're looking through starry eyes and a lovesick heart. You won't die from a broken heart or broken dreams, even though it may feel like you will. You will probably even look back one day and think of the lyrics to Garth's song.

Look for the guy that makes you starry eyed and gives your heart flutters, but if it shouldn't work out, try to think about the two tears floating down the river. If it does work—well, let's cross that bridge when we get there!

Pray with me:
Lord, You know what the answer to our prayers should be. Help us to trust your judgement more than ours. Amen

Patty B. Williams

June 9th
(Amanda's birthday)

Friends Of Worth

"A man of many companions may come to ruin, but there is a friend who sticks closer than a brother." Proverbs 18:24 (NIV)

A British author by the name of Ben Johnson wrote a little message that I read from a calendar. The message was, "True happiness consists not in the multitude of friends, but in the worth and choice." He is so right, as I know you know already.

I am happy that you have a multitude of friends. That speaks well of who you are and what type friend you are in return. What I'm proud of most, however, are the ones you have chosen to be your closest friends. You have looked for qualities that are much more valuable than the surface things that we often make the mistake of looking for first. That has resulted in a different level of friendship that will most likely last a lifetime.

Does this mean that you should limit your other friendships? I certainly hope not. Different friends satisfy different needs or wants. I'm sure God gave us friends as a gift, each with their own special wrapping. I know, too, that you like lots of gifts, so you keep right on adding to your list. Just remember, to have a good friend, you have to be a good friend. Remember, too, that just because you don't pick someone as a friend, she may pick you, so leave that door open.

Pray with me:
What a wonderful blessing to have many friends. Help us to cherish those relationships and remember to take care of them. Amen

Clean Underwear, Wild Elephants and the Princess

June 10th

Looking For A Major

"For great is your love, reaching to the heavens." Psalm 56:10 (NIV)

I know you have struggled with trying to declare a major. I suppose one problem is too many choices. Another problem is that you haven't had enough life experiences to help you make the decision. By that I mean, there are many folks that if they could go back now after living life and working in some capacity, they would change their major.

Henry Drummond, an early 20th century writer, said, "You will find, as you look back upon your life, that the moments when you have really lived are the moments when you have done things in the spirit of love." I think he has the right idea.

While you're trying to make a decision about your major, think about those things you've done that have made you "really live". Then determine if you can find a related profession. Think about the reasons you did those things that really made you feel good. What merit did the outcome have? Did you help someone? Did you make the way to do something easier for others? Did you make someone laugh? Did you fix something that was broken? Did you make someone feel good about his or her self? Think about your motivation, too. Did you do the things you did primarily for money or because you just wanted to do it? Were your efforts out of obligation or out of the spirit of love? Remember that none of these reasons are wrong. They all have their place. Just consider which ones work best for you and make you the happiest in day-to-day living.

I'm not worried. I know you will be successful in whatever major course of work you decide to pursue, and I know by the time you decide, you will have given it a great deal of thought and tried to make the best decision. That's all I ask.

Pray with me:
Lord, thank you that we have the opportunity to make choices. Help us to make the best of the opportunity and not leave you out of the decision. Amen

Going Out On A Limb

"When I am afraid I will trust in you." Psalm 56:3 (NIV)

I read something one time that said, "Don't be afraid to go out on a limb—that's where the fruit is." Going out on a limb can pertain to a lot of things. It could be something you try to do, a relationship, an investment, or a move. The relationship you and Gabriel had would certainly qualify for going-out-on-a-limb status, don't you think? I'm sure you were afraid, too, at least to some degree. Do you regret it? Was it worth what you both had to endure? Even though the relationship has changed now, was the "fruit" there? My guess is your answer is "Yes", and I probably agree with you.

You will most likely have many other "limbs" to consider, not necessarily in terms of relationships, but in terms of risk in business decisions, decisions about your career, decisions about money. I hope you'll approach them all with a question that seems quite popular these days—WWJD (what would Jesus do?) If you do that, it will make you think a little deeper if nothing else.

I know you have a certain amount of confidence in yourself already, but I know you are still working on it in many respects. I hope that you will get to the point one day that your confidence in taking risks, when appropriate, is easy. I hope also that your confidence is great enough to say "no" to the risk when that's appropriate, too. I'm counting on you to make the right choice in both cases. I have enough gray hair!

Pray with me:
Father, when we've made the right decision to go out on a limb, please keep us steady and guide our footsteps. Amen

Patty B. Williams

June 12th

Brotherly Love

"He who loves his brother abides in the light, and in it there is no cause for stumbling in him." 1 John 2:10 (NKJ)

It's heart-warming for me to see you and Michael together enjoying one another's company. There were times in your lives together that you did *anything but* enjoy one another. I'm glad those times have changed. There are times, too, that I know you wish you were closer in spirit and in your day-to-day relationship, but I think for now you are going to have to be satisfied with the part of his heart and time that you have, a part that I'm certain is much greater than he lets you see.

How close the two of you become will probably depend more on you than it will on him, just because he's a typical guy and won't think about your relationship in the same way or as often as you will. Try not to be offended about that or let your pride get in the way of being the one who does the most calling or the most thoughtful gestures of love. On occasion he'll surprise you with his show of affection and genuine love. Don't get me wrong; if you're doing all the giving and getting nothing in return, then it's o.k. to tell him so. You can even tell him Mom gave you permission! Chances are he'll be oblivious to what he has been doing and will appreciate your lovingly keeping him on track and the two of you close.

Actually, this modus vivendi (a way of living or coping) may well be a way that works with boyfriends and husbands, too. They are, you know, all related. Keep up the efforts I know you make. They are Biblical, and knowing that should make the task a little easier.

Pray with me:

Thank you, Lord, for brotherly and sisterly love. Keep us diligent in our efforts to make it all that you intended it to be. Amen

Brooke and Michael

Patty B. Williams

June 13th

Take The Bus

It is a trap for a man to dedicate something rashly and only later to consider his vows." Proverbs 20:25 (NIV)

I know you like Oprah Winfrey. I do, too. I also like something I read that she said: "Lots of people want to ride with you in the limo, but what you want is someone who will take the bus with you when the limo breaks down." Now that's not such a profound statement, but it sure is one to think about.

Remember the story Ganddaddy told you about the two sisters he dated and how one of them always asked what car he was driving before she would go out with him, and the other sister would go out with him regardless of which car he was driving. Maybe Oprah and Grandddaddy know the same sisters!

When you take your wedding vows one day, you will most likely repeat those words that go "for richer, for poorer, in sickness and in health." You could even add, "in a Lexus or a hooptie car." Isn't that what Aunt Debbie called the ole junk cars?

Anyway, you get the picture. You need to think about Oprah's statement. It's easy to love and be loved when times are good, things are easy, compromise is unnecessary, and great effort is not required. Unfortunately, that is not realistic in any relationship of significance, including your relationship with God. Think about it.

Pray with me:
Lord, help us to look for the things that are truly important in a relationship and to keep all the other things in proper perspective. Amen

June 14th

Sleepy Head

"Do not love sleep or you will grow poor; stay awake and you will have food to spare." Proverbs 20:13 (NIV)

Are you surprised that there is such a verse in the Bible? Interesting statement, isn't it? I can remember not long ago when I could have used this verse with you. Maybe I still could, but with your schedule, I'm not sure you have much time to fall in love with sleep.

Don't take the verse wrong. God knows you have to have a sufficient amount of sleep to function at your optimum level and stay healthy. With your asthma, it's even more important that you pay attention to the amount of rest and sleep you get.

I think the essence of what the verse is saying is that if you waste time sleeping when you should be awake and productive, you'll have to reap the consequences of lost opportunities. I don't want that to happen.

I think, too, that if you're sleeping more than you need, you might want to examine the reasons. Are you depressed? Are you having a difficult time getting started on an assignment? Are you avoiding having to think about or face a situation that's uncomfortable? Are you stressed? Ask yourself these questions if you're the one sleeping too much. If the person sleeping too much is a friend, think about talking to him or her and finding out what's going on in their life. Maybe you can help and maybe they need someone to help them recognize the signs of possible problems.

Pray with me:
We are so thankful, Lord, for warm, cozy beds to crawl in at night, but when it's time to be up, help us to remember that you want us to have "food to spare." Amen

Patty B. Williams

June 15th

Hot Coffee

"Whoever obeys his command will come to no harm and the wise heart will know the proper time and procedure." Ecclesiastes 8:5 (NIV)

I will never forget a time when you were about three years old and we were at a Wednesday night dinner at church. I was talking to someone and you or I knocked a cup of coffee over spilling it on your leg. Instead of reacting like we both should have by jumping up, screaming, and seeing what damage had been done, we calmly cleaned it up, I kept talking, and you didn't cry, both of us embarrassed by the incident. We left shortly after that and of course you began crying the minute we were out the door. You can imagine my horror when I took off your little jeans and saw this huge blister on your leg. Saying I felt awful would be the understatement of the year.

It's not that the blister would have been any less severe had I or you reacted differently at the time of the incident, but when I looked back on it, I thought I certainly could have done more than I did. If you had cried, I would have realized it was worse than I thought.

It's incredible the things we do or don't do because of embarrassment or how we think others may react to it. I think I have matured a little in my thinking since the coffee incident, and I'm sure you would react differently today if someone spilled hot coffee on you. My point in this story is that there is a right time and a right way to respond or react to most things that happen or things that are said. Don't let embarrassment or the fear of what others might say or think keep you from reacting in a way that you should. Don't have regrets for missing an opportunity that could make a difference. It may be difficult at times, but if you react with the right motivation and the right heart, you will be on the right path.

Pray with me:
Lord, give us courage to respond to others when a response is the right course of action, and give us wisdom to respond in the right way. Amen

Patty B. Williams

June 16th

Character

"And now, my daughter, don't be afraid. I will do for you all you ask. All my fellow townsmen know that you are a woman of noble character."
Ruth 3:11 (NIV)

I read something one time that a guy by the name of Frank Outlaw was credited as having said. He didn't say it exactly like this, but you'll get the gist of it. He said, "You need to pay attention to the thoughts that you have because those thoughts will become words." You need to be careful of the words you say because those words will become actions. You should watch your actions because they may become habits. Those habits, if you aren't careful will become your character. And most importantly, you need to pay attention to your character because it will become your destiny."

I think he is right on target. Think about those people you know who always seem to be thinking about negative things, about how bad things are, how bad this person or that person is, or the person who always sees the glass half empty instead of half full. Is that the type of personality you want to be around often? I don't think so.

Think also about the person who is the opposite, the one who is upbeat most of the time, has a positive attitude, sees the glass half full. What does this say about their character?

It's easy to be upbeat when things are going well; it's more difficult to stay that way when things are not going so well. That's where the character part comes in. Work on it continuously by controlling your thoughts, words, actions, and habits in both the good times and the bad.

Clean Underwear, Wild Elephants and the Princess

Pray with me:

Father, help us to strive to have the character that you exemplified, especially in those times that are most difficult. Amen

Patty B. Williams

June 17th

Think Good Thoughts

"Brothers, stop thinking like children. In regard to evil be infants, but in your thinking be adults." 1 Corinthians 14:20 (NIV)

I read something one time that said, "Look for similarities, and you will see similarities, look for differences, and you will see differences." I suppose the same thing could be said about good and bad in people. If you look for what's bad in someone, you'll probably find it. If you look for what's good, you'll most likely find that, too.

That message seems pretty simple, doesn't it? Actually, the message is simple, but it's not always simple to look for the good instead of the bad or the similarities instead of the differences, especially if we have already programmed ourselves to thinking we're going to find the other.

Think about that new professor you're going to have that you've heard so many bad things about already, how difficult she is, how moody, how rude. Think about the girl that dated your best friend's boyfriend, the guy that likes classical music, wears glasses, and is always reading. Preconceived ideas about others without getting to know them may cause you to miss out on a great friendship. Try not to put yourself in that situation.

Strive to have a pact with yourself to always look for something good in a person first, regardless of who he or she is, under what circumstances you meet them, or what things you heard about them previous to your meeting. Now, that would be a good thing to write home about!

Pray with me:
God, we have the ability to direct our thinking. Help us to choose the right direction. Amen.

Patty B. Williams

June 18th

Be Prepared

"Preach the Word; be prepared in season and out of season; correct, rebuke and encourage—with great patience and careful instruction." 2 Timothy 4:2 (NIV)

You've heard the Boy Scout motto "Be Prepared" haven't you? It's a good motto. It could literally save your life one day. Think of all the fire drills you've had to go through at school during your life. You even went through tornado drills, didn't you? When you get on a plane and the stewardess starts the drill about what to do in case of an emergency, do you pay attention? When you stay in a motel, do you look for the closest stairwell before you go to bed at night? My guess is, you don't.

When you are going to a party that you're a little uncomfortable about, do you think of preparing for a legitimate reason to leave? If you don't drive yourself, are you prepared with another way home? Does someone know where you're going so that if you don't make it home at a reasonable time, someone will look for you?

I think about all those young teen books that tell you how to prepare for peer pressure. It makes sense, you know. If you aren't prepared to handle the situation, the situation may get out of hand in a hurry.

Even God tells us to be prepared. He knows the dangers and temptations we're going to face daily, and he wants us to be able to handle them. How do we do that? Well, we pay attention when we're being taught; we think about potential situations and plan ahead, we read what experts tell us, and we study God's word.

I hope all your preparations make you confident in your ability to handle emergencies or uncomfortable situations, and I'll pray that you are never tested.

Pray with me:
Help us to recognize the value of being prepared, Lord, and protect us from those things that test our preparedness. Amen

Patty B. Williams

June 19th

Awesome God

"When I consider your heavens, the work of your fingers, the moon and the stars, which you have set in place, what is man that you are mindful of him, the son of man that you care for him?"
Psalm 8:3 (NIV)

I know the title of this devotion reminds you of Mountain Top and the songs you sang at night. If I remember correctly, the lyrics about an awesome God were from one of yours and Michael's favorite songs.

If you've never taken the time to spend a few minutes alone on the beach, outside in the back yard on a starry night, or sitting on the porch watching the wind and rain, you should. You will find yourself in awe of God's creations. To think, as some do, that all those natural wonders came in to being without an awesome God in charge is beyond my comprehension.

I certainly have my questions and limits of understanding when it comes to all the facets of God, his being, and his creations, but I don't have a problem trusting that he is in charge and that he is perfectly aware of everything about me. If he weren't, how would he find those parking places for me that I pray for on occasion?

I hope as you continue to grow in your spiritual life that you will take time to think about the awesome things around you that we all take for granted. It's those things that we can't figure out that keep bringing us back to God. Continue to search for understanding, but don't lose faith when you don't find all the answers.

Pray with me:
Thank you, God, for all your creations. Help us to continuously seek understanding of your awesomeness but to be satisfied with knowing we will never fully understand. Amen

Patty B. Williams

June 20th

How Do You Love?

"Christ's love is greater than any person can ever know. But I pray that you will be able to know that love. Then you can be filled with the fullness of God. Ephesians 3:19 (NCV)

We will never fathom the depth of the love God has for us because we try to imagine his love like the love we know, and our kind of loving is so different. So much of our love is conditional. We love because others love us. We love out of passion. We love because of the way someone makes us feel or what he or she can do for us. We don't love because we are filled with God's spirit, yet that's exactly the kind of love for which we should be striving.

Can you imagine loving that friend who just betrayed you, the boyfriend who dumped you, the professor that failed you, or the person who just did $1,000 worth of damage to your car and can't pay for it? I don't think Jesus had to worry about professors failing him in class or someone crashing into the back of his car, but he sure had a lot of people doing a lot of bad things to him.

Loving with the spirit of God's love is difficult. Actually, I think it is impossible without God's help. You have to be able to get beyond a lot of different feelings—anger, hurt, disappointment, pride, jealously, embarrassment.

Does loving with the spirit of God's love mean you don't get angry, you don't hurt, you aren't disappointed, have no pride or jealously, or don't get embarrassed? No, it just means that you can love through it all. It's a tough assignment. Yet, it is our assignment. It is what we are to strive for daily.

Pray with me:

Lord, fill us with your spirit so we are capable of loving others as you love us. Amen

Patty B. Williams

June 21ˢᵗ

A Cheerful Giver

"Each man should give what he has decided in his heart to give, not reluctantly or under compulsion, for God loves a cheerful giver.
2 Corinthians 9:7 (NIV)

I think when people read this verse they may think only of money, and I'm not sure the message was meant to be just in terms of money.

Every day we have the opportunity to give something. That something may be money, it may be material possessions, it may be time, or it may be talent. It could just be a sweet smile or a hug.

I think what Paul, the writer of Corinthians, was trying to say is that whatever you're giving, you should give it with the right attitude and the right heart. That's what pleases God. If you give money to church and begrudge giving it, you might as well keep it. If you give of yourself with your time, your talents, or your hug and you're doing it for the wrong reasons, I think God would tell you to hold off giving until you've worked on your attitude.

There will be instances, of course, when you may need to give and you haven't had time to work on your attitude. For instance, there is a project at church that needs immediate financial assistance and you're called upon to give more when you've already given your share. Know that God understands those times and will wait for your prayer asking for a follow-up cheerful spirit. I've seen your cheerful spirit on many occasions, and at other times I've seen that not so cheerful spirit. It's for sure you've seen both in me. As we both grow spiritually, we'll pray that there's more cheerful than not-so-cheerful giving in the future.

Pray with me:
Work on our hearts and attitudes where they need it the most, Lord. You know our weaknesses. Amen

June 22nd
(Weston's Birthday)

Weston

"But Timothy has just now come to us from you and has brought good news about your faith and love. He has told us that you always have pleasant memories of us and that you long to see us, just as we also long to see you." 1 Thessalonians 3:6 (NIV)

It saddens me at times when I think of you and Weston not being as close as you once were. You were such wonderful playmates when you were little and playing in your pretend world of hair salons, grocery stores, offices, and pine straw houses. Those times together at Nanny's and Granddaddy's, St. George Island, the trussel, and in ole Blue won't be forgotten easily. I hope you realize, too, how precious those memories are, not only for you and Weston, but also for so many others in the family.

Remember that just because you and Weston are far apart in miles, and just because you might be far apart in interest right now, you don't have to be far apart in heart. Remember that your family will always be a common bond, as will the special memories you built together.

Don't let too much time go by without being in touch with one another, even if it's only a card to say, "Hi, just a note to let you know you're in my thoughts today." You may be surprised how much that little card could mean if one of you were having a lousy day.

Certainly on this day, his 16th birthday, we will both be thinking about him. Let's say a prayer that he's safe, happy, and walking in the path God has planned for him.

Pray with me:
Thank you, Lord, for special cousins and precious memories. Help us to continue our growth together as friends, family, and as your children. Amen

Brooke and Weston

Patty B. Williams

June 23rd

Gandhi's Advice

"And he said: I tell you the truth, unless you change and become like little children, you will never enter the kingdom of heaven."
Matthew 18:3 (NIV)

Gandhi said, "Be the change you want to see in the world." That's pretty good advice even for today, don't you think?

I'm sure you remember some of the talks we've had about things that shouldn't be that are, such things as racism, immorality, disrespect for others, unkindness, and apathy. Some you've had more experience with than others. Some you've probably been guilty of yourself and later regretted. I know I have.

Too often people see something like racism or immorality as being such a big problem that they don't even consider what they can do to prevent it, or at least make it better, so they don't even try. I'm sure you won't fall into that way of thinking, and I hope you will encourage your friends to be positive about doing their part, too. We certainly would have been in a mess if Jesus had decided that we were too big a problem to do his part to change the world, wouldn't we?

Even if it's a statement you make against racism to someone who is telling a mean-spirited joke, or a stand you take against doing something immoral, or an apology you make for someone else who has been disrespectful to another, it is a start. Try to remember Gandhi's words and pass them around every chance you get. He would be proud.

Pray with me:
Lord, we know change is needed in the world. Help us to do our part to make it happen. Amen

Clean Underwear, Wild Elephants and the Princess

June 24th

Many Kinds Of Love

"We love because he first loved us." 1 John 4:19 (NIV)

I'm glad to hear about those times you meet new guys that you think are "hot." I think we used to call guys, "tough." Whatever they are called, we know what the descriptions represent, don't we?

I hope you have the opportunity to date a lot of different guys, to experience different kinds of love, to know what it's like to have someone touch your heart and someone to leave footprints on it. I don't want you to have your heart broken, but chances are you will and will break a few yourself. That's just the way it is most of the time.

I think I have experienced most of the type loves you think about—puppy love, first love, crush love, romantic love, physical attraction love, love at first sight, forbidden love, marrying love, and even lost love. Most I can recommend, but some you will do well to avoid.

My one hope in all the loves that you will experience is that you never get to a point that you love so deeply that you lose yourself. That could be devastating both physically and mentally, and I don't think that is what God wants for us. Try to keep that in mind. If you find yourself getting to that point, step back and examine what's really going on with your feelings and why. Don't let it get out of hand. Love is supposed to feel good. It should be easy and make you happy. If it's not, then something is wrong with the picture. Do something about it, girl!

Pray with me:
Lord, help us to use our heads as well as our hearts. Help us to love the way you would have us to love. Amen

Patty B. Williams

June 25th

Yesterday, Today, And Tomorrow

"Listen, I tell you a mystery: We will not all sleep, but we will all be changed." 1 Corinthians 15:51 (NIV)

This is about the time of year we were making big plans to go to St. George Island with Nanny and Granddaddy, Uncle Billy, Aunt Debbie, and the boys. Gosh, it seems in many ways that that was only yesterday!

Do you remember our first summers there when we used to stay at the Buccaneer Inn and you all played on that little concrete courtyard and in the pool? Then remember the first summer we went to 300 Ocean Mile? That was certainly a transition. Then there was the fantastic three-story house where we stayed. I think that was the first summer Weston had his head turned by a girl. Miss Jamie certainly made a big impression, didn't she?

I don't think you kids ever really thought much about the differences from year to year as you all began to get older, but it was interesting watching the transition. Isn't it incredible when you think about how much has changed since those first summers?

I want you to always cherish the memories of the years gone by with family and friends, but I want you to always look forward to the changes that time brings, too. Don't get stuck in the past with disappointment for having to move on. God gives us yesterday, today, and tomorrow. He wants us to enjoy each equally. Take what you learned and enjoyed yesterday to make today and tomorrow even better. It's a good plan.

Pray with me:
Father, thank you for such wonderful yesterdays. Help us to always look forward to today and tomorrow with as much enthusiasm as we remember the past. Amen

Clean Underwear, Wild Elephants and the Princess

June 26th

Keeping It Balanced

"The boundary lines have fallen for me in pleasant places; surely I have a delightful inheritance." Psalm 16:6 (NIV)

I think you finally are beginning to see the necessity of keeping your checkbook balanced. A few returned checks with twenty-dollar penalties make the point much better than I ever could.

When your checkbook is balanced, you know what you have and what you don't have. You may be disappointed that the balance is low and you want to go shopping or buy groceries, but at least you aren't stressed because you don't know if you've written a bad check. You know your boundaries.

Life is kind of like a checkbook. You need to keep it balanced. When you work hard, you need to take time to play hard, too. When you spend hours studying, you need to take time to relax and let your brain rejuvenate. If you eat too much today, then eat less tomorrow and exercise. If you're spending too much time with a guy and letting all your other relationships fall by the wayside, you'll have a really difficult time adjusting if he decides to do his own thing one day. When you fill your mind with only worldly things and no spiritual things, your perspective about life will be limited just as it would if you only filled your mind with spiritual things and ignored what was going on in the world.

Keeping everything balanced in your life will not always be within your control. That's why it's important to keep those things that you can control as balanced as possible. God wants that for you and so do I.

Patty B. Williams

Pray with me:
Lord, it's so easy for us to get off balance. Steady us when we need it and help us to look to you for help when we falter. Amen

Clean Underwear, Wild Elephants and the Princess

June 27th

Independence

In the Lord, however, woman is not independent of man, nor is man independent of woman. 1 Corinthians 11:11 (NIV)

You will study about independence in terms of history and what it meant for our country. You may also think about it in terms of yourself now that you're away from home. Maybe you even think about how your college education will enhance your independence one day. I hope so.

I think all parents want their children to grow up and be able to take care of themselves. I am no different. I don't ever want you to feel like you have to get married because you can't make it on your own, nor do I want you to have to depend on your dad and me forever. That's why we are helping you to get the education you need now.

Just remember, however, that even though you are striving for independence, you will never be totally independent of others. If you end up in a career making tons of money or win the biggest lottery, you'll still depend on others for things money can't buy. I think God planned it that way.

Therefore, continue to work hard on that college education and the independence it will bring you, but don't strive for independence void of God, family and friends. Remember that Eve was created as a helper for Adam. God never intended for us to be totally independent.

Pray with me:
God help us to learn to take care of ourselves, but help us to be willing to seek help from others and especially from you when it's needed. Amen

Patty B. Williams

June 28th

Adjust The Sails

"Preach the Word; be prepared in season and out of season."
2 Timothy 4:2 (NIV)

I like the little saying, "We cannot direct the wind, but we can adjust the sails." That is so true.

When a hurricane is on the way, there's not a whole lot we can do other than get prepared for it or leave. When a teenager does something against her parent's instructions or wishes, the parents only have control over how they respond afterward. They can either adjust the teenager's sails or adjust their own. When you've failed a test, there's not much you can do about it then, but you can certainly make the necessary adjustments to not let it happen again.

The older I get the more I see life changes for many of my friends. A spouse dies, a parent has a stroke, a divorce occurs, a child abuses drugs, and the list goes on and on. It's amazing to see how easy it seems for some to adjust their sails and how difficult it appears for others. Surely a close walk with God helps when those challenges come along.

We have been fortunate as a family when it comes to life challenges. We haven't had to face some of the most difficult challenges. Should those challenges and hard winds come in the future, I hope, with God's help, that we will be able to adjust our sails. Let's remember to pray for that ability now so we will be prepared.

Pray with me:
Lord, keep us alert to the possibilities of changing winds at any time, and help prepare us to adjust our sails when necessary. Amen

Clean Underwear, Wild Elephants and the Princess

June 29th

What It Takes

"Then you will have success if you are careful to observe the decrees and laws that the Lord gave Moses for Israel. Be strong and courageous. Do not be afraid or discouraged." 1 Chronicles 22:13 (NIV)

I know you want to make good grades. I know a semester with a 4.0 would be a great accomplishment and make you very proud of yourself. Of course it would make me proud, too, but it's not something I'm pushing you toward. It's more important to me that you learn what it takes to make that 4.0 and know that you can do it if that's your goal.

A man by the name of Charles Kendall Adams said, "No one ever attains very eminent success by simply doing what is required of him; it is the amount and excellence of what is over and above the required, that determines the greatness of ultimate distinction." Though he said it much more eloquently, that is what I've always tried to explain was the difference in good grades and great grades—going beyond what is required. It's also the difference you will experience in your success at work, the difference in your relationships with friends, and the difference in a mediocre marriage and a great marriage.

I know you will always strive to do a good job regardless of whether it's at school, on a job, or within a relationship. What I want you to think about are those things that are important enough that you will work hard at attaining that greatness of ultimate distinction of which Charles Adams speaks. Only you can decide if you are willing to go over and above the required in whatever you do. I will be your cheerleader.

Patty B. Williams

Pray with me:

Give us confidence, Lord, in knowing that we can be successful if we choose to be. Help us to know, too, that you are our greatest strength when we need assistance. Amen

Clean Underwear, Wild Elephants and the Princess

June 30th

Who's On The Ladder?

"Be strong and very courageous. Be careful to obey all the law my servant Moses gave you; do not turn from it to the right or to the left, that you may be successful wherever you go." Joshua 1:7 (NIV)

When you went through sorority rush, you knew that I would have been tickled if you had pledged Delta Zeta since that was my sorority. Hopefully you also knew that I wanted you to pledge where you felt comfortable, the place where you felt most at home. When you chose Kappa Delta, I was happy for you. I wasn't disappointed at all.

The other organizations that you have chosen to become associated with are the ones you hopefully feel good about and think you belong. Hopefully neither status nor prestige were your motivating factors for any of the choices you've made.

As you continue to climb the ladder of success in college and later in your career, I hope you always remember that your position on the ladder of success is not near as important as who you're climbing the ladder with and how you're climbing it.

I hope in making those steps up the ladder that you remember that no amount of money or recognition can take the place of your peace of mind or that feeling in your heart of hearts that you are where you should be. I'll be here to listen and give counsel if you want it, but start with prayer. God's directions will always be better than mine.

Pray with me:
Thank you God for the freedom of choice that we have in so many things. Help us to use our freedoms wisely. Amen

Patty B. Williams

July 1ˢᵗ

Reading

"Afterward Joshua read all the words of the law—the blessings and the curses—just as it is written in the Book of the Law." Joshua 8:34 (NIV)

There are a lot of things I could encourage you to do that I wish I had done better as a young person. Reading more is one of them; studying beyond the assignment is another. You have said so many times that you wish you were smart like Kelly. Reading is one of your best ways to get there. Of course, reading just romantic novels and the latest *Seventeen* magazines won't do the trick.

It's good to have pleasurable, relaxing reading, but if you really want to broaden your horizons and have the reading be helpful in developing your mind, you need a variety. One of the things I regret is never having read the classics. They aren't all fun type reading, but you would learn a lot about people and life from the most gifted writers in history. Best-selling novels are good because so many people read them. They become a topic of conversation, and their stories often take you away to a place you know nothing about.

When you read the Bible, and I hope you will, start with a study Bible that tells you about the author, gives you background information and a theme so you will better understand what's going on. One of the reasons many people have difficulty relating to what the Bible says is because they don't understand the context from which it comes.

Read about current events, too. Be aware of what's going on around you. Know who the best candidates are so you can vote intelligently. At least read enough to know who they are and their major platforms. God gave you beautiful eyes and a good mind. Use them both to get you closer to where you want to be.

Clean Underwear, Wild Elephants and the Princess

Pray with me:
Lord, remind us of our own resources. Keep us always looking for opportunities to grow in wisdom, knowledge and love. Amen

Patty B. Williams

July 2nd

Peace That Passes Understanding

"And the peace of God, which transcends all understanding, will guard your hearts and your minds in Christ Jesus" Philippians 4:7 (NIV)

As you get older, you will see friends or family go through really difficult times and will feel at such a loss as to how to help them. How will you console a friend who loses a child, a parent, a boyfriend or girlfriend? I know we've talked about being there for that friend, about what to say and how to act, but there is another thing that I think will be as helpful as anything you can do. As a matter of fact, I think this is where you should start.

Pray for that person and ask God to give him or her inner spiritual peace, that peace that passes all understanding, the peace of God that protects believers hearts and minds in spite of the turmoil that is going on around them.

Haven't you seen some people who seem to always keep it together regardless of what they're going through? They are the ones that continue to smile, continue to do the things that need to be done, console others when they should be the ones being consoled. They defy logic and rationale. Those are the ones that I think have that inner peace.

I've prayed that prayer for you and many others, as well as for myself. It's amazing how different you can feel the next morning about a big decision, a big test, a spoiled relationship, a frustrating situation, once you've asked God to give you the peace only he can give. Try it sometime.

Pray with me:
Lord, help us to remember that you are our greatest source of peace and strength. Amen

July 3rd

A Loaf Of Bread

"Jesus answered, 'It is written: Man does not live on bread alone.'" Luke 4:4 (NIV)

I know you have had relationships before that have been romantic at one time but your feelings changed. You no longer wanted the relationship to be romantic. Friendship was enough, at least for you.

The problem, however, is when the other person involved isn't at the same point as you. That makes it very difficult, especially if you truly care about the person.

I read something that explained the point pretty well. It said something like, "when you offer a man friendship when what's in his heart is love, it's like giving a loaf of bread to someone who is dying of thirst." I think that pretty much hits the nail on the head.

Just because you are at a certain point, doesn't mean the other person can jump right in there and be at the same point. That's pretty evident by the number of suicides and murders related to romances having gone bad.

What I want to remind you of is to treat everyone's heart tenderly; don't expect someone to be able to change gears quickly just because you do, and don't push a friendship if the friendship is not something they can handle at the time. Be patient. It may be able to grow at a later time when their feelings aren't so vulnerable. I think you are aware of this, but it may not hurt to be reminded.

Patty B. Williams

Pray with me:

Help us, Lord, to be sensitive to the needs and feelings of others. Help us to treat others as tenderly as you treat us. Amen

Clean Underwear, Wild Elephants and the Princess

July 4th

The Forth Of July

"You, my brothers, were called to be free. But do not use your freedom to indulge the sinful nature; rather, serve one another in love." Galatians 5:13 (NIV)

I hope today, as you celebrate Independence Day, that you will take time to think about all the freedoms you have. Say a little extra prayer of thanksgiving. Remember some of the things Erika told us about her country and their way of living compared to ours. She thought the US was wonderful. Can you imagine leaving your country at her age for a whole year to go somewhere you could barely speak the language and knew practically no one?

Think about what it means to be free from the rule of another country, to be able to participate in choosing your leaders, your religion, who you will fall in love with and marry. We definitely take these things for granted, don't we?

Remember the price that many paid to gain the freedoms we have, and work hard at not abusing those freedoms or let others abuse them.

When you enjoy the festivities of the day, see the beautiful fireworks at night and our flag flying high, I hope you get a little lump in your throat thinking about what it all truly represents.

Pray with me:
Father we are blessed beyond measure. Thank you for the freedoms we enjoy. Keep us ever mindful that they come with a great price. Amen

Patty B. Williams

July 5th

Improve Your Aim

"And I trust that you will discover that we have not failed the test."
2 Corinthians 13:6 (NIV)

Gilbert Arland said, "When an archer misses the mark, he turns and looks for the fault within himself. Failure to hit the bull's eye is never the fault of the target. To improve your aim—improve yourself."

When you perform really badly on a test, what are your first thoughts? Do you blame the teacher for making the test so hard? Do you blame the fact that you had two other tests to study for or a sorority function you were required to attend the night before the test?

My guess is that if you truly analyzed the reasons why you didn't do well, being unprepared would be on the top of the list. Chances are you didn't devote the time to studying that you should have throughout the semester, you didn't spend quality time reviewing the material the day or two before the test, and you procrastinated overall in getting prepared.

If you're going to improve your grades, your work ethic, your relationships, your willpower, or anything else, then you have to look at improving yourself. Don't look for others or other things to blame for something that you can control. You have all it takes to make your aim at anything successful.

Pray with me:
God, keep us honest with ourselves. Teach us to look at ourselves when we miss the mark. Then help us improve our aim. Amen

July 6th

For The Record

"It is God's will that you should be holy; that you should avoid sexual immorality." 1 Thessalonians 4:3 (NIV)

I'm not sure we've ever specifically talked about how I would feel if you decided to live with a guy before marrying him, although I'm sure you know without discussing it. For the record (or should I say for the book), let me tell you so there will be no question.

I do not think that living with someone without the benefit of marriage is God's plan, nor do I think it will enhance your chances of having a better marriage or not divorcing. In fact statistics say just the opposite.

What I do think it does is give both parties involved an easy way out of commitment. True, you may be committed to one another in terms of a monogamous relationship, but there is so much more to commitment in a marriage than just commitment in terms of a sexual partner.

I certainly don't have all the answers when it comes to what is right or wrong in relationships; that's why I depend on someone much wiser than me for guidance. God's word is pretty clear on what he thinks about the matter; so if you have questions, check your Bible. Then my guess is you won't have to ask me what I think.

Pray with me:
Lord, sometimes we think our wisdom is so much better than yours, our maker. When we start thinking that way, please bring us gently back to you. Amen

Patty B. Williams

July 7th

The Man In Rome

"We love because he first loved us." 1 John 4:19 (NIV)

"Thanks be to God, the world is wide, And I am going far from home. And I forgot in Camelot the man I loved in Rome."

I wonder if this was a personal experience of the author, Edna St. Vincent Millay. You may never go to Rome and fall in love, but if you fall in love and it doesn't work out, I hope you get to Camelot quickly.

Break-ups are the pits. I know you've already experienced that once or twice and will probably experience a few more. I just hope that as you go through the hurt and all those other feelings that you will have, that you keep the right perspective, that you know you will make it, and that time is a great healer.

I don't believe there is only one person that God has planned for us and there are no others. I do believe, however, that He has a plan and knows what is best for us. Our responsibility is to seek knowledge of that plan. If it doesn't come together in Rome, then maybe Camelot is a better place to look.

My prayer is always that God will help you find the right person, not just the cutest, the richest, or the brightest. I hope your prayer is the same. Remember, the world is wide, don't get left in Rome with a bad break-up. Pack your bags for Camelot!

Pray with me:
God, help us to always seek your guidance in all that we do, especially when that guidance has to do with the opposite sex. We need all the help we can get. Amen

July 8th

From Dresses To Jeans

"... and you will be changed into a different person."
1 Samuel 10:6 (NIV)

In reading some of the letters I have written you over the years, it's interesting to see how you have grown and changed. I can remember when you were a little girl and I could very seldom get you out of a dress. Then as you got older I wondered if I'd ever see you in a dress again.

In reading one of the letters I'd written you when you were eleven, I made the comment that you had always been fairly timid and not keen on venturing out in the world to find the new and different. You liked knowing where you were, what to expect and how difficult it was going to be to get something done. Your comfort zone was in the routine. That doesn't exactly describe you now, does it?

Change is good sometimes. Sometimes it's not so good. Most of the time, however, it's difficult, regardless of whether or not it's good or bad. I hope you remember that, not only as you grow and change personally, but also as you get into a profession, a marriage, as you start a family, and as you start to lose friends and family through moves, changes in life style, marriages, and even death.

Remember that nothing is forever—at least not here in this world. Enjoy where you are now so you have no regrets for having missed something that you took for granted. Be prepared, however, to work through the changes that come along in your life. Try to think of them as new doors opening instead of old ones closing. I'm sure you'll do fine whether it's in your jeans or a dress!

Patty B. Williams

Pray with me:
Lord, be with us through all the changes of our lives. Help us remember that you are in charge, and we need to relax. Amen

Clean Underwear, Wild Elephants and the Princess

July 9th

"Goodnight, God"

"What other nation is so great as to have their gods near them the way the Lord our God is near us whenever we pray to him?"
Deuteronomy 4:7 (NIV)

I know you will remember being tucked in every night and saying your prayers, but do you remember telling God, "goodnight" instead of "amen" at the end of your prayers? God and I remember.

I hope as you say your prayers as a nineteen-year-old instead of a three-year old that you still say what you want God to hear, that you don't just say a rote prayer.

College life will offer you lots of opportunities to take concerns, frustrations, hurt, and anxieties to God. If you learn how to communicate well with Him, it will make your college life much easier.

Think of God as one of your best friends. Talk to him like you would to them. He knows you better than they do. You don't have to hide any thoughts.

Don't save your prayer time for only those times when you are distressed. I think some of my best prayer times have been when I was thanking God for the good things in my life. You don't share just the difficult times with your best friend, do you? God should be no different.

I'm glad those tuck-in times were special for us. I hope each night as you crawl into bed 300 miles away from me that you know I'm still tucking you in with my thoughts and prayers.

Patty B. Williams

Pray with me:
Lord, teach us to communicate with you as though you were visible right beside us, and help us to listen for your response. Good night—

Clean Underwear, Wild Elephants and the Princess

July 10th

Curiosity

"Whenever the rainbow appears in the clouds, I will see it and remember the everlasting covenant between God and all living creatures of every kind on the earth." Genesis 9:16 (NIV)

I think my favorite age with you was three. Not only were you cute, but you were so much fun. You were so expressive and talkative, and it was hard not to laugh in the middle of some of your serious conversations. You were also very curious and could ask all kinds of questions like, "What happens if you push the brake and accelerator at the same time?" and "Does it rain in heaven?"

I hope you will always remain curious because being curious is what makes you learn about things. Don't ever be afraid to ask questions if you don't understand something or if you just want to know for the sake of knowing something.

People will normally be glad to answer your questions if they are sincere, primarily because your questions indicate that you are paying attention to what they are saying and that you are interested. Think about that in terms of your classes. Professors are, for the most part, normal people. How will they know you are interested in what they are teaching if they don't get some feedback? Think what it does for their self-esteem when you ask questions, and they have the answer.

As for your answer to the question "Does it rain in heaven?" I think the answer is, yes, but I think the caveat to that response is that it rains just the right amount, not too much and not too little. The sunshine, the rain, and wind are all perfect. Does that satisfy your curiosity for now?

Patty B. Williams

Pray with me:
Keep us curious, God, about everyday life so we continue to grow in wisdom and knowledge. Keep us curious about heaven so we continue to study your word. Amen

Clean Underwear, Wild Elephants and the Princess

July 11th

Self-Confidence

"I am glad I can have complete confidence in you."
2 Corinthians 7:16 (NIV)

It's been interesting and encouraging watching your self-confidence grow over the years. I remember times when you were much more dependent on others than you were on yourself. I'm glad that has changed.

Self-confidence helps you try things you might not otherwise try. It reduces anxiety when you are in situations where others aren't around and you have to take care of yourself and make decisions on your own.

I hope you will always have enough self-confidence in yourself that you won't let others intimidate you, that you won't be afraid of failure, or afraid to make a mistake.

Remember, God made us all. He doesn't put one of us higher than another, nor should we. Wouldn't this be a wonderful world if we could all get it together with that one concept?

Continue to work on all those things you want to improve about yourself, but know that you are already a work of art—God's art. You have every reason to be self-confident.

Pray with me:
For who we are, Lord, we give you thanks. For loving us the way you do, we are blessed. Keep us confident in ourselves and in who you are to us. Amen

Patty B. Williams

July 12th

Intimacy

" . . . a time to embrace and a time to refrain." Ecclesiastes 3:5 (NIV)

While in college I'm sure the word intimacy will come up on numerous occasions. It may be in some social science class, it may be sitting around talking with a bunch of girls, or it may be with a special guy. My understanding of what it means has changed over the years, and maybe you can benefit from what I've learned.

First, I've learned that sex is a very intimate thing, but having sex doesn't mean, necessarily, that you are intimate with that person. Marriage is also no guarantee that you'll have intimacy with your spouse.

You see, I think intimacy means that you can be your true self, who you really are beneath all your defenses, masks, and fears. You can even show the side of yourself that you aren't proud of and want changed. You can be truthful, unafraid to show your vulnerability, and feel safe with a person knowing your innermost feelings.

You can, of course, have an intimate relationship with a friend, whether male or female. You don't have to be married. I think, however, that God planned for marriage to be the ultimate, intimate relationship between a man and woman, and that relationship takes time and trust. Think about that when you start getting stars in your eyes and flutters in your heart. It takes time, my child, time. Don't rush it!

Pray with me:
Lord, help us to understand what true intimacy is and what it is not. Help us to strive for it in all our relationships but most importantly with you. Amen

Clean Underwear, Wild Elephants and the Princess

July 13th
(Granddaddy's Birthday)

A Legacy Of Love

"For great is your love, higher than the heavens; your faithfulness reaches to the skies." Psalm 108:4 (NIV)

Today is your Granddaddy's birthday, and I'm sure I won't need to remind you to call him and let him know you're thinking about him. I know he's in your thoughts every day.

Granddaddy has been such an important part of your life. I can't read one of the letters I've written you over the years without Granddaddy or Nanny being part of the story. Granddaddy was one of yours and Weston's greatest playmates. He was your best customer at your store, your best beauty salon client, and your best phone customer at your office. He helped you, Weston and Justin blaze many trails through the woods and over the streams and rocks at the trussell. He's ridden many waves with you in the ocean, rode hundreds of miles with you either riding or driving ole blue, bought you junk at the Handy Way, and told you the story about the red-eyed raccoon too many times to count.

As you've grown up, he's become your confidant, your beach buddy, your counselor, your traveling companion, and anything else you ever asked. He has always been your security blanket just like he has been mine. His love for you is beyond measure. That's a nice feeling, isn't it? When God gave us Granddaddy on loan, he gave us the best of the best.

Pray with me:
Lord, you could have given us riches or fame, a castle or a kingdom;

instead you gave us a legacy of love. We are blessed beyond measure. Amen

Brooke and Granddaddy

Clean Underwear, Wild Elephants and the Princess

July 14th

Laughter

"Our mouths were filled with laughter, our tongues with songs of joy . . ." Psalm 126:2 (NIV)

Do you remember all those ValueTale books I bought when you and Michael were little? We have a whole set of them. I think the one that was both of your favorites was *The Value of Believing In Yourself,* the story of Louis Pasteur. I think the reason you both liked it so much was because it was scary when a little boy almost died with rabies after being bitten by a mad dog.

There is another of those books called *The Value of Laughter,* that is the story of Lucille Ball. I suppose you know who Lucy is, surely you're not too young to remember her. She certainly made millions of people laugh over the years and became a household word while doing it.

Life is much too short not to enjoy it and share times of laughter with others. One of my dearest friends, Smitty, has brightened my life over the years with his wonderful laughter. I would miss that laugh so much if I couldn't hear it every now and then.

You also have an infectious laugh. Well, I guess it's more a chuckle than a hearty laugh like Smitty's, but whatever it's called, it's unique, and I love it. I always look forward to hearing it, and then when you leave, I miss it terribly.

I hope, since you can't be here, that you are sharing that laughter and brightening someone else's day at UCF. God wants joy and laughter for all of us. We do others and ourselves an injustice when we don't use it more often to lighten our load or the load of someone else.

Patty B. Williams

Pray with me:
Lord, keep us high in spirit, full of your love and the joy and laughter you want for us. Amen

Clean Underwear, Wild Elephants and the Princess

July 15th

Broken Vows And Promises

"When a man makes a vow to the Lord or takes an oath to obligate himself by a pledge, he must not break his word but must do everything he said." Numbers 30:2 (NIV)

Three years ago this was such a special day. It was the day Bill and I were married. It was perfect, we thought, in so many ways. Now three years later, that picture of perfection doesn't exist. What happened in such a relatively short period of time? How could two intelligent people who knew the meaning of commitment, who loved one another, who loved God, and who had so many things going for them, blow it? I wish I knew.

I know divorce was not God's plan. It never is. He's disappointed that we didn't try harder, that we took our eyes off him, that we unintentionally hurt one another and made poor choices in responding to each other's needs. Are we broken? Maybe we are in spirit for a while, but it won't be forever.

Can God use this brokeness for good even though it wasn't his plan? My guess is he can. Did either of us grow through the times of happiness and the times of heartache? I hope so. Were others touched by us when we were together or when we parted? I certainly hope that, too.

My point in all this is to remind you of three things: marriage is serious business, don't jump into it; true commitment is difficult, know what you're doing; and God is great; he can mend broken hearts and broken dreams, regardless of the circumstance.

Patty B. Williams

Pray with me:

Lord when we botch things up, remind us that you are there to help. Forgive us for our mistakes, mend our hearts, and make us whole again. Amen

Clean Underwear, Wild Elephants and the Princess

July 16th

Leadership

"Give me wisdom and knowledge, that I may lead this people, for who is able to govern this great people of yours?" 2 Chronicles 1:10 (NIV)

I remember when you were little I used to be concerned that you would be a follower and not a leader. Some of that reasoning came from the fact that you were timid and a little clingy for a while. My, did that change!

As you got in to high school you certainly did your share of following—and sometimes in the wrong direction! You, like most other teenagers, succumbed to peer pressure and did things you wouldn't normally have done on your own. Then, gradually, I began to see a change. I'm not sure what caused it, but I was happy to see it.

I think leadership shows character. It shows confidence in who you are, and often determines where and how far you'll go in life. It gives you wonderful opportunities to influence others and make a difference in your corner of the world.

Don't pass up opportunities to lead when you get them, and if you don't get them, then go look for them. You have too much to offer to let your potential go untapped.

Remember that picture of you and Brittany where she's standing in front of you with her little head tilted way back looking up at you? I love that picture. It says so much. I think one of the things it says is, "I'm looking up to you, Brookie Bear; lead me wherever, and I'll follow." Is that an awesome responsibility or what?

Patty B. Williams

You have proven that you are a good leader. Brittany is in good hands. I'm not concerned any longer.

Pray with me:
Help us to lead, Lord, in the direction you would have us to go. Amen

Clean Underwear, Wild Elephants and the Princess

July 17th

Foresight

"Since no man knows the future, who can tell him what is to come?"
Ecclesiastes 8:4 (NIV)

Although it has been frustrating to you to not know the area in which you want to major, it's been encouraging to see you think about it and try to figure out what it is you want to do with your life.

I wish I had had the foresight that you are exhibiting. It's not that I haven't liked what profession I ended up in, it's just that I wonder where I'd be had I given it as much thought as you.

Foresight is important in a lot of areas besides choosing your life's work. Using foresight can help you avoid a lot of relationship problems, financial problems, and day-to-day living problems.

If you don't have enough foresight to take care of the minor things that go wrong with your car, you're sure to have more expensive problems further down the road.

If you don't have enough foresight to know that you have to budget your money and delay gratification on some things, you will always be broke.

I'm proud of the maturity you are showing in trying to make your education beneficial instead of just trying to obtain a degree. Keep up the good work. You're doing the right thing.

Pray with me:
Father, help us to be wise in looking ahead to prepare for our future, but help us to also be wise enough to enjoy the moment. Amen

Patty B. Williams

July 18th
(Amy's birthday)

Calm, Cool, and Collected

"If a ruler's anger rises against you, do not leave your post; calmness can lay great errors to rest." Ecclesiastes 10:4 (NIV)

I don't ever remember your having a temper when you were little like Michael did. That doesn't mean, of course, that you didn't have your moments. You certainly did.

It's interesting to see how different people react to anger. Some react aggressively, trying to fight back, some retreat out of fear, and others handle it with just the opposite of anger. They calmly listen to the ranting and raving and then speak softly with calmness as they try to help the one angered through their tantrum.

Does that mean that showing a calm spirit is always the right response? I don't think so. Even Jesus got angry enough to overthrow the tables of the moneychangers in the temple courts when they were using the courts for a market to sell cattle, sheep and doves and gouging the worshippers.

It's just that often when one stays calm when another has lost it, the situation doesn't escalate into something worse. One reason for that is the element of surprise. An unexpected calm reaction may make the other person listen closer to themselves or at least change their thought pattern for a few minutes while they try to figure out how the other person can be so mellow. Try it sometime. I think you will be surprised.

Pray with me:
Lord, help us to keep our cool when others may be losing theirs all around us. Give us the words and demeanor to calm even the greatest of outrages. Amen

Patty B. Williams

July 19th

Homosexuality

"Do not show partiality in judging; hear both small and great alike. Do not be afraid of any man, for judgment belongs to God."
Deuteronomy 1:17 (NIV)

Society has, over the years, begun to accept or at least tolerate homosexuality much more than it did when I was young. I think that is good, not from the standpoint of thinking it is morally right or wrong, but thinking more in terms of leaving the judging to God.

You know I have a friend who has chosen to live a different lifestyle. Regardless of that decision, she is still my friend. Does it affect our relationship? No, it doesn't, but I suppose it could if we lived closer. I might not feel comfortable sharing time with her friends just as she may not feel comfortable sharing time with mine.

At this point in time, we do not know all the causes of homosexuality, whether it's a conscientious decision one makes or whether it's a physical or mental condition that a person doesn't control entirely. For that reason alone, we need to be cautious of how we react to it.

I have good Christian friends who have had to face the fact that their child was homosexual. It was probably the hardest thing they ever had to do in their lives. The conclusion they came to was that they loved him unconditionally. Were they proud of it? Of course they weren't. Were they disappointed? I'm certain they were. Did they leave the judging to God? I'm sure they did. Any other course of action would have been less than God expected.

You will be faced with this issue and will hear many opinions about it. You will, most likely, even hear or see some very ugly reactions to it. I am not concerned about your feelings; I think I know your heart. I just want you to have courage enough to speak your mind about it if a situation calls for it. God made us all and loves us all. He asks us to love, too. Judging is not loving. Don't ever be afraid to say that.

Pray with me:
Lord, it is so much easier to love those people we understand and who are like us. Help us remember your commandment to love everyone. Amen

Patty B. Williams

July 20th

The Internet

"Do not conform any longer to the pattern of this world, but be transformed by the renewing of your mind. Then you will be able to test and approve what God's will is—his good, pleasing and perfect will." Romans 12:2 (NIV)

The Internet has certainly broadened our research capabilities, hasn't it? I'm convinced that regardless of what we want to know, if we know how to search the WEB, we can find it.

The Internet, like most other things in life, can be used for good or for bad. There's good information out there and there is a tremendous amount of harmful, bad information, too. Sometimes people look for it, and sometimes they inadvertently find it while searching for something else.

E-mail certainly changed the way we communicate, too. It has opened lines of communication to people all over the world that before we would never have dreamed of trying to contact. Yet, it too can be used in the wrong way.

I know as you continue your college education you will be required to use the Internet more and more, and as you begin getting more friends on line and higher phone bills, you will start using E-mail more frequently. You know I try to encourage you to learn all you can about computers and computer programs because you'll need it when you start working. I want to encourage you to use the Internet for purposes that you would be proud of if someone checked the sights you visited or E-mails you sent. Think about the ugly jokes you may receive. You may not be able to control receiving them, but you can control what you do with them. If you accidentally get to a bad site, it won't take you long to figure that out. Then you decide what to do and whether or not to share it.

You have much too good a mind to fill it with things that are useless, tasteless, and against God's will. I have no doubt that you are aware of that. You might, however, have an opportunity to influence others, and for that reason, thinking about it ahead of time will help.

Pray with me:
Lord, temptations are everywhere, and now we have the Internet. Keep us mindful that you are always looking over our shoulder. Amen

Patty B. Williams

July 21st

Joyful Memories

"These things I have spoken to you, that my joy may remain in you, and that your joy may be full." John 15:11 (NKJ)

I will never forget the afternoon and early evening we waited for the phone call that would affirm your making cheerleader in Middle School. I'm not sure you've ever wanted anything as much as you wanted that phone to ring and you and Melissa to be cheerleaders together. Then, when the call finally came along with the tears of joy, I remember the look on Roy's face as he shared the moment of watching us together. He was touched and it showed. What a great memory for all three of us.

Think about the scripture above. Understand that the feeling of joy we shared that evening is how God would like us to feel all the time. Wouldn't that be wonderful? Think how much more you could get accomplished, how much you could lift the spirits of others and how differently you could handle the stresses of daily life.

Strive to get where God wants you. When you start to feel joyless, try to think about all the positive things in your life that bring you great pleasure—walks on the beach, a day at the mall—with money, a home cooked meal, a cozy bed to crawl into at night, the list could go on and on. You get the idea. Joy is God-made, available, and attainable. You don't have to wait for a telephone call or a fulfilled dream. Just look up, ask, and then do your part!

Pray with me:
Thank you, Lord, for those special times of ecstatic joy, but thank you, too, for the everyday joy that being filled with your spirit brings. Amen

Clean Underwear, Wild Elephants and the Princess

July 22nd
(Cindy's Birthday)

Sending Messages

"I also want women to dress modestly, with decency and propriety, not with braided hair or gold or pearls or expensive clothes, but with good deeds, appropriate for women who profess to worship God."
1 Timothy 2:9-10 (NIV)

I can remember when I was about 13 or 14 I had this dress that I thought was super sexy. It was white, short, and had the sides cut out. Of course that was second only to the white, pink-trimmed, eyelet pants and top I had when I was your age. It showed my whole midriff! I was just too cool. Then as you grew up, my conservatism set in. We certainly didn't always agree on what was appropriate dress, did we?

I'm not sure what the test should be to determine if you should or shouldn't wear something, or whether or not it's appropriate for a particular occasion. Perhaps the question to ask is, "what message am I going to send," or "what message do I want to send about myself." I think that is a fair question. We wear conservative, blue or grey suits to interview, red when we want to appear powerful, dark when we go to a funeral, and white at our wedding. Surely what we wear, the style of dress, blouse, or pants, says as much about us as color does.

I think we might have the wrong idea about sexy clothes anyway. To me, some of the sexiest clothes were those in Civil War times. Those dresses were long, with tons of undergarments, and often the collar was up around the neck, almost like a turtleneck. Maybe leaving something to the imagination is the sexiest of all. Think about that!

Anyway, I will trust your judgement to use appropriate discretion in your dress and the messages you send. I know you know your mom's view.

Pray with me:
Lord, help us remember that we honor you not only in what we do and say but also in what we wear. Let the message we send be one pleasing to you. Amen

Clean Underwear, Wild Elephants and the Princess

July 23rd

Overload

"For the sun rises with scorching heat and withers the plant; its blossom falls and its beauty is destroyed. In the same way the rich man will fade away even while he goes about his business." James 1:11 (NIV)

I know you have a busy schedule when you work, go to school, and participate in sorority life and other campus activities. I'm very happy that you are getting involved and making UCF a good memory.

I know, too, that you have a tendency to get on overload at times, and you need to prevent that as much as possible.

Sometimes it's good to just stop and evaluate where you are spending your time, what you are enjoying most and least, which activities are most worthwhile, and which if you were living your last days would be the things you wish you'd done more of instead of something else. I certainly don't think I would be saying I wish I had spent more hours at the office.

Time is precious, even though you don't realize it as much when you're young. Try not to waste it on frivolous things that don't really matter. Take time on occasion to re-evaluate where you are and what you're doing. Then make any changes that are necessary and get right back in the swing, but with a better perspective.

Pray with me:
Lord, help us to determine the things that are most important and be willing to put those less important things aside. Help us to stay balanced so we don't get on overload. Amen

July 24th

A Big Order

"If you love those who love you, what credit is that to you? Even 'sinners' love those who love them. And if you do good to those who are good to you, what credit is that to you?" Luke 6:32-33 (NIV)

It is easy to do nice things for people who always do nice things for us, isn't it? We often buy gifts, not necessarily to get a gift, but knowing that most likely we will get one in return. It's also a lot easier to care for someone who we feel cares the same for us, don't you think?

Jesus tells us that we should be concentrating more on those persons who don't necessarily do nice things for us, or buy reciprocal gifts, or care as much for us as we do for them.

I suppose that means I need to continue remembering that friend's birthday that doesn't remember mine. I need to continue efforts to reach out in friendship even though the friend seems to make no effort. I need to love the unlovable, and treat everyone as I want to be treated. Whoa—that's a big order! Have you tried anything like this lately? Well, if you haven't, I can assure you, it's not easy. I struggle with it all the time.

Remember though, we don't have to struggle alone. We can ask for help. There will be rewards, even though we might not be able to experience them on our timetable.

I know times you have loved the unlovable. I'm proud of you for that. Keep up the good work.

Clean Underwear, Wild Elephants and the Princess

Pray with me:
Father, you know how difficult it is to love the unlovable, to do good to those who aren't necessarily good to us, place in our hearts your love that we might find our loving easier. Amen

Patty B. Williams

July 25th

What's That In Your Eye?

"Why do you look at the speck of sawdust in your brother's eye and pay no attention to the plank in your own eye?" Luke 6:41 (NIV)

This is such an excellent question. If we had a little angel flying around and stopping at the beginning of each gossip session and asking the participants this question, I bet it would quickly change the mood of the gathering.

It's so easy to criticize others, isn't it? Why can we see so clearly the faults of others but not see our own? How can we miss our own weaknesses that are the same as those we easily see in others?

I think a good plan of action might be to ask ourselves these questions before we start complaining about or criticizing others. If nothing else, it will make us at least think before we speak. Now isn't that a radical idea?

Pray with me:
God, forgive us of our trespasses as we forgive others, and lead us not into the temptation of criticizing others when we should be criticizing ourselves. Amen

Clean Underwear, Wild Elephants and the Princess

July 26th

Staying Connected

"Remain in me, and I will remain in you. No branch can bear fruit by itself; it must remain in the vine. Neither can you bear fruit unless you remain in me." John 15:4 (NIV)

You and Michael have been raised in the church. You had different church experiences, and in some ways I think Michael's experiences were more positive for him than yours were for you. There were probably several factors contributing to that, but none of which caused you to have different basic Christian values or beliefs. It's just that he may have had more fun being involved in church activities over a longer period of time than you did. I always regretted that but never knew what to do about it.

As you both get older, it concerns me when I know you aren't participating in some type church activity or church itself. Jesus tells us that we must stay connected to him. He knows how important that is. We exercise to keep our bodies healthy. We read and study to keep our brains working well. We write and call our friends and families to keep our relationships in tact. Is it not just as important to keep our spiritual life healthy? What would happen to our bodies if we didn't exercise regularly, our brains if we didn't do anything to enhance them, our relationships if we made no effort to maintain them? Again, our spiritual life is no different. If we let it wane (fade) it becomes more difficult to lead a Christ-centered life. It becomes easier to live by societies norms instead of those required by God.

I don't expect either of you to be in church every Sunday, but I do hope you will see the necessity of staying connected. You can do that by attending church when you can, continuing relationships with Christian friends, getting involved in activities such as Fellowship of

Patty B. Williams

Christian Athletes, or Bible study groups. You just need to make the effort. I know because I have to make the effort, too. There are many Sundays I would prefer to stay in bed or do my own thing. I promise that if you will make the effort, you will reap benefits from it.

Pray with me:
Lord, life is tough. Help us recognize the importance of staying connected so we don't have to face it alone. Amen

Clean Underwear, Wild Elephants and the Princess

July 27th

Great Minds

"The entrance of your words gives light; it gives understanding to the simple." Psalm 119:130 (NIV)

"Great minds discuss ideas; average minds discuss events; small minds discuss people." Smart minds are able to use others' words of wisdom to make their point!

I don't know who penned the above statement about minds, but I remember that the first time I read it I was impressed by it and never forgot it. Think about it. It's so easy to talk about people, whether it's gossip or just facts you're passing along. To discuss events you have to at least be knowledgeable from book learning, reading or listening to other people, but think what it takes to discuss ideas. You have to use your brain—at least you do if you're going to formulate those ideas to any degree in your head before you discuss them.

Think about the great philosophers and inventors you study about in school. Many are credited as being the great thinkers of the world. What we study about is their ideas.

One of the reasons I encourage you to read and pay attention to what's going on in the world is so you will have a variety of things to choose from when you start or enter into a conversation. Does that mean you should never talk about people? I certainly hope not, or I'm in big trouble. I think it means that you need a broader spectrum of things from which you can choose. Many times the person or persons you are having conversation with will dictate what you discuss, but often you will set the stage for your conversations. When those opportunities arise, use that great mind I know you have!

Patty B. Williams

Pray with me:
Whatever we decide to talk about, Lord, help us to remember that you are listening. Help our thoughts and words to be pleasing to you. Amen

Clean Underwear, Wild Elephants and the Princess

July 28th

The Thunder Rolls

"That night the Lord appeared to him and said, I am the God of your father Abraham. Do not be afraid, for I am with you . . ."
Genesis 26:24 (NIV)

I've told you many times about your timidity when you were a little girl. Now, even though you are so confident and unafraid about so many things, it's interesting how one bolt of lighting or a clap of thunder will send you seeking the safety and security of your dad, me, or anyone else close by that can make you feel safe.

Actually, I suppose that makes me smile a little in my heart of hearts. It makes me think for a moment that maybe you do still need me on occasion, and maybe I haven't totally lost my little girl.

There will be times, as you know, that neither your dad nor I will be there when you're frightened. Sometimes there may be no one you can reach out and touch or run to for comfort. I hope when that happens that you will quickly reach out in prayer to God and ask for safety and a feeling of security. Remember who is in control.

Pray with me:
Lord, you never expected us to live life without you, especially in our times of need. Help us remember that you are only a prayer away. Amen

Patty B. Williams

July 29th

Get Organized

"But everything should be done in a fitting and orderly way."
1 Corinthians 14:40 (NIV)

There are days at work that I seem to do so much, yet at the end of the day, I don't seem to have anything to show for it. My desk is still full, my mind is cluttered, the stress level is up, and I'm pooped!

That's when I know it's time to stop and get reorganized. To feel like I've accomplished something, I have to know where I am and where I'm going. That's when I look for the notepad to make my "to-do" list, the folders to rearrange the papers in some semblance of order, and the calendar to write down reminders of when I'm to do something, or be wherever.

Being organized is a wonderful attribute. It helps you stay focused. It helps you to meet deadlines, and it ultimately helps you to be more productive. It also reduces stress tremendously.

I know you have a busy schedule with your classes, sorority life, work life, and your personal life. That's why it's so important that you keep a handle on it so it doesn't get you stressed out or make you unproductive. I know, too, that you know how to get organized. You are very good at it. It just takes discipline. So, go to it, girl. Get the job done!

Pray with me:
Thank you, Lord, for the many activities that keep us busy and happy. Give us the necessary discipline to keep them all in order. Amen

Clean Underwear, Wild Elephants and the Princess

July 30th

"Beautiful, Beautiful, Brown Eyes"

"Then all the nations will call you blessed . . ." Malachi 3:12 (NIV)

Although you don't seem to think so, I think God blessed you with beautiful, expressive eyes. They are one of your prettiest features. They sparkle with your smile when you're happy, they show your pain when you're sad or hurt, they twinkle when you are being coy, and they give you away when you're trying to be less than 100 % honest,

I hope you will learn to use them as the asset they are. Let them show your sincerity when you're trying to make a point. Use them to show your interest in someone when they're talking to you. Let them make contact with another's who are less confident than yours or filled with tears so you can lift them up. Use them to show disappointment when others do things that you know are not right.

Use them also to see the things around you that need to be changed, the people that need your help, the good things that need to be emphasized. God gave you an added asset in those big brown eyes. Use them to your advantage and to His. If they help you in flirting with that cute guy in the seat next to you, that's o.k. but use them also to see the things God wants you to see.

Pray with me:
Lord, help us to use the assets you gave us, not only for our purposes, but for your purposes, too. Amen

Patty B. Williams

July 31st

Watch For His Presence

"You will search for me. And when you search for me with all your heart, you will find me!" Jeremiah 29:13 (NCV)

How often have you had things happen like a phone call from a friend, unexpected money appear, a particular incident that happened at the right moment, or maybe one of these daily devotionals that discussed just what you needed at the time? Did you immediately chalk it up as coincidence, or did you think instead that it might be another one of God's small ways to show you his presence in your daily life?

Surely all those parking places that I've prayed for over the years that appeared, the obstacles that fell in the way of great temptations, the feelings of peace in the midst of heartache and sadness weren't all coincidence. There have been times that I have laughed out loud when things have happened to me that I knew were from God. One day I will tell you about one of those particular incidences.

My point is to remind you again that you don't have to look for God just in the Bible, or in church, or at some moment of crisis. Pay attention to your daily life, to your answers to prayer (which may be an answer you don't want at the time), to God's timing, and in some of my experiences, even God's humor in showing his presence. You will be in awe when you stop and think about it.

Pray with me:
Lord, in our times of doubt and in our times of faith, show us your presence in the little things and help us to recognize that you are a part of our daily lives. Amen

Clean Underwear, Wild Elephants and the Princess

August 1st

College Goals

"Listen, my dear brothers; Has not God chosen those who are poor in the eyes of the world to be rich in faith and to inherit the kingdom he promised those who love him?" James 2:5 (NCV)

Other than your goal to get a degree and hopefully a ticket to enter the world of a professional career, have you thought about what college is doing for you? Are you thinking it is going to make you rich one day? Is it going to change who you were before you entered classes that first day almost a year ago? Do you need it to make your life successful? Some of the wealthiest people around are not educated beyond high school.

I hope that college does help you begin a professional career faster than if you had decided not to attend. I hope it will help you become richer in many ways, not just monetarily. I hope it opens your eyes to other ways of thinking, to other cultures, to opportunities to interact with many different people and in various situations. I hope it teaches you how to take care of yourself and to take care of others.

Rich is not one of the top things I hope you are looking for with the degree you will earn. Does that mean I want you to be poor or to struggle financially all the time? I think you know the answer to that. I just want "rich" to be in its proper place in your thinking. Some of the poorest people are the richest in spirit, in living life, and in loving others. Some of the richest are the poorest in all those same things.

Think about your goals. Use your college experiences to help you get there. Don't worry about which major will give you the most opportunities for wealth, look for the one that will help you make a difference

Patty B. Williams

in your life and the lives of others. You are rich already in the things that matter most.

Pray with me:
Help our goals, Lord, to match those you have planned for us. Amen

Clean Underwear, Wild Elephants and the Princess

August 2nd

Well-laid Plans

"Do not boast about tomorrow, for you do not know what a day may bring forth." Proverbs 27:1 (NCV)

"The well-laid plans of mice and men often go astray". This is a quote I've heard all my life, but it never made me feel any better when my plans fell through or had to be altered.

How do you handle it when your plans are spoiled or have to be altered? Do you pout? Do you get really upset, or do you roll with the punches? I know you have had some experience with this, and I know that one way you have learned to handle it is to not really count or plan on something until it happens. That way you don't get disappointed as often as you might if you counted on the plans more than you should.

I think the way I most often handle plans that go astray is to think there must be a reason for it, and if I can't get the plans back on track, I might as well get over it, and move on. I figure that somebody wiser than me is in control. Does that mean I never pout? I don't think so!

How do you think God would want us to handle it? My guess is He wants us to keep it in perspective. In other words, how major is this change in plans in relationship to more important things that are going on in life? Is it worth getting terribly upset over? Is it going to alter what's really important in your life? God doesn't expect us not to have reactions of disappointment or possibly even some agitation, but He doesn't want us to give the event more importance than it deserves. You got it?

Pray with me:
Lord, help us to accept changes in plans the way you would have us accept them. Amen

Patty B. Williams

August 3rd

Quick Witted

"To make an apt answer is a joy to a man, and a word in season, how good it is!" Proverbs 15:23 (NCV)

I have often wished I were as quick-witted as your Aunt Shirley. She seems to always be able to come up with an appropriate response to most any comment. My brain just doesn't work that fast.

Maybe she's just a good listener or pays more attention to others' responses and can remember them, or maybe quick wittedness is just one of her God-given gifts.

Wouldn't it be nice to not only be quick witted but to also be quick with the right words, for the right situation, at the right moment? If someone needs good advice, don't you want to be able to give it to him right then, right when he wants and needs it? When someone needs lifting up or consoling, don't you want to make him feel better on the spot?

I'm not sure how we develop this skill, but my guess is it takes practice, possibly a little reading or research, courage to speak out beyond the fear of saying the wrong thing, and patience.

God wants us to be able to communicate well with others. He made us that way. It's up to us to develop those communication skills.

I am glad you are taking some classes that will help you to do just that. I know God has some special plans for you, young lady. Keep up that good work!

Pray with me:
Father, teach us how to help ourselves so we can help others, as you would have us to do. Amen

Patty B. Williams

August 4th

Don't Panic

"He should say, Listen, Israel! Today you are going into battle against your enemies. Don't lose your courage or be afraid. Don't panic or be frightened." Deuteronomy 20:3 (NCV)

Don't panic; that's good advice. I hope you'll take it.

You will have situations, as I'm sure you've had already, that will be frightening, frustrating, or at minimum, tense. The best way to handle all of them initially is, don't panic, think instead. Stop, take a deep breath, say a quick, "please help me, Lord", and then use your head to think the situation through before acting too hastily.

I really have to work on that. I am impatient and want to jump right in to take care of the problem without taking a few seconds or minutes to think the whole situation through. What that causes many times is extra effort, doing something that isn't necessary, doing the wrong thing, or making the situation worse.

If you give your brain time to get into gear, you'll also be giving yourself time to calm down and get a grip. That way you can think clearer and thus make better decisions.

Don't sell yourself short either. Don't think you can't handle a situation just because it's new to you. You have a lot of brain cells that are untapped. Just because they are untapped doesn't mean they aren't there. Scary, tense, or unpleasant situations will often get your brain search engine working faster and better than it does under normal conditions. Remember, too, you also have something even greater than brainpower to help, so don't forget to use it.

Clean Underwear, Wild Elephants and the Princess

Pray with me:

Lord, when we start to panic, help us remember our greatest source of power. Calm us and help us to use you first and then the brains you gave us. Amen

Patty B. Williams

August 5th

Happy Birthday

"Every good and perfect gift is from above, coming down from the Father of the heavenly lights, who does not change like shifting shadows." James 1:17 (NCV)

This is your birthday, the day our princess was born! I can't imagine a greater feeling unless it will be the day my first grandchild is born or the day you have a daughter. Of course if that never happens, I will still have been blessed with God's greatest gift in you and Michael.

Today you are nineteen. I can hardly believe it. Your birth in so many ways seems like only yesterday. You were such a perfect little girl. I could not have made a special order any better. You did all the "girly" things as well as Michael did all the boy things. There was never any gender confusion with either of you. Now you have grown into the perfect young lady—even after those couple of teenage years when I had my doubts!

I know that your experiences and knowledge gained during your college years will help you become that perfect adult, that perfect employee, that perfect wife, and perfect mother God has planned. I hope you will keep those goals in focus and not get sidetracked by anything less than what God wants for you. Remember those wild elephants. They are huge distracters. They can ruin a lot of dreams and goals.

Know on this special day how much you are loved, how much joy you have brought to others, and how very proud your Dad and I are of you. You and Michael have made our lives complete.

Pray with me:
Lord, how truly blessed we are. Thank you for life, love, and health. Thank you for birthdays that are remembered and friends and family to share them with. Amen

Patty B. Williams

August 6th

In Everyday Life

"Can you fathom the mysteries of God? Can you probe the limits of the Almighty? Job 11:15 (NCV)

I think you know from your own experience that these devotionals have touched others beside yourself. One group of my friends that I've shared them with has been the Extra Point Club. As chaplain this year, it gave me the opportunity to read one page at each of our meetings. I picked them randomly, yet on occasion, I felt like God led me to the right one for that day.

I often had ladies come up to me after the meeting saying how much they either liked them, felt they needed that particular message, or knew someone they would like to send a copy to. They also, of course, gave me encouragement at times when I was getting writers block or when I just needed to hear encouraging words.

I hope by now you see how God works in mysterious ways in all walks of our lives. It doesn't have to be the big things. It's in the day-to-day things like a devotional or a word of encouragement. He sends us signs all the time. We just need to stay alert to spot them.

I look forward to the day when you tell me you laughed out loud when you realized God stepped in to your everyday life to get you back on track, to help you find that parking space, or to get your attention. In the mean time . . .

Pray with me:
Thank you, Father, for being with us through the words and actions of others and through the feelings you place in our hearts. Keep us attuned to you in our everyday life. Amen

Clean Underwear, Wild Elephants and the Princess

August 7th

Street-wise

"The person who trusts in himself is foolish, but the person who lives wisely will be kept safe." Proverbs 28:26 (NCV)

When I was a teenager, one of the times I got into the most trouble was when I didn't come in until 2:00 in the morning. It wasn't the time that was so bad, it was the fact that I didn't call and let Mama and Daddy know where I was and that I was safe.

To this day, if I'm going to be over an hour and a half late, I call to let Daddy know I'm okay and running late. If I don't call, he's likely to be out looking for me or having someone else look for me.

I suppose some people might think this is a little overboard, that it infringes on one's freedom or privacy. I like to think of it in different terms. I like to think of it as having someone love and care about me enough to want to know I'm safe.

Think what a difference an hour could make if you weren't safe. Think about being out in the middle of the night, on a dark highway, alone, with a flat tire or a broken fan belt and a cell phone with a dead battery. Wouldn't you like to know that someone would be out looking for you before dawn?

Always, always let someone know where you're going and when you plan to return. If you don't know, give as much information as you do know, and then call later when you have more information. If no one is home when you leave, write a note or leave a phone message. Don't put yourself in an unsafe situation by not taking time for precautions.

Patty B. Williams

Pray with me:

Make us street-wise, Lord. Teach us to discipline ourselves to practice safety in our daily lives so that we don't alter our lives by our carelessness. Amen

Clean Underwear, Wild Elephants and the Princess

August 8th

The Ants

"Ants are creatures of little strength, yet they store up their food in the summer." Proverbs 30:25 (NCV)

I admire people who are organized, who know how to plan for the future and have the discipline to stick to their plan. It makes life so much easier when you know where you are and what it will take to get where you want to go.

Just because you may not have all the money you want, it doesn't mean that you can't make plans for what you do have. Just because you may not be an officer in the sorority doesn't mean that your vote or opinion doesn't count. Just because you haven't found Mr. Perfect to marry doesn't mean that you can't prepare to be a good wife and mother in advance.

We should learn from the ants. They are wise little creatures. If they're smart enough to know the importance of preparation, doesn't that have something to say to us, God's highest creatures?

You are showing more and more maturity as you continue college life away from home. I hope you will continue the path you seem to be taking. Plan and work your budget so you don't live your life in constant turmoil not knowing when, or if, you can pay your bills. Study well in advance for the exam so you don't panic the night before, or the day of, the exam. Pay attention to the ants! Don't hibernate like the bear and think things will work out on their own when you decide to wake up one day!

Pray with me:
Lord, it's not always easy or fun taking the time to plan. Motivate us when we need it most, and then help to keep us on track. Amen

Patty B. Williams

August 9th

Children

"But Jesus said, Let the little children come to me. Don't stop them, because the kingdom of heaven belongs to people who are like these children." Matthew 19:14 (NCV)

You and I share the love of children just as Nanny did. I don't know if that was "handed down", but we sure all have the baby bug.

I think one of the things I love the most about little children is their innocence and integrity. Little boys hold hands; little girls hug each other. They all kiss one another and sit close with no reservations. Color doesn't matter; looks don't matter. Money doesn't matter, and for sure status doesn't matter. A three-year-old may walk out in a room filled with other children with their pants down around their knees needing help with a zipper or button and never think twice about it. I just love that innocence.

It's a shame we have to lose that innocence and childlike integrity. This old broken world would be such a better place if we could preserve them both. Think what a difference there would be if we saw no color difference in one another or no status differences.

God never wanted us to lose our innocence or integrity. He didn't want that for Adam and Eve and he didn't want it for us. We're the ones that blew it! So what can we do about it at this point? I suppose not a lot in terms of the world, but we can start with ourselves and how we look at things. You are further along in the seeing no color than my generation is. Your children will be even better than you. We can encourage our guy friends to hug each other without reservations if a hug is warranted, and we can pass up the Tommy Hilfigger jeans for a less status seeking pair of Lerner's jeans, and we cannot "fudge" on our timesheets or our income taxes.

For anything to get better, someone has to begin. It might be with a word, a small deed, or something big. Keep this in mind. Think about it. Then the next time you see an opportunity to make your small contribution, you'll recognize it.

Pray with me:
Lord, forgive us for botching things up. Help us to do our part in trying to make the world better, even if it's in small ways. Amen

Patty B. Williams

August 10th

Larie

"I thank my God every time I remember you." Philippians 1:3 (NCV)

Today is the birthday of the first little girl I ever baby-sat. It was the first babysitting job for which I was paid. She would have reminded you a little of Cassidy, blonde, little, and she loved me like Cassidy loves you. She also had a different name like Cassidy. Her name was Larie. I just loved it.

Now, Larie is a mommy herself with three children, and when I saw pictures of her daughters when they were little, it brought back such memories of her when she was that age. What sweet thoughts.

It is incredible how fast time goes by when you're an adult. Babysitting as a pre-teen seems like only yesterday. Yet when I think of all that has happened since those days, it seems like forever.

I think one of the reasons I have written you and Michael letters to include with your baby books over the years is because I don't want you to forget anything. God has given you both such a good life. I want you to have the notes to jar your memory when you start writing letters or books to your kids about your lives growing up.

I hope you will keep your own notes, too, even if it's only a sentence or two a day. You'll be surprised what it will mean one day. So find that notebook, girl, and get busy!

Pray with me:
Thank you, Father God, for a life we want to write about and remember. Rescue those children who are living lives they want to forget. Amen

August 11th

Digging A Hole

"He who digs a hole and scoops it out falls into the pit he has made." Psalm 7:15 (NCV)

"He's digging his own hole". I know you've heard that saying before. Did you know it was in the Bible? I think one of the feelings that I get when I find something like this in my reading is a feeling of validation. It helps me know that God is in our everyday life, that he tries to guide our thoughts and actions by giving us encouragement, words of discipline, and words of wisdom. Still, however, He lets us make our own decisions.

If we don't take care of our bodies, we dig our own hole for old age. If we don't discipline ourselves to study, we dig our own hole when exam time comes. When we don't take care of our friendships, our thank-you notes, those little actions that show our appreciation for what others have done or mean to us, we dig our own hole of alienation from them.

I think, in essence, digging our hole is God's way of letting us punish ourselves for bad choices. He'll let us dig that hole as big as we want, and lie in it as long as we want. The good news, however, is that he'll also help us dig out if that's what we want, as long as we don't wait too long.

We all make poor choices at one time or another. My hope for you will always be that as soon as you recognize a poor choice that you will do what you need to rectify it. Avoid digging those holes as much as possible, but if you find yourself there, start with a prayer and then get the heck out of the dirt!

Patty B. Williams

Pray with me:

Sometimes we have a tough time, Lord. The dirt looks fun. The hole doesn't look too deep, and we lose our balance. Please help us to avoid falling in the pit. Amen

Clean Underwear, Wild Elephants and the Princess

August 12th

Journey's End

"The priest answered them, Go in peace. Your journey has the Lord's approval." Judges 18:6 (NCV)

We're almost at the finish line, at the end of the journey we have had together over the past year. We've covered some territory, haven't we? Has the trip been meaningful? Will having read the book help you to tell your children and grandchildren more about me one day than they might have learned otherwise? Now that's a scary thought! Has God spoken to you through any of the scriptures, the subject matter, or the prayers?

The journey has been a real challenge for me in many ways. It has required discipline, prayer, thoughtfulness, and in some cases it's caused me to relive old hurts and have sadness for things I wished for but couldn't have. On the other hand it has caused me to reflect on some very sweet memories about you, about our family, about people who have touched our lives and made imprints that will last forever. It has made me, once again, count my blessings and recognize the joy and happiness that have been in my life.

I hope the journey has given you some things to think about, to discuss with your friends. I hope that some of the letters have awakened your senses to things you may have taken for granted, like safety and caution in everyday situations, like different feelings and ideas unlike your own. I hope it has given you food for thought in your prayer life and your relationship with God.

It's been a good trip. I hope you'll plan to take the same one with my grandchildren one day in the not too distant future.

Patty B. Williams

Pray with me:

Thank you, Father, for special times together. Keep us close always in mind, body, and spirit with each other and with you. Amen

Clean Underwear, Wild Elephants and the Princess

August 13th

The End

"Listen to advice and accept instruction, and in the end you will be wise." Proverbs 20:20 (NCV)

When you get to the end of a project, you normally have a lot of different feelings. One might be exhilaration, one might be exhaustion, one might be sadness, and one might be a combination of all three. I think for me it's the latter of the three.

I have thought and thought about what I wanted this last page to say to you other than how much you are loved and how proud I am of who you are and who you are becoming. I have wondered what last bit of wisdom I might bestow upon you that would sum up most of what I've tried to say over the past year. I'm not sure I can do that, but let me try.

In all your relationships, remember to treat others in a way that is consistent with God's great commandment to love others as you love yourself. In bad situations, remember to look in God's book of instructions for guidance and use the values you have learned at home. For safety, use your head more than your heart. To love, use your heart more than your head! When you're struggling, know you have a supportive and loving family you can always count on. You never need to run away from problems. Remember to have friends you have to be one. Take care of those friendships. Don't disappoint those who look up to you. Count your blessings. Count them again!

I look forward to our continued journeys together, whatever form they may take. You have started college life exactly as I would have planned it for you. You have made me very proud. Keep up the good work! I love you.

Patty B. Williams

Pray with me:
Oh, Lord, let this time together have benefits long past this one year. Thank you for your blessings on this work and on our lives. Use them both to glorify You and touch others for Your sake. Amen

Epilogue

The *Princess* graduated (on time) May 5, 2001 from the University of Central Florida. Along the way she made good grades, played hard and worked hard. As anticipated, she broke a few hearts and had hers broken. She avoided the most serious *Wild Elephants*, found her passion in Social Work and Health Education and will continue in graduate school at Florida State University in the fall. She grew intellectually, emotionally, and spiritually and is striving daily to find God's will for her life. As we knew she would, she made her mark at UCF, made her family and friends proud and continues to bless our lives. Stay tuned . . . .

Index of Subjects

A Big Order	24-Jul
A Cheerful Giver	21-Jun
A Cute Message	17-Feb
A Desire To Know The Future	30-May
A Greater Plan	20-May
A Heavenly Resource	27-Aug
A House Divided	15-Feb
A Legacy Of Love	13-Jul
A Loaf Of Bread	3-Jul
A Mother's Joy	3-Apr
A New Baby In The Family	2-Jan
A Tear Floating Down The River	8-Jun
Acceptance	19-Apr
Adjust The Sails	28-Jun
Afflictions	28-Jan
An Attitude Of Gratitude	18-Jan
Angel Kisses	22-May
Angels	25-Oct
Anxiety	10-Sep
Anxiety And Worry	12-Dec
Are The Differences Important?	19-May
Are You Bored	14-Apr
Arguments	13-Mar
Ask Not What Your Country Can Do	11-Jan
Asking For Guidance	7-Nov
Asking For Help	22-Aug
Asking God For Direction	7-Oct
Assumptions	4-Apr
At Peace With Who You Are	10-Mar
Aunt Debbie	17-Mar
Aunt Dolly	6-Oct
Aunt Mary Ella And Terrie	19-Jan

Patty B. Williams

Aunt Mary Jane	2-Dec
Avoiding Sorrow And Sadness	5-Jan
Awesome God	19-Jun
Be Prepared	18-Jun
Be Yourself	14-Aug
Beautiful, Beautiful, Brown Eyes	30-Jul
Because I'm Breathing	14-Nov
Being Content	29-Nov
Being Happy	13-Oct
Being Loved	15-Jan
Being Tired	7-Jan
Being True To Yourself	16-Jan
Belonging	21-Feb
Bragging	14-Mar
Breaking The Routine	22-Jan
Brittany's Horse	26-Apr
Broken Vows And Promises	15-Jul
Brokenness	17-Oct
Brotherly Love	12-Jun
Call My Dad	24-Sep
Calling The Guys	14-May
Calm, Cool, And Collected	18-Jul
Celebrating Life And Death	27-Jan
Challenges	13-Feb
Chance To Bloom	17-Aug
Changes	26-Dec
Character	16-Jun
Children	9-Aug
Christianity	28-Oct
Christine	4-Dec
Christmas	25-Dec
Church	30-Jan
Clean Underwear	28-Aug
Cleaning Out Your Heart	25-Mar

College Goals	1-Aug
Commitment	8-Oct
Communication	4-Mar
Compliments	23-Aug
Conformity	16-Apr
Confronting Others	15-May
Constructive Criticism	27-Sep
Contentment	19-Mar
Crying	28-Mar
Curiosity	10-Jul
Dad's Birthday	2-Jun
Date Rape	2-Sep
Destiny	6-Feb
Devils And Angels	28-Sep
Differences	5-Dec
Different Friends	5-Oct
Different Kinds Of Families	20-Dec
Digging A Hole	11-Aug
Disappointment	25-Nov
Disciplining Children	18-Dec
Discrimination	27-Feb
Disney World Excitement	12-Nov
Disputes	22-Apr
Do It Well	7-Feb
Do These Things	29-Mar
Do Unto Others	5-Mar
Do What You Can	6-May
Do Your Best	17-Apr
Don't Break A Shin	6-Jun
Don't Break 'Um	4-Jun
Don't Miss The Message	7-Jun
Don't Panic	4-Aug
Drinking	4-Nov
Emily And Ellen	22-Dec

Encouragement	24-Feb
Enjoying God's Nature	23-Oct
Experiences	3-Dec
Failures	10-Feb
Faith	7-Sep
Fall	4-Oct
Familiar Voices	5-Feb
Family	19-Feb
Family And Friends	28-Nov
Fearful	19-Aug
Finding The Right Guy	6-Jan
Finding The Right Profession	11-Dec
Fixing Things	21-Sep
Fooled Again	2-Apr
For The Record	6-Jul
Foresight	17-Jul
Forgive And Forget	25-Aug
Freedom	16-Sep
Friends Of Worth	9-Jun
From Dresses To Jeans	8-Jul
Fruit	9-Sep
Funerals And Parties	8-Jan
Gandhi's Advice	23-Jun
Get Organized	29-Jul
Getting Back On Track	19-Nov
Getting Beyond The Actions	23-Nov
Getting Even	31-Jan
Getting Ready For Christmas	19-Dec
Getting Started	2-Feb
Gifts	24-Aug
Give Me A Sign	26-Jan
God And I Together	6-Sep
God Knows	21-Mar
God's Job	31-Oct

Clean Underwear, Wild Elephants and the Princess

God's Plans	30-Dec
Going Out On A Limb	11-Jun
Good Health	26-Feb
Good-Byes	19-Oct
Goodie Two-Shoes	18-Sep
Goodnight, God	9-Jul
Gossip	12-Sep
Gossips And Busy Bodies	18-Feb
Governed By The Spirit	26-Nov
Granny	15-Oct
Great Communicators	21-May
Great Minds	27-Jul
Greatness	8-Feb
Greed	8-Sep
Grief	12-Apr
Guilt	27-Mar
Hanging In There	8-Nov
Hansel And Gretal	1-Jun
Happy Birthday	5-Aug
Having To Be Right	12-Oct
Healthy Bodies	25-May
Heart Conversations	11-Mar
Held Accountable	13-Nov
Helping Others	14-Dec
Holding The Keys	17-Dec
Home Cooking	7-May
Homecomings	10-Jan
Homosexuality	19-Jul
Honesty	22-Oct
Hot Coffee	15-Jun
How Do You Love?	20-Jun
Humbleness	16-Feb
I See The Moon	9-Oct
Idols	27-Oct

Patty B. Williams

Improve Your Aim	5-Jul
In Everyday Life	6-Aug
In Full Bloom	9-Nov
Independence	27-Jun
Inside And Outside	14-Jan
Instructions To The Rich	23-Apr
Intimacy	12-Jul
Intimidation	28-Feb
It Gets Easier	27-Apr
It's The Pits	15-Apr
JB's Barbecue	16-Nov
Jen	29-Aug
Jim And Jason	29-Jan
Journey's End	12-Aug
Joyful Memories	21-Jul
Judging	18-Oct
Just Having Fun	1-May
Karen	25-Jan
Keeping It Balanced	26-Jun
Keeping Things Inside	22-Mar
Kindness	13-Dec
Knowing The Right Thing To Do	18-Mar
Knowledge	5-Nov
Larie	10-Aug
Laughter	14-Jul
Laziness	10-Oct
Leadership	16-Jul
Life Is Tough Sometimes	29-Sep
Life Puzzles	9-May
Listening	22-Sep
Little Eyes	3-Oct
Lives Changed Over Night	21-Oct
Living Within Your Means	15-Sep
Long Hair	25-Feb

Clean Underwear, Wild Elephants and the Princess

Looking For A Major	10-Jun
Looking For Mr. Perfect	18-Apr
Love	29-Dec
Love Your Enemies	24-Mar
Make Me Strong	5-Jun
Making a Difference	20-Sep
Making Commitments	24-Nov
Making Mistakes	3-Sep
Making Transitions	28-Dec
Man is Limited; God is Not	1-Nov
Managing Your Time	17-Sep
Many Kinds Of Love	24-Jun
Mistreatment	5-Apr
Mom Bigham	1-Apr
Money	13-Apr
Mr. Irwin	14-Sep
My Prayer	12-May
Names	10-Dec
Nanny	6-Mar
New Beginnings	31-Dec
New Year's Resolutions	1-Jan
No Place Like Home	13-May
Not Doing The Things I Should Have Done	3-Nov
Not My Will	3-Feb
Obstacles	11-Feb
Old Baggage	3-Jun
On Golden Pond	29-Oct
On Loan	26-Oct
On Your Own	18-Aug
One In A Million	4-Jan
Opportunity	20-Apr
Our Partnership	11-May
Over-commitment	3-Mar

Patty B. Williams

Overload	23-Jul
Paying Attention	11-Oct
Peace And Harmony	13-Jan
Peace That Passes Understanding	2-Jul
Peanut Butter And Jelly Toast	18-Nov
Pearl Harbor Day	7-Dec
Perseverance	15-Nov
Pick A Pumpkin	20-Oct
Planning	2-Mar
Pookie Bear	11-Apr
Pray, Don't Worry	6-Nov
Prayer	20-Jan
Pre-marital Sex	30-Aug
Promises	26-Aug
Proud Parents	1-Sep
Public Speaking	30-Oct
Questioning God	15-Dec
Questioning God's Existence	24-Oct
Quick-Witted	3-Aug
Reading	1-Jul
Recognizing Dreams	30-Sep
Remember Me	24-Apr
Remembrances Of You	19-Sep
Respect	3-Jan
Richard	1-Oct
Riches	20-Aug
Roommates	15-Aug
Sadness	21-Aug
Saying Your Blessings	14-Oct
Saying You're Sorry	23-Feb
Sean	5-May
Seeking God's Will	30-Apr
Self-Centeredness	9-Mar
Self-Confidence	11-Jul

Clean Underwear, Wild Elephants and the Princess

Send Me A Sign	26-Jan
Sending Messages	22-Jul
Set The path	26-May
Show Your Appreciation	18-May
Shredded Wheat	8-Apr
Silence	31-May
Sinful People	22-Nov
Sleepy Head	14-Jun
So Wrong, Yet It Feels So Right	16-Dec
Special Friends	22-Feb
Special People	20-Nov
Spiritual Maturity	9-Apr
Stained Glass Windows	4-May
Staying Connected	26-Jul
Stepping Up	23-May
Stone Throwing	9-Jan
Street-Wise	7-Aug
Study Habits, Discipline, And Balance	24-Jan
Suffering For Doing Right	11-Sep
Susan's Shells	10-Nov
Swearing	1-Feb
Take The Bus	13-Jun
Tattle-Tale, Tattle-Tale	4-Feb
Tested Faith	27-Dec
Thank Goodness	28-May
Thanksgiving	27-Nov
That Thorn In Your Side	20-Mar
The Aged	12-Feb
The Ants	8-Aug
The Bad Apple	23-Mar
The Christian Scientist	26-Mar
The Company You Keep	21-Apr
The Devil	7-Mar
The End	13-Aug

Patty B. Williams

Title	Date
The Forth Of July	4-Jul
The Game	21-Nov
The Greatest Of Life's gifts	20-Feb
The Heart Doesn't Lie	31-Aug
The Heart Part	6-Apr
The Internet	20-Jul
The Man In Rome	7-Jul
The Need To Know	3-May
The Night Before Christmas	24-Dec
The Perfect Son And Daughter	23-Dec
The Present	10-May
The Princess	16-Oct
The Right Equipment	25-Apr
The Spirit Within Us	2-Oct
The Thunder Rolls	28-Jul
The Twins	1-Mar
Think About Rabbits	16-May
Think Before You Speak	28-Apr
Think Good Thoughts	17-Jun
Think Upon This	8-Mar
Those Who Help Shape Us	10-Apr
Those Who Inspire Us	17-May
Time	7-Apr
Times Alone	6-Dec
Timing Is Everything	12-Jan
Tithing	13-Sep
Transcending Differences	21-Jan
Treating Everyone Equally	2-Nov
Tug At Our Hearts	30-Nov
Uncle Billy	23-Sep
Under The Circumstances	21-Dec
Understanding Your Parents Desires	17-Jan
Valentine's Day	14-Feb
Walk The Talk	9-Feb

Walking With The Wise	5-Sep
Walking To The Edge	25-Sep
War	11-Nov
Watch For His Presence	31-Jul
Welcoming Strangers	15-Mar
Well-laid Plans	2-Aug
Weston	22-Jun
What Do I Say	2-May
What Happened To Yesterday?	29-Apr
What It Takes	29-Jun
What Keeps Us Sane	29-May
What Makes You Beautiful	12-Mar
What's That In Your Eye?	25-Jul
When The Time Comes	1-Dec
When We're Apart	27-May
When You Become Weak	16-Mar
Who's On The Ladder	30-Jun
Who's Responsible?	31-Mar
Whose Interest Is It?	24-May
Wild Elephants	23-Jan
Wisdom	8-Dec
Words And Actions	16-Aug
Words Of Instruction And Wisdom	9-Dec
Work	4-Sep
Work Your Best	30-Mar
Working Where It Counts	8-May
Worrying	26-Sep
Yesterday, Today, And Tomorrow	25-Jun
Youth	17-Nov

Index of Characters

Adams, Charles Kendall	6/29
Albom, Mitch	2/20
Arland, Gilbert	7/5
Balazs, Erika	7/4
Baker, Danny	11/14
Barber, Patsy	10/21; 11/24
Barrett-Browning, Elizabeth	2/14
Beetles, The	12/29
Bender, Karen Hodge	1/25
Bigham, Aunt Debbie	8/20; 12/25; 1/2; 3/17; 6/13,25
Bigham, Bill (Granddaddy)	9/2,7,18,23; 10/9,19,24; 11/11,12; 12/7,8,9; 1/2,4,10,12,23; 2/12,26,28; 3/6; 4/1,24; 5/11,17; 6/1,2,13,22,25; 7/13; 8/7
Bigham, Grace (Nanny)	9/18; 10/19,23; 11/12; 12/8,9; 1/2,4; 2/28; 3/6; 4/1,24; 5/11,17,20,22; 6/22,25; 7/13; 8/7
Bigham, Justin	3/1; 7/13; 8/9
Bigham, Mom & Pop	4/1
Bigham, Uncle Robert	4/1
Bigham, Stephen	1/2; 2/5
Bigham, Uncle Teddy	4/1
Bigham, Uncle Billy	8/20; 9/23; 12/25; 1/2; 3/17; 5/11; 6/25
Bigham, Weston 9/4;	12/11; 3/1,17; 6/22,25; 7/13
Bohnstengel, Ellen	11/7; 12/22; 2/14
Bohnstengel, Emily	11/7; 12/22; 2/14
Boom, Corrie Ten	3/8
Brooks, Adam	10/3
Brooks, Alyssa	10/3
Brooks, Garth	9/30; 6/8
Bryan, William Jennings	2/6

Patty B. Williams

Buckner, Colleen Cain	12/20
Burns, Robert	8/2
Callan, Jen	1/29
Carnegie, Andrew	2/9
Chaires, Jackie	1/21
Clemons, Mary	2/14
Churchill, Winston	2/8
Cohen, Alan	10/13
Conner, Doug	9/18; 3/1
Corbett, Terrie	10/29; 1/19
Covington, John	12/20
Cranford, Terry	5/9
Crawford, Mike	8/24
Cruise, Tom	8/20
Culbreth, Carol	8/28; 10/21; 2/19
Culbreth, T.C.	8/28; 10/21
Delta Zeta Sorority	1/25; 6/30
Deyo, Bill	9/21,23; 10/16; 1/6; 7/15
Deyo, Obie	9/28
Douglas, Jean	1/4
Douglas, Mike	9/18
Driver, Ann (Aunt Punkie)	12/10
Drummond, Henry	6/10
Duncan, Doug	12/20
Eliot, George	5/31
Eubanks, Mary Roe	9/28
Extra Point Club	8/6
Falcon, Donald	9/18; 3/1
Fields, Benny	4/8
Finley, Susan	11/10
Ford, Henry	2/10,11
Fossum, Mavis & Merle	10/12
Gandhi, Mohandas Karamchand	6/23
Gibson, Don	4/15

Green, Brittany	4/26; 7/16
Green, Cassidy	12/24; 8/10
Green, Cindy	1/10
Green, Don	1/10; 3/1
Green, Doug	3/1
Green, Emily	2/5; 3/6
Green, Johnnie	1/8,15,27
Green, Aunt Mary Jane	9/23,29; 10/20; 11/9; 12/2,9,24; 1/8,15,26; 3/17; 4/1,24
Green, Spencer	2/19
Griner, Harold	4/4
Griner, Ramona	4/4
Hamilton, Mark	1/16
Hardee, Honey & Daddy Hardee	9/23
Hardee, Uncle Les & Aunt Mary Ella	1/19
Harrell, Aunt Dolly	10/6; 1/4
Harter, Amy Deyo	9/28; 2/14
Henderson, Casey	5/14
Hendley, Aunt Shirley	8/3
Irwin, Carrol	9/14
Irwin, Harriet	12/22
Irwin, Jim	12/22; 1/29
JB's Barbecue	11/16
Johnson, Ben	6/9
Jones, Deborah (Green)	10/20; 3/25
Kappa Delta Sorority	9/30; 12/4; 2/15, 21; 6/30
Katanich, Sharon	2/22
Kelly, Roxanne	5/9
Kennedy, John	11/22; 1/11
Kubler-Ross, Elizabeth	5/4
Landers, Ann	9/24
LaRosa, Adam	11/23
Lester, Bobbi	12/27
Livingston, Amanda	4/10

Patty B. Williams

Long, Christine	12/1,4; 2/14
Long, Jeff & Carole	11/28; 12/4
Long, Matt	12/1; 2/14
Lubbock, J.	4/17
Luther, Jim	1/14
Lyons, Mitch	12/1; 2/14
Mares, Nicole Batchelor	9/25; 1/18
McCloud, Gabriel	12/28; 2/27; 6/11
MacDonald, George	5/8
Mehr, Vicki	10/13
Millay, Edna St. Vincent	7/7
Mortman, Doris	3/10
Myers, Glenda	5/5
Myers, Larie Temple	4/10; 8/10
Newton, Howard W.	2/7
Nivelle, Robert	6/5
Nobles, Phyllis	9/18
Norley, John	4/27
Outlaw, Frank	6/16
Overton, Patrick	9/25
Parrish, Regina	9/23
Patton, George S.	2/13
Perkins, Terry	12/20
Presley, Elvis	12/16
Rhodes, Jamie	6/25
Rhodes, Roy	7/21
Roosevelt, Eleanor	7/27
Roosevelt, Franklin D.	5/6
Shanks, Jim	5/5
Shanks, Sean	5/5
Shropshire, Kelly	7/1
Sparks, Shane	2/14
Spears, Peggy & Del	5/17
Stuckey, Smitty	7/14

Sundberg, Alan Carl	12/27
Temple, Jimmy	4/10
Tillman, Paula	2/22
Tindale, Bob	10/28; 3/14,20,31; 12/21
Turner, John and Nancy	10/29; 11/20
Unknown or Anonomous Authors	9/21,22; 2/17; 5/10; 6/11,17,28; 7/3; 9/21,22
Vepraskas, Nancy & Mark	3/17
Wainwright, Richard	4/12; 10/1
Warfel, Jen	8/29; 2/14
Weedn, Flavia	10/26; 4/6
White, Jason	1/29
Williams, Barbara (Granny)	10/15; 2/12
Williams, Ivan (PaPa)	2/12; 3/19
Williams, Kenny	8/18; 9/1,2,19,22,25; 10/14,19; 11/6,11,16; 12/9,13; 1/28; 2/4; 4/4; 5/5, 20,21; 6/1,2,27; 7/28; 8/5,9
Williams, Kim Turner	11/20
Williams, Michael	9/1,2,19,23,28,30; 10/3,25,26; 11/1,2,9,12,16,18,20; 12/1,2,4,7,9,10,13,14,18,23; 1/6,17,19,24,28; 2/4,14,29; 3/1,4,6,12,28; 4/3,9,10,11,13,24; 5/7,9,11,12,20,21,22,30; 6/12,19; 7/14,18,26; 8/5,10
Winfrey, Oprah	6/13
Zapata, Gloria	10/6
Zapata, Melissa	7/21